MUSIC AND MUSICIANS

AN INTRODUCTION

DONALD D. MEGILL
Mira Costa College

Prentice Hall, Englewood Cliffs NJ 07632

Library of Congress Cataloging-in-Publication Data

Megill, Donald D.
  Music and musicians: an introduction / Donald D. Megill.
      p.   cm.
  Includes index.
  ISBN 0-13-034919-4
  1. Music appreciation.   I. Title.
MT6.M44135M9   1994
  780 — dc20   92-38407
                                                        CIP
                                                        MN

Editorial/production supervision: Keith Faivre
Acquisitions editor: Bud Therien
Interior/cover design: Thomas Nery
Page layout: Maureen Eide
Production coordinator: Bob Anderson
Photo researcher: Cindy Joyce
Photo editor: Lori Morris-Nantz
Cover art: Tom Voss/Stockworks

 © 1994 by Prentice-Hall, Inc.
A Simon & Schuster Company
Englewood Cliffs, New Jersey 07632

Printed in the United States of America

10 9 8 7 6 5 4 3 2 1

ISBN 0-13-605668-7
{TEXT ONLY}
ISBN 0-13-034919-4
{TEXT WITH 2 CASSETTES}
ISBN 0-13-103698-X
{TEXT WITH 2 COMPACT DISCS}

Prentice-Hall International (UK) Limited, *London*
Prentice-Hall of Australia Pty. Limited, *Sydney*
Prentice-Hall Canada Inc., *Toronto*
Prentice-Hall Hispanoamericana, S.A., *Mexico*
Prentice-Hall of India Private Limited, *New Delhi*
Prentice-Hall of Japan, Inc., *Tokyo*
Simon & Schuster Asia Pte. Ltd., *Singapore*
Editora Pentice-Hall do Brasil, Ltda., *Rio de Janeiro*

*To Cynthia, who faithfully supports all of my "projects,"
and to David, with whom I share vision in all things.*

CONTENTS

Chapter 6   THE RENAISSANCE PERIOD: *1450 to 1600*   68

Chapter 7   THE BAROQUE PERIOD: *1600 to 1750*   81

PART III: TOPICS: *Musical Ideas and Developments* 205

LISTENING EXAMPLES IN ORDER OF APPEARANCE

PREFACE

Music and Musicians: An Introduction offers a *one*-semester study toward the appreciation of music. It is not designed to expose any particular style at the expense of another, but rather discusses musical styles as diverse as classical, rock, jazz, and studio. This study draws lines of similarity within these worlds of music. History is a continuous process in which students must determine their place.

The goals of this book are:

- to develop an appreciaiton of music in light of style and period;
- to realize the cultural relevancy of music, both in history and in the present;
- to free musical perception from bias and personal taste;
- to see music as an expressive art form representative of its time and place.
- to see music as a continually developing art form; and
- to use historical periods as a backdrop for topical discussions of musical concepts and concerns.

This study exposes the growth and development of music. In light of this, who are the Bachs and Beethovens of today? How are they different from each other and from earlier musicians? How are they the same? These interesting and important questions will be addressed in the pages that follow.

"Prelude to Appreciation: Music and Culture" presents and discusses some questions that are inherent to a general education course in music appreciation. The framework for future study is explored and left open for development and growth. These questions are provocative and establish an environment for critical thinking necessary for the study that follows.

Part I, "The Language of Music," presents, *in a reference format,* the language of music from traditional notation to tape and computer. The definition-like style of presentation allows students to return to this section and review basic definitions and musical forms. Teachers can elaborate on these fundamental definitions. Traditional and nontraditional instruments are grouped by family and ensembles, and compositional structures, ranging from a simple popular song to the sonata-allegro form, are compared. For additional explanation of these terms the *Oxford Dictionary of Music* is recommended. For more elaborate discussions of the elements of music, musical structures, and musicians, refer to the much larger *The New Grove Dictionary of Music and Musicians*.

Part II, "Stylistic Periods in Music," looks at music in history. Each period overview begins with an outline of the essential musical aspects of that period. Dateline biographies of composers and descriptions of their music help articulate the terms and concepts particular to each period. The relationship of jazz and rock is discussed in the appropriate period surveys.

Part III, "Topics," deals with concepts in composition that thread through history. This part sews together the historical periods by tracing continuously developing musical events and, in light of the historical overview studied in Part II, will be of particular interest. Students will naturally review styles from Part II while studying the topics in Part III. Composers from different periods are compared, and their commonality of purpose and motivation is emphasized. *The topics in Part III can be studied in any order* and are easily expanded to present other important musical topics, favorite composers, and musical comparisons across styles. There is no need to use all the topics, and additional topics can be added or replaced by the teacher. These provocative topics lend themselves to stimulating tangents and discussions.

Also featured in this text are *listening notes,* including *timed listening guides* for the students' listening in class and at home. Intentionally not technical in nature and patterned after program notes, these notes help to focus attention on large musical elements without suggesting that the students must be able to recognize sophisticated structural elements. They allow the student to listen at a level of success and enjoyment. The notes are designed to be models for notes written by the students for assigned listening.

All terms pertinent to the discussion are in bold type and most are defined in the margins. *All* terms, however, can be found in the glossary at the end of the book. The *extended glossary* is a vital part of this text, offering expanded definitions and references to works discussed. Terms that reappear in bold in later chapters (Part III) should be reviewed.

Ancillary Materials

1. A teacher's manual, which presents topic discussions and activities, chapter summaries, paper topics, and materials for testing, is available. Listings of world events for each historical period and a bank of test questions are also included.

2. A student manual containing objective and subjective study materials as well as study questions designed to focus on the listening is available for out-of-class assignments.

3. A set of five compact discs containing fifty-two listening examples discussed in the text is available. An alphabetical listing of these examples is printed on the inside back cover of the text. Those few examples discussed in the text but not included on the recordings are marked with an asterisk in the Table of Contents. Most of these examples can be found on the *Smithsonian Collection of Classic Jazz;* others are readily available in record stores.

4. *Either two cassettes or two compact discs are available with the student text.* A recording of Benjamin Britten's *The Young Person's Guide to the Orchestra* begins the selection, introducing students to the instrument families and to two formal structures: variations and fugue. The recordings also include examples from each musical period. Students should listen to these selections many times so that a point of perspective can be established for each period. An alphabetical listing of these selections is printed on the inside front cover of the text.

MUSIC AND MUSICIANS

PRELUDE TO APPRECIATION:
Music and Culture

 Introduction

Music is everywhere. We cannot visit a supermarket, the dentist, the bank, or many public places without hearing music. Tucked-away speakers broadcast music of every conceivable style. Most of the music you hear during this course will sound similar to something you have heard before. You are probably not aware of the many styles of music you have passively stored in your head over the years. All these styles are related and only the difference makes the difference; that is, variables in the basic parameters of each style differentiate one from another. Sometimes the differences enhance or support specific activities, allowing music to serve many purposes. Music accompanies work and play, it supplies the framework for dance, it is the underpinning of musical soundtracks for stage and film, it helps in advertising and business, and it can change one's mood.

We commonly use music to fill space and time and accompany other activities, but we rarely focus on the elements of style and technique that can further enrich the listening experience. Music as an art form consumes one's complete attention. The interface of melody, harmony, and rhythm in a world of tension and release becomes an intricate drama unfolding in a progression of musical colors.

Music styles, whether classical, folk, jazz, rock, country, pop, or commercial, share a common heritage using similar sounds and ideas. To isolate one style from another diminishes them all. The more we know about one style, the more we know about all styles. The ability to perceive the aesthetics within one style opens the door to appreciate music in other styles.

Everyone has a favorite musical style. Arguments abound as to which style or performer is technically or musically the "best." Such arguments, although entertaining or frustrating, miss the point of the reasons or need for music and musicians. To foster an attitude of positive openness before a study of music can be undertaken, a few questions must be addressed and discussed but not necessarily answered. Only then will the music of all styles come alive.

The following questions are presented to consider and carry throughout this study of music. Listening success requires that you be open to new sounds and styles and unencumbered by preconceptions or bias. Use these questions to discover what background you will bring to the music discussed in this book. Under conditions of openness music history is exciting.

This photograph shows Eugene Ormandy conducting the Philadelphia Symphony Orchestra. His face is full of the passion and love for music born of his understanding and appreciation of the craft. One can only speculate if his expression is a result of an idea about to happen, the very moment, or the memory of a sound played moments ago. Regardless of the reason, he is celebrating an exciting musical idea and sound.

🎼 *What Is Music Appreciation?*

When I hear music, I flutter, and am the scene of life, as a fleet of merchantmen when the wind rises.
— Henry David Thoreau, *Journal* (1841)

The term *appreciation* has been used by teachers and students for years and generally, it is thought to mean that one who appreciates music also likes music. This is a common misconception. Appreciation of anything is a complex relationship born of a four-step process. The process, if exercised, brings about new appreciations and, if neglected, screens out what is unknown.

1. You must first be exposed to the sound and performance of music. You cannot expect to find an immediate affection for even the greatest work of art; toleration is sometimes the first and only step to understanding. Listening attentively to music provides the background necessary to compare and contrast sounds intelligently. The music and its sound are the point of beginning. Without exposure music remains meaningless and distant.

2. After exposure comes analysis and criticism. To be critical does not mean to find negative aspects of a composition or performance. To look at and listen to music critically requires that you look at the stylistic elements and compositional details of the music. Criticism should be viewed as an investment that yields an understanding of a composition and its composer.

3. Understanding is the byproduct of exposure followed by criticism. Understanding a composition and its composer develops a respect for the process and the sound. Appreciation is the combination of respect and knowledge derived from an evaluation of the music's quality and significance.

4. The last stage in this process is taste. Following exposure, criticism, understanding, and appreciation, what impact did this music have on you?

🎼 *What Constitutes Musical Taste?*

Wagner's music is better than it sounds.
— Mark Twain

Realizing the steps involved in developing an appreciation of music, you will naturally continue the process of appreciation (exposure-criticism-understanding) with personal taste. Do you like what you have listened to, analyzed, and appreciated? Is it wrong or nonintellectual to like or not like the final product? What value must be placed on this encounter with a work of art?

It is not necessary for everyone to love all great works of art. Personal opinions will not diminish its greatness or value; likewise, the worth of the individual who holds a negative opinion of a specific composition, composer, or performer will not be devalued.

Every kind of music is good, except the boring kind.
—Gioacchino Rossini, 1973

Many pieces of music are considered "good" or "bad" because of the situation in which they were heard. For example, to people falling in love love songs seem to have special meaning and often become lifelong favorites. ("Oh, honey! Our song.") Musical taste can also be shaped by visual effects. Due to their association with a story or picture, songs from soundtracks to movies are effective (remember the Strauss waltz from the movie *2001*?). In today's world of music videos it is common to hear statements such as, "I hated the song until I saw the video," or "What a strange song; did you see the video?" Such statements raise the question of the role of video and music. Many things and conditions can influence musical taste, and not all of them have to do with music and its language.

In the old days we had sensible popular songs like "Daddy wouldn't buy me a Bow-wow" and "TaRaRa Boom De Ay."

—Anonymous

Not all works of art are attractive. Some are full of tension, conflict, confusion, or even anger. The expression still stands and its impact on each listener varies. The personality of the listener must encounter the expression of the composer. Honesty in these encounters is paramount to understanding one's self as well as the expression of the composer.

What Is the Role of Composers, Performers, and Listeners?

The requisites of a singer—a big chest, a big mouth, ninety per cent memory, ten per cent intelligence, lots of hard work, and something in the heart.

—Enrico Caruso

Everyone enters the world of music as a listener. Sounds excite and stimulate both composers and listeners to explore and create musical possibilities. Composers take and nurture ideas in hope that they develop into something substantial without evaporating before something magical happens.

Composers are usually involved, to some degree, with the performance of their music; they may be the soloist or conductor. There are, however, composers who write music for others to perform and, in fact, are not even present for the performance. Today some composers skip the actual step of writing down the music in traditional notation. Music generated in the studio, for example, is often performed in layers and, through the aid of a computer, played together at another time. Performers can become composers instantly when improvising, the process of inventing melodies, harmonies, and rhythms. This mixture of composing and performing draws the attention of all musicians. Even though improvisation has been an important element of music creation throughout time, today such instantaneous composition and interpretation is most commonly associated with jazz.

Listeners can feel the spirit of composition and performance through continued listening and study. Communication between composer, performer, and listener is a vital link to most musical styles. What is communicated is always difficult to say; however, the language seems to cross many cultural and historical lines.

 *When Does History Begin?*

Nations are destroyed or flourish in proportion as their poetry, painting and music are destroyed or flourish.

—William Blake, *Jerusalem* (1804–1820)

The end of each day gives birth to another historical moment. However, there seems to be a greater sense of awe when considering musical works that are "really old." Although the music and lives of Bach and Beethoven retreat further and further into history, they are still studied with intensity. Until Mendelssohn rediscovered the music of Bach, the musical public functioned quite well without Bach's music. Due to an increased emphasis on history, Bach is more widely known today than at any other time; it seems impossible to think of a musical heritage without Bach. The effect of history on us shapes our thinking and growth. If Bach were not represented in history, someone else would take that position, yielding different influences on today's music.

The study of music history has traditionally remained centered on music that elicits a universally accepted feeling of beauty. As we move further in time from these works it is increasingly difficult to find musical threads that tie today's music to the past.

Historical styles develop from the broad brush strokes of composers, wielding new and bold ideas. We naturally assume that there are composers today who will prove equal to their predecessors. For the student, music history becomes a tool for understanding today's musical developments.

When Does "Old-Fashioned" Become History?

Every intelligent product must be judged from the point of view of the age and the people in which it was produced.

—Walter Pater (1839–1894)

Music from the recent past, for example, ten years ago, is difficult to evaluate objectively. In fact, its place in history is yet to be established and, as a result, is often set aside until later for final evaluation. Likewise, the excitement of newness tends to elevate the importance of some music unrealistically. The period of time that lies between the past and

Edward Hopper, *Nighthawks* (1942). Oil on canvas. 30″ × 60″.
Is the subject of this painting old-fashioned? Historical? For many people this scene enlivens nostalgic memories. To others, it is far removed from any personal experience and is associated with another generation. Both responses are certainly valid but are very different. Due to the varying backgrounds of those who ponder the painting it is difficult to be artistically objective about so ''recent'' a topic. (The Art Institute of Chicago. Friends of American Art Collection. Photo © The Art Institute of Chicago. All rights reserved.)

the present is often considered nostalgic rather than historical. However, once left alone long enough and tested by time, it will remain in the minds of historians and musicians purely on its inherent musicality or significance.

"Old-fashioned" applies most often to styles that were associated with recent memory. An old-fashioned style is most commonly attributed to one's recent past, whereas a stylistic period commands more breadth, perhaps fifty to 100 years. For example, disco is a rock style that may disappear when the stylistic period of rock covering 100 years is remembered. Such brief stylistic windows are not insignificant; they are just too brief to command much attention. In the spectrum of music history, a 100-year period may be called Baroque, or Romantic; however, realize that each period was comprised of shorter and often very well-defined styles that were at one time considered to be old-fashioned. If remembered at all now, they are considered "historical."

 ## *What Are the Features of a Musical Style?*

I only know two tunes, one is "Yankee Doodle" and the other isn't.
—Ulysses S. Grant

Musical styles differ in structure, sound, and performance. Composers write music that is stylistically associated with their place in time and is reflective of their personal perceptions. A composer's music can be recognized and identified because of elements common to his or her other compositions. By discovering elements common to other works written at the same time a composition can also be associated with a historical period. Styles change when compositional practices and techniques change, and such changes can take place suddenly or over a long period. On one hand, the stylistic differences between the works of Bach and those of The Beatles are easily recognized by most people, although the reasons stated for these differences may be as diverse as the styles themselves. On the other hand, the works of Haydn and Mozart may "sound the same" to many first-time listeners; works of the same historical period share many stylistic features, and one must look closely to find the composer's unique differences.

What is it that makes unnoticed differences obvious? Differences are amplified by an awareness of detail. Just as the voice of Pavarotti, in all its beauty, sets a standard for operatic styles, the voice of Louis Armstrong set standards within its style. Details specific to any style are first used to imitate the style, then further to develop the style, eventually leading to its mutation.

René Magritte, *Personal Values* (1952). Oil on canvas. 31½ × 39″.
What is important in this painting? Things that are normally small are very large here and demand our attention. There is a shift in priorities. Are we indoors or outside? This painting redefines what is important in this room. Is this perception incorrect? Unrealistic? A new importance is given to the shaving brush, wine glass, matchstick, comb, and bar of soap. Did you notice the crack in the ceiling? Is it important? (Herscovici/Art Resource.)

The details of construction, performance, instrumentation, melody, harmony, and so forth add definition and uniqueness to a musical style. The elements of music are the building blocks needed by composers, and the composer's positioning of these blocks establishes the detail of style. With an awareness of these basic building blocks of music, there is excitement in plotting stylistic development through history, of which we are merely a part.

What Musical Styles Influence the World Today?

Music oft hath such a charm
To make bad good, and good provoke to harm.
—William Shakespeare, *Measure for Measure*
(1604–1605)

Merely listing the styles remembered throughout history will not tell us which musical styles influence the world today. The importance of each style compared with all the others is also not an answer. A more realistic answer is the relationship of all the different styles and how each developed from the one before. Early composers (A.D. 900–1100) were associated with and supported by the church; today, however, most composers of traditional concert music are associated with, and

Hyacinthe Rigaud *Louis XIV* (1701). Oil on canvas. 9′1″ × 6′3″.
This baroque painting shows fashions of the French royal class. Our recent past has traditionally focused more colorful and ornamental fashions onto women's clothing. This painting shows that flamboyance with delicate detail was once high fashion for noble men. Stylistic ideas seen in this painting have not disappeared entirely and are again popular for men in today's pop culture. Notice the long, flowing hair, the ornamental shoes, and the cane. A sword tucked into the large cape is a masculine symbol that seems to contrast the delicate stockings and high heels. Think of the cult heroes in rock today, their jewelry and their flamboyant dress. One could argue that any similarity is merely coincidence or an aesthetic circle. (Louvre Museum, Paris.)

supported by universities. As patronage shifted over the years so did musical styles.

Besides the mainstream of concert music today, there are vast numbers of active composers: songwriters, composers for film scores and musical theater, jingle writers for television and radio commercials, and composers of background music. In addition to these front-line musicians are the many tangent careers, from instrument builders and sound engineers to theater managers and promoters. The spectrum of musical activity is so wide that the U.S. music business has become one of the largest in the world. It is no wonder that to a large segment of our society cultural heroes arise from the musical entertainment business. For example, most of us have some knowledge of Madonna or Michael Jackson whether we like that music or not; however, it may be difficult to find a significant percentage of our society who could name the current secretary of state.

Compare the posture of this model with the painting of Louis XIV. The acceptance of contemporary style adds relevance to each image. The portrait of Louis XIV clearly identifies with the very elite. This photo, however, invites viewers to adopt immediate comforts associated with the middle class. It is impossible to draw lines of empirical taste with such divergent cultural identities. Taste is conditional and momentary.

Each student of musical development is obliged to remove the sometimes convenient boundaries between the large musical periods to see that each musical style was alive and forever changing. In fact, composers often changed stylistically within their own lifetimes. To overdefine each period reduces compositions to static entities. Dynamic composers in history were solving musical problems, creating new sounds, breaking down old structures, and inventing new ones.

Realizing the fluid nature of stylistic development brings the many styles known from history and those of today into perspective. Music does not progress. It is not "getting better." It is changing and will continue to change, expressing the needs and ideas of those who compose, perform, and listen.

What Styles Should Be Included in a Definition of Music as Art?

Music is the universal language of mankind—poetry their universal pastime and delight.
Henry Wadsworth Longfellow, *Outre Mer* (1833–34)

Defining music as an art form has led to many pages of discussion and consideration. Regardless of how complicated the definition, its most basic foundation must include the following elements.

Music is

1. expressive of both the composer and performer;
2. representative of its time in history;
3. an extension of culture and heritage;
4. a product of skill and concept expressed through technique, measured by sound and sometimes compositional technique;
5. a language involving sound and notation that is capable of communicating numerous levels of feeling, emotion, and meaning.

Therefore, the various periods of concert and popular music qualify, to some extent, as pillars of the musical arts. There is a place for Renaissance, Baroque, Romantic, jazz, rock, dance styles, and concert styles. Details may vary but the similarities are undeniable. To say that one musical style is less important than another in the greater definition of the musical arts would be misleading. Instead, the balance of all the historical and active styles defines the whole.

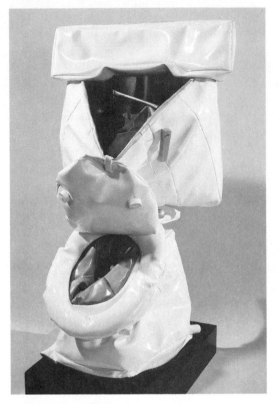

Claes Oldenburg, *Soft Toilet*
(1966). Vinyl filled with kapok
painted with liquitex, and wood.
52 × 32 × 30″.
Much about this pop art sculpture
flies in the face of tradition. Rather
than carving stone, Oldenburg
shaped vinyl for this project. It is
not a true representation of reality,
and the subject matter is offensive
to some; however, it is expressive
of an attitude toward "traditional
artistic concepts." Is this art? Is it
an insult to established definitions
of art? Oldenburg desired that his
art make strong statements both
politically and socially and not sit
forever in some museum; ironically,
many of his works have found just
such a place. (Collection Whitney
Museum of American Art, N.Y. 50th
anniversary gift of Mr. and Mrs. Victor
W. Ganz.)

 Imitation or Unique Expression?

If a man does not keep pace with his companions, perhaps it is because he
hears a different drummer. Let him step to the music which he hears,
however measured or far away.
— Henry David Thoreau, *Walden* (1854)

Historical periods are naturally grouped by time, common traits, and
similar beliefs. It is easier to explain stylistic development in history by
setting models and drawing associations to these models. However, the
excitement of history comes with the deviations from tradition.
Beethoven expanded musical structure; we remember him. Berlioz
envisioned new orchestrations; we remember him. Wagner redirected
the scope of opera and we remember him.

History has become a science of recording first those individuals
who moved away from the norm. At the same time, as in the case of Bach
and Mozart, it applauds those who recognize tradition and work to

develop it. How about the many excellent composers and performers who have been overlooked by historians merely because they were excellent but not innovative? Today composers and performers work to add their own unique expression to the music that has existed before them. They do not see themselves as imitating the past but as individuals adding expression to great ideas.

Some musicians are so unique to the historical flow that they cannot be easily explained. If statements of individuality cannot be classified by existing style categorizations, then there is always the temptation to eliminate them from discussion. However, it is the uniqueness of creation that brings the joy of study. Music history requires a posture of investigation to see developing differences and to expose the expressions unique to each composer and performer. Structural forms and cultural trends may set direction, but it is the individual composer who

Salvador Dali, *The Persistence of Memory* (1931). Oil on canvas. 9½ × 13″.
This painting has both imitative and unique ideas. The subject is clearly beyond reality. One watch is covered by insects, and three other watches hang limply in a barren environment. The objects do not match their surroundings; instead the subject puts familiar objects in a strange juxtaposition. The images are clear and understandable, but at the same time they appear dreamlike, a mixture of the known and the unreal. (Collection, The Museum of Modern Art, N.Y. Given annonymously.)

sparks the imagination and teases the senses. Music flows through variation. Without decisive statements of change and variation, music is destined to become nostalgic and eventually stagnant. We look for aggressive, unique statements of change to stimulate and direct culture.

Every composer important to us has an aura of uniqueness and excitement. History is merely an exposure of this development.

Why Is Music Considered a Fine Art?

Music must take rank as the highest of the fine arts—as the one which, more than any other, ministers to human welfare.

—Herbert Spencer, *Essays on Education* (1861)

In the days of Bach and earlier, musicians were to play the music they composed. It was common for a composer's music to die with the artist. To borrow another's musical ideas was a compliment, a symbol of the originator's importance. Music was less important than the function it supported; in fact, the scholarly study of music was the last of the fine arts to be accepted into the academic community. Music supported social functions and was not lauded as an art form in its own right. Until it reached the educational arena, music played a more practical role in society with little regard to its history. But over the centuries, focus on the music itself gave new identity to its place in the world of fine arts.

In the developing definition of music as a fine art, debate constantly arises about the role of commercial music versus classical music. It is common for music to slip into the fine art category as it becomes older. An example of this would be the very popular Strauss waltzes. They have grown in stature over the years, from dance music to concert music. Music is a fine art in that it is crafted with care and detail, representing a long development of techniques associated with composing, performing, and listening.

Today more than ever musicians not only compose and perform but study the theory, literature, and history of music. Musicians are becoming more knowledgeable of music styles around the world. The refinement of today's music is a study in itself; the finery of the various stylistic periods is continually examined and explored for its complexity and beauty.

🎼 *What Is An Art Period?*

Every work of art adheres to some system of morality. But if it be really a work of art, it must contain the essential criticism of the morality to which it adheres.

—D. H. Lawrence, *Study of Thomas Hardy* (1936)

Finally, music as a fine art is brought into historical focus when common elements of cultural and musical thought draw certain composers and performers together. An art period is necessarily defined after the fact. Once history, the similarity of condition, technique, procedure, and thought identify works as homogenous. As stated earlier, music is constantly in transition, but many such transitional activities blend into a larger whole, encapsulating a unified musical or art period.

An art period encompasses several smaller styles represented by several composers. All the smaller styles eventually merge into a period epitomized by common technique and thought. It is important to maintain an awareness of the fluid transformation of musical style within an art period while simultaneously perceiving the larger movement from period to period. The stability of a well-defined period can then be compared to the instability of change between periods. The boundaries between periods are difficult to draw exactly, and rightfully so. Change is not limited to one or two activities between periods. Within a period there are changes taking place constantly.

Periods in music history help articulate large periods of similar identity. Composers were seldom aware of what period they were a part of and wrote music to satisfy themselves and those around them. As musical styles fade and disappear, new ones are born, often as a result of the very same activity.

Part I
THE LANGUAGE OF MUSIC

Treat this part as your reference section. To some degree, all musical styles involve most of the terms and concepts described in these early chapters. Instruments and instrumental groupings are explained. There are diagrams of large and small musical structures that appear in works discussed later in the text. These terms, ideas, and structures will become more familiar as you study the music in parts II and III. You will need to refer back here, and to the Glossary, as you work your way through later chapters.

Use *Young Person's Guide to the Orchestra* at the end of this part to practice your listening skills. Listen to this example several times so that the instruments and the forms become familiar.

Chapter 1

SOUND:
The Foundation of Music

The emotional power of music has been attributed to many different sources. When the sound from a pipe organ caused the stones of an old church to vibrate, observers took it as a sign of divine approval. Science, and physics in particular, has explained much about sound over the last 100 years. For example, musicians have known for centuries that two notes played together can create tension **(dissonance)** or they can blend in a pleasing fashion **(consonance)**. Physical laws govern the resulting sound of combining notes. What remains difficult to explain is how dissonance and consonance together in the same composition move the listener emotionally.

The physics of sound shows us that a single tone produced by any sound source has many different but related tones as part of its total sound. The **fundamental pitch** is the loudest and draws your attention. But many other, softer pitches vibrate simultaneously with the fundamental pitch which flavor and give identity to the sound. The combination of all these tones is called the **overtone series**.

The notes in an overtone series for the single note C are written out on the music staff (Figure 1-1).

dissonance
a combination of notes that seems unrelated or harsh. Too many dissonant sounds make most listeners uncomfortable.

consonance
the pleasing sound of two or more notes. Consonant sounds are stable and do not create tension.

fundamental pitch
the primary pitch. The lowest pitch heard in an overtone series is the fundamental, and also the loudest, pitch.

overtone series
the combination of pitches that are based on the same fundamental pitch. Every note has several related pitches, or overtones, from low to high, that vibrate at the same time.

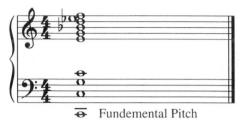

Figure 1-1

🎼 Sound Waves

synthesizer
a tone generator, often a keyboard. Using a synthesizer, sounds imitating acoustic instruments or new and unique wave forms are created.

amplitude
the volume of a sound. Amplitude is measured by the height and depth of its wave form.

frequency
the length of a sound wave or the number of vibrations per second. Every pitch has a specific frequency; for example, the note A above middle C vibrates 440 times a second.

intonation
accuracy of pitch. Good intonation or being "in tune" is the exact sounding of a specific pitch without being slightly above or below the standard.

tune up
bringing two or more instruments in agreement on pitch. Once instruments are tuned, the music can better be controlled by the musicians.

Sound moves through the atmosphere in waves as molecules of air bump into one another. When these waves of molecules bump into your eardrum, you perceive the movement and hear pitch by the speed of the waves. These waves of sound have many shapes, depending on the complexity of the overtone series above the fundamental pitch. An infinite number of variables are possible in a sound wave, and each gives rise to a unique sound. The violin, for example, does not sound like the clarinet because their respective wave forms are different. (See Figure 1-2.)

Today's electronic instruments allow musicians to invent new sounds by inventing and changing the shape of sound waves. On modern keyboards, called **synthesizers**, musicians and composers are free to manipulate the very essence of a sound by varying the shape of the sound wave.

The height and depth of a wave shape tells us how loud the pitch is, that is, its **amplitude**. The length of the wave shows the actual note's pitch **(frequency)**. (See Figure 1-3.)

Thus the term A440, for example, the international standard for the note A above middle C, simply means that the pitch A has a frequency of 440 vibrations per second. Each note vibrates a different number of times and for this reason is given a letter name. The same note played on any instrument vibrates the same number of times per second. Lower notes have longer sound waves. For this reason, longer or bigger instruments play lower notes than shorter or smaller instruments.

Intonation is the matching of one instrument's pitch to another's so that each note on one instrument will match the other exactly. Instruments **tune up**, usually to A440, so that they all produce the same frequency when playing the same note. When they are out of tune, disruptions in the sound wave create unintended dissonances. Even

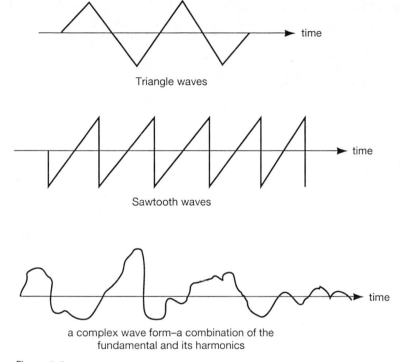

Triangle waves

Sawtooth waves

a complex wave form—a combination of the
fundamental and its harmonics

Figure 1-2

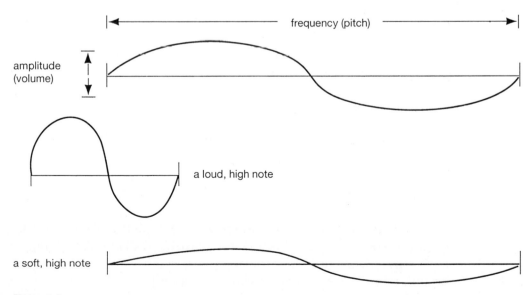

frequency (pitch)

amplitude
(volume)

a loud, high note

a soft, high note

Figure 1-3

small variations in the length of the sound waves between two instruments are quickly perceived as "wrong" or out of tune.

 ## Sources of Sound

The most common sounds we hear are those that occur in nature. Familiar sounds such as the rustle of leaves, the songs of birds, the pounding of surf, and the silence of a cave give us a sense of peace and order. Other sounds invade this world of natural sound: the roar of traffic, the whine of lawnmowers, the boom of stereo systems, the shouts of people.

The difference between musical and nonmusical sounds is not easily described. Traditional sounds of music are based on familiarity. All instruments, when first invented, found resistance because they produced unfamiliar sounds. Only time made them part of the accepted musical world, if they were accepted at all. Contemporary composers use all kinds of sounds in their compositions, even those over which they have little control such as sounds of nature. Any sound used in musical composition is "musical" by definition; when used to color a song the sound of ocean waves or of a jet taking off can be perceived musically. The sounds of motors were used in a short-lived experimental style called "industrial music." It is not uncommon for composers and performers to try to incorporate all sorts of sounds into expressive musical structures.

The most recent instrument in the musician's toolbox, the synthesizer, generates newly discovered sounds as well as familiar ones through the manipulation of wave forms. The re-creation of previously created wave forms through **sampling** is perhaps the most exciting new possibility. The wave form of sounds produced by an acoustic instrument, for instance, can be analyzed, or sampled, and plotted; then that sound can be rebuilt to match the sound produced by the instrument exactly. A modern keyboard can therefore call up these sampled sounds stored on a computer and can sound amazingly like the instrument it sampled.

Sound is now explored and explained by both the scientist and the musician. The musician who tries to control and manipulate sound to make music is now required to have an understanding of how sound is created, moves, and combines with other sounds.

sampling
the re-creation of existing wave forms. Any sound can be analyzed and its wave form plotted. The synthesizer can then read out this code and from it re-create an exact copy of the original sound.

Chapter 2

MUSICAL INSTRUMENTS:
Traditional and Nontraditional

Ever since humans discovered that they enjoyed the sound of banging on a hollow tree or shaking a dried seed pod or blowing through a hollow reed, they have been trying to vary and improve upon the sounds they could make to communicate with one another and give pleasure. Different cultures have chosen vastly different kinds of instruments to bring life to their musical ideas. The Western European tradition from which most of our music is derived uses instruments that fall into four groups: stringed, woodwind, brass, and percussion. Similar instrument groups appear in other cultures; however, the specific instruments within each group have developed quite differently. The development of those instruments familiar to us from the Western European tradition can be traced by looking at the changes in the orchestra from 1600 to the present.

Since the beginning of orchestral literature many changes have taken place. It is difficult to pinpoint when the first orchestra was developed; however, as instruments were developed and accepted by the musical community, they were brought into existing ensembles, adding new elements of contrast and blend. Within the modern symphony are families of instruments that share the same means of creating sound.

Each family of instruments is capable of producing very high as well as very low pitches. The larger, longer instruments create longer frequencies, producing lower notes than the smaller, shorter instruments.

 ## The Four Instrumental Families

1. Stringed instruments. Musical instruments in the string group have strings of varying lengths and widths that are made to vibrate by drawing a bow across them or by plucking them. The sound resonates and is amplified by the wooden body of the instrument. The length of the strings determines the range of the instrument. To get sound from a stringed instrument the player draws a bow across the string with one hand and with the other hand shortens the length of the string by pressing the string down on the fingerboard. As the length of the string changes, so does the pitch. The longer the string, the lower the note. Thus smaller instruments have shorter strings and play higher than larger ones. The violin, viola, cello, and string bass are the most common bowed stringed instruments today. These instruments can also be plucked, a technique called **pizzicato**.

pizzicato
plucking a stringed instrument rather than bowing it.

Guitar, lute, mandolin, banjo, and even the harp are stringed instruments that are not bowed but are plucked and strummed. Plucking

The New York String Orchestra performing at Carnegie Hall.

and strumming these instruments give the sound a percussive and rhythmic quality unique to this subgroup of the string family.

2. Woodwinds. The wind instruments, that is, instruments whose sound comes from being blown through, were at one time made of wood. Although not the case today, for example, flutes are now made from metal alloys and not wood, the name woodwinds has stuck.

To activate the tone of the woodwinds, the performer blows air into them. Within this category are instruments that require a single cane reed such as clarinets and saxophones and those that do not use reeds such as flutes and recorders. Double-reed instruments such as the oboe, bassoon, and English horn have two cane reeds that vibrate against one another to create the sound. The keys on the instruments cover holes that, when closed, cause the air to go farther down the body of the instrument, thereby lowering the pitch. This activity effectively changes

Woodwind instruments

the length of the air column inside the instrument and in turn changes the pitch of the sound being produced.

3. Brass instruments. Brass instruments are long and tubular and use the buzzing motion of the lips within a small metal cup or mouthpiece to generate a tone. The player makes changes of pitch by "buzzing" faster or slower to play different notes within a single overtone series. Many notes can be played without changing the length of the instrument. Early brass instruments had no keys or valves to help change notes.

Valves to change notes appeared in the early nineteenth century. The depression of a valve opens up more tubing, and this changes the length of the instrument. With valves, brass instruments can play notes that are outside the overtone series of the earlier instruments. The slide of a trombone also changes the length of the instrument, allowing for greater pitch flexibility. Varying lengths and bores of tubing enable larger brass instruments—trombones, baritones, and tubas—to play very low,

The Canadian Brass Quintet

Percussion instruments

and smaller ones—trumpets, flugel horns, and French horns—to play very high.

4. Percussion instruments. Whether made from a natural or an artificial substance, any sound source that is struck falls into the category of percussion instruments. One of the earliest forms of pitched percussion was the wood drum over which animal skin was stretched and struck for tone. Many different and exciting drum shapes and sounds have been derived from this basic plan.

Wood blocks, shakers, tambourines, and hollow wood drums are all percussion instruments. As soon as techniques for forging metal developed, people began to make instruments such as cymbals, bells, triangles, and gongs that could be played by striking them. Other percussion instruments such as steel chimes, glockenspiel, xylophone, vibraphone, marimba, and tubular bells provide well-defined pitches. The harp, piano, and harpsichord are stringed instruments that require either plucking or striking motions to make their sound. Thus they share identities with both the string and percussion families.

 Instrumental Ensembles

Instruments from the same family naturally blend with one another and, for this reason, are grouped into small ensembles with high- and low-pitched instruments. For example, the string quartet has two violins playing the higher parts, one viola playing in the middle range, and the cello playing the lowest part. There are comparable brass and percussion

Hans Burgkmair, *Maximilian with His Musicians* (1505-16).
This woodcut shows a variety of instruments used in the sixteenth century during the Renaissance. In the lower right corner on the floor are two drums, a sackbut (brass instrument), and a trumsheit (stringed instrument). Flutes, recorders, a viola da gamba, and a krummhorn lie on the table. Musicians are playing a small organ (left), harp (center), and a small keyboard (on the table). In the background another musician plays a cornet (brass) and seems to be reading music that is being discussed by three others who are, perhaps, musicians? Composers? Even though they appear to be dressed for a performance the setting looks like a rehearsal. Most of the instruments shown have been discarded or been greatly modified and developed over the last 500 years. Some musical societies today, however, still perform music of the Renaissance using these original instruments. (Metropolitan Museum of Art. Gift of W. L. Andrews, 1988.)

ensembles. Large ensembles such as an orchestra incorporate instruments from each family. Each instrumental family brings contrast to the sounds of the others.

Composers naturally favored popular instruments in the music of their time. As instruments faded from favor, composers reflected the change by focusing on other, more currently popular instruments. For example, for 200 years the harpsichord dominated musical composition; today it is used very little. For this reason, music from different historical periods can often be identified by the instruments and their groupings.

Instruments in the Early Orchestra (1600-1700)

Early in the seventeenth century viols, among the earliest bowed stringed instruments, were replaced by violins, violas, and violoncellos. The earlier lute gave way to the guitar. Recorders (predecessors to the flute), along with the oboe and bassoon, dominated all other wind instruments up to the eighteenth century. Military trumpets and kettledrums and, more rarely, the bass drum and side drum made appearances for military, marchlike music. An underpinning of harmony, rhythm, and even percussion came from the harpsichord, a predecessor to the piano.

Instruments New to the Modern Orchestra (Since 1700)

Performance techniques and the design of the instruments themselves developed rapidly. Sections in the orchestra expanded until all the woodwinds were paired, a move that added two flutes and two clarinets. By the end of the Baroque era (1750) the recorders were gone. By 1780 the orchestra usually had two flutes, two oboes, two clarinets, and two bassoons.

In the late nineteenth century, alto and bass flutes, the bass clarinet, and the contrabass bassoon further expanded the orchestra. By then a typical brass section had two trumpets, three trombones, four French horns, and last of all, a tuba. The percussion section grew dramatically to include the triangle, cymbals, orchestra bells, bass drum, snare drum, and kettledrums. The harpsichord disappeared in the late eighteenth century; keyboard instruments would only appear again as solo instruments.

The string section grew in size, outnumbering all other sections combined. The string section is still made up of violin, viola, cello, and double bass.

The New York Philharmonic

The Duke Ellington Orchestra, 1940

Instruments in Jazz

Orchestra instruments appeared in popular music early in the twentieth century. Wind instruments were favorites as melodic instruments. Clarinet, cornet or trumpet, and trombone were the first to appear in Dixieland jazz. The saxophone quickly assumed and still maintains a dominant role in jazz and popular styles.

Jazz rhythm sections grew from banjo and tuba to piano alone or with guitar, string bass, and drums. The string bass has remained an important voice throughout jazz history, the only member of the string family to do so. Most recently, synthesizers, controlled by keyboards, guitars, and wind instruments, have become very popular.

The larger jazz bands, starting in the late 1920s, began grouping instruments into four sections:

1. The reed section consists of five saxophonists who also play clarinet and flute.
2. In one brass section, four or five trumpeters use various mutes to modify their sound. These performers also double on flugel horn, a larger-bore instrument shaped like a trumpet.
3. In the other brass section four or five trombonists also use mutes to transform their tone.
4. The rhythm section is comprised of four different percussion sounds: piano, guitar, string bass (or electric bass), and drums.

Instruments in Rock and Commercial Music

Over the past fifty years instruments used in folk music such as the guitar have been dramatically transformed into powerful melodic and rhythmic instruments in rock and commercial music. The use of amplification to propel the sound has given this music genre a distinctive nature. Sound amplification and electric manipulation have also profoundly influenced jazz and even modern classical music.

Rock and commercial music ensembles are essentially enlarged rhythm sections without a large wind or string section as found in classical or jazz ensembles. Along with the dominant voice of the electric guitar, the ensemble contains the bass guitar, keyboards capable of many unique sounds, an enlarged drum set, and auxiliary percussion drawn from Latin American countries. Music for film can use a vast array of ensembles ranging from modified orchestras to rock bands or just a single musician using highly developed synthesizers.

MIDI *(Musical Instrument Digital Interface)*

The familiar sounds of a drum machine playing the various sampled sounds from a drum set have replaced many of the "live" drummers on commercial recordings. Along with the many other sampled sounds from synthesizers these sounds are now controlled from a single keyboard. Keyboard controllers, drum machines, and sound generators are now commonly tied together through a computer to supply contemporary studiolike sounds such as echo and delay. Once a musician plays a part on the drum machine or keyboard, the computer stores the decisions made by the performer and, upon command, will replay those decisions on any synthesizer at any speed.

sequenced
music as the product of electronically processing all the musical parts of a composition. The parts are played separately and stored as data in a computer. The data are combined and organized by the computer to be played together later.

MIDI
acronym for Musical Instrument Digital Interface. This process transmits data between several electronic instruments so that they all communicate and play together.

When the music is finally performed as a whole, all the decisions are assembled and coordinated **(sequenced),** just as a composer organizes the sounds in an orchestra. Instead of several musicians assembled together to play several different parts, the parts are first played separately and later combined. Composers who use **MIDI**

Musician using a MIDI keyboard along with a drum machine to compose, record, and play back music directly from his computer

techniques feel they have complete control over the music from concept to performance. Very often, the composer plays all the parts; therefore a performance of many parts can be the product of a single musician. This is very common in studio recordings and film soundtracks.

 ## *New Concepts in Instruments*

There is no specific reason for the development of an instrument. Why a violin, bassoon, or tuba? In the realm of instrument development, musicians continue to be experimental; that is, they are open to harnessing new sounds regardless of how the sounds are acoustically or electronically generated. At times an image of a new sound or combination of sounds will drive a composer or inventor to modify, disregard, or invent new sounds. In the twentieth century this goal became a substantial part of modern composition. There have been, and will continue to be, new designs for sound production, and some will fade without adoption. Composers and performers are always searching for technical improvements, and they will continue to expand the capabilities of the instruments. The "ideal sound" changes from one age to the next.

Any sound used in music composition must first be controlled in such a manner that, upon request, it will produce the desired sound. Sounds not in traditional ensembles such as a rattle in a car door or a squeak in a hinge or the thud of a book dropping onto a table could, with a little refinement, be used quite effectively. The possibilities of new sounds are endless.

John Cage's prepared piano

Chapter 3

FLEXIBLE MUSICAL ELEMENTS

Various elements of composition and performance shape and define each musical work. They not only separate one work from another but also draw works into stylistic groupings where these elements are used similarly. In the same manner as an artist paints, composers manipulate the elements of music to fill **musical space.** Where the artist considers color, blend, and texture to fill a canvas, a musician might think of rhythm, tone, and harmony to create a world of sound. The three fundamental elements basic to all music are

> **musical space**
> the range of sound filled by the music elements motion, pitch, harmony, texture, and tone.

1. **motion,** comprised of rhythm, meter, and tempo,
2. **pitch,** expressing frequency and instrument range, and
3. **tone,** established by instrumental color and orchestration.

In addition to these three basic elements, two additional elements have been important in western European music of the last 1000 years:

1. **harmony,** a combination of several pitches interacting simultaneously, and
2. **texture,** resulting from various degrees of simultaneous activity.

 *Motion*

The ongoing pulse of music is the primary element of motion. **Rhythm** is the ongoing of time measured by an audible or implied pulse, often called the **beat.** Different note values can serve as the beat; in fact, any rhythmic value (quarter note, half note, whole note, and so forth) can be called one beat. The beat is assigned to whatever the composer chooses to count. Following is a table of rhythm values showing their relationship to one another.

The progression of beats is further organized or grouped into larger units. The clicking of a clock is an even rhythm without grouping. If the pulse were grouped into even, predictable sounds such as TICK-toc, TICK-toc, then a **meter** would be established. In this case, a meter of two is established because of the **accent** on the first of the two pulses. If for some reason the clock sounded TICK-toc-toc, TICK-toc-toc, then the meter would be three. Such meter groupings organize musical sounds into definable rhythmic units called **measures** that, when written in notational form, are visually separated from one another by the vertical lines in the music staff called **bar** (measure) **lines.** Measured music is essential for creating rhythmic styles as identifiable as a waltz (groups of three) or a polka (groups of two). All dances are designed around regular groupings. Most contemporary dance forms today are based on groupings of four beats.

The symbol for meter is represented in notation by a meter signature or, more commonly, the **time signature.** The top number is the number of beats in each group and the bottom number is what note value will be assigned the beat. Time signatures appear at the beginning of the printed musical line along with the **key signature** (discussed later). In Figure 3-1, the time signature indicates that there will be four beats in each measure and that the quarter note (♩) will be assigned the beat.

rhythm
the regularly recurring pulses or beats that are arranged into regularly recurring groups consisting of multiples of two or three pulses that establish meter. Rhythm refers to the frequency of chords and the activity of the melody, hence harmonic rhythm and melodic rhythm.

meter
the number of beats grouped in each measure. For example, ¾ meter means 3 quarter notes per measure; 6/8 means 6 eighth notes per measure, and so on. Various meters form the bases of dance forms; for example, a waltz is written in groups of 3 (¾ time), and cha-cha is in groups of 4 (4/4 time).

measures
small equal units of a composition that contain a determined number of beats. Measures are separated in written music by vertical bar lines.

time signature
the two numbers at the beginning of written music indicating the number of beats per measure and what note value will be counted as one beat; for example, ¾, 6/8, 4/4.

key signature
a group of ♭'s or ♯'s representing the tonal area of a song; for example, the key of A, or the key of B-flat. The key signature is written on the staff at the beginning of a composition.

Figure 3-1

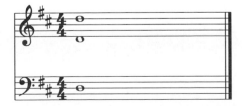

Pitch

range
the distance between high notes and low notes on an instrument. Also the distance between loud and soft, fast and slow.

envelope
the four elements that make up the sound of a note: attack, decay, sustain, and release (ADSR). *Attack* is the sound of a note as it begins, *decay* is the sound of a note as it softens immediately after the attack, *sustain* is the time a note sings after the attack and short decay, and *release* is the ending of the note.

melody
a logical series of notes that expresses a musical thought. There are two basic types of melodies; **conjunct** melodies move by step and small intervals, and **disjunct** melodies move by larger skips.

Pitch is the fundamental element of music vital to both melody and harmony and is very important in defining the **range** of notes possible for each specific instrument. Range governs each instrument's place in a large ensemble. Every instrument can play many notes; however, not all instruments are capable of playing all the notes we can hear. Each instrument has a specific range; for example, a flute, which plays notes in the high range, cannot produce the low notes associated with a tuba. Within the limit of each instrument's range are different qualities. A note, C for instance, played up high on a trumpet will be filled with tension and energy, whereas a C played low in the trumpet range will have a more relaxed and effortless sound. Astute composers are well aware of these changes and choose each pitch in accordance with an instrument's particular range and quality.

Every pitch has four elements that make up its sound: *attack, decay, sustain,* and *release* (ADSR). When we hear a note played by any instrument, it has this **envelope** of activities. Every envelope can be described by listening to the sound of the note as it begins (attack), softens from the peak of the attack (decay), sustains, and stops (release). Figure 3-2 shows the four activities of a single note.

Imagine and compare the envelope of a harp to that of a flute. The differences are dramatic evidence of the musical family each represents and the uniqueness of each instrument.

Melody is merely a logical progression of pitches. Melodies are often evaluated by their tuneful qualities. However, many great melodies are just the opposite: angular, disjointed, and difficult to sing. The song

Figure 3-2

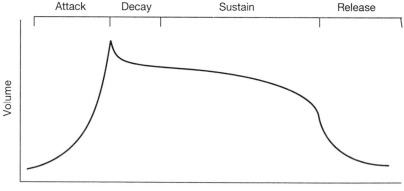

Billy Apple, *Untitled* (1967).
The lines of this light sculpture suggest progression and unity. It flows from a beginning point to a logical conclusion. Unlike the lines of a signature, these lines do not have a universally specific meaning; they only have meaning in the eyes of the viewer. Melody carries similar logic. Melodic lines can sweep and bend in interesting directions unified by a common sense of direction and goal. It is the listener who finds meaning in the flow of a melodic line. (Courtesy of the artist)

"Mary Had a Little Lamb" is a simple conjunct melody, while "When You Wish Upon a Star" is a disjunct melody. The first has notes that move small distances either up or down, and the second has large skips that move the melody over a much larger range.

The character of a melody can be shaped further by markings, placed above or below notes, indicating special treatment for that note. These **articulation markings** tell the performer to add emphasis or expression. For example, the marking ">" above a note means to accent that note, to make it louder than the ones before and after it. To shorten a note, separating it from the ones around it, a dot is placed above the note; this is called *staccato*. The opposite of staccato is *legato* (smoothly connecting the notes). There are many symbols to aid the performer in interpreting the character of the melody. Figure 3-3 is a written melody with several markings above the notes to help define the character of each note.

articulation markings symbols above or below a note to indicate special treatment such as *legato* (smooth and attached) or *staccato* (separated, detached).

Figure 3-3

Following is a list of the most common markings above notes and their meanings.

·	*staccato,* separate or shorten its sound
-	*tenuto,* hold the note to its full length
⌣	*legato,* connect the notes encompassed by the symbol (tie)
>	*legato* accent, emphasis this note above the ones around it
ʌ	*staccato* accent, emphasis this note but separate it from the ones around it
s ff	*sforzando,* very heavy accent

Tone

Every musical instrument has a unique quality of sound within which there is a variety of tonal qualities. A voice can sound round and rich, nasal and thin, airy and weak, or strong and profound. The tone of a single instrument can be modified by adding its sound to a second instrument; for example, a harp sounds different when a flute plays in unison with it. The possibilities of tone manipulation are infinite and impact both texture and harmony. **Orchestration** is the process of combining such variables of instrumental color and tone. There is an unlimited number of sounds and colors in the orchestra just by adding and subtracting the unique tone qualities of various instruments.

Composers manipulate the elements of music, filling the space of a composition to give life and expression to otherwise mathematical realities. Each element of music is very flexible and when combined, an infinite number of interplays is possible. If not, we would have exhausted all the melodies, rhythms, and harmonies long ago. However, the composer must share musical control of these elements with the performers. To enhance the expression of the music the conductor and performers provide interpretation. The **tempo** or speed of the music and the **dynamics** or volume can be controlled. Tempo and dynamics alone can change the character of a composition. Although often taken for granted their effect is tremendous. Faster tempos and louder dynamics make music increase in intensity. Volume and changes in volume add drama to melodies and vary the musical textures.

orchestration
the process of assigning instruments to musical ideas. Orchestration is part of the compositional process, important to the mood and spirit of a work.

tempo
the speed of a musical composition. The basic rhythmic pulse can be slow or fast or change gradually between fast and slow.

dynamics
various volume (loudness) levels, as well as gradual changes in volume. Italian terms describe the various volume levels between *piano* (soft) and *forte* (loud).

Dynamics are notated by using symbols ranging from soft to loud. The range of dynamic markings is as follows:

pp	*pianissimo*	(very soft)
p	*piano*	(soft)
mp	*mezzopiano*	(moderately soft)
mf	*mezzoforte*	(moderately loud)
f	*forte*	(loud)
ff	*fortissimo*	(very loud)

These terms are performed relative to one another; there is no exact volume level at which each should be played. Rather the relationship between them creates the difference between loud and soft.

Judgments to determine appropriate tempo and volume are necessary in each performance. The goal is to enhance each performance using tempos and dynamics specific to the moment. For this reason tempos are often indicated in terms that allow for variation such as ***allegro,*** meaning lively or fast, or ***grave,*** meaning seriously or slow. In the case of *allegro,* the music must have a tempo where it will be lively and seem fast. Beginning in the nineteenth century composers sometimes indicated the exact speed of the music by specifying how many beats should be played per minute; for example, the marking will show a *note value = beats/minute.* A metronome is a device used by musicians to determine specific tempos. A metronome marking of 120 means that there would be 120 beats each minute; by setting the metronome to 120, there would be a series of clicks at that exact tempo. Some common tempos are as follows:

allegro
stylistic term meaning fast or lively.

grave
a stylistic term indicating the mood and possible tempo of a performance; very slow, seriously.

prestissimo	as fast as possible
presto	very fast
vivace	fast, lively
allegro	brisk, fast
allegretto	moderately fast, lightly
moderato	moderate
andante	walking tempo, moderately slow
adagio	slow leisurely
grave	very slow, seriously
largo	very slow, broadly

Performers, using dynamic and style markings, are therefore required to make decisions that help interpret the composer's intent within a realm of musicality.

 *Harmony*

chord
the simultaneous sounding of three or more notes. In tonal music chords have specific harmonic relationships to one another, and chords are used to accompany melodies.

Chords are the combined sound of three or more notes, which, when played together, form a logical relationship. There are many different chords in a single composition; each chord assumes a relationship to the other chords in the same piece. Consonant chords are made up of notes that blend and dissonant chords contain notes that create tension when played together. The relationship between consonant and dissonant chords helps give music a feeling of building tensions and resulting resolutions. The progression of chords and the manner in which they move determines the greater concept of harmony. While harmony often goes unnoticed, it creates mood and fills the texture. Along with rhythm and meter, chords create motion by changing in a regular pattern or rhythm **(harmonic rhythm).** As chords move one to another, they reinforce the meter and shape each **phrase** or unified musical thought. Some phrases end like a simple sentence, others like a question.

harmonic rhythm
the frequency and regularity of chord changes in a composition. A pulse is established by the regular movement from one chord to another.

phrase
the musical equivalent of a spoken phrase, clause, or sentence; a melodic statement with a recognizable beginning, middle, and end.

 *Texture*

As pitch, harmony, and motion interact, there is a resulting activity level that runs the gamut from simple to complex. As each element of music intensifies, it further thickens the overall texture. It is the very balance of all these variables that characterizes the different textures within a single composition.

Change in activity is not the only element of textural change. Change in pitch and dynamic range also affects the overall texture. Texture fluctuates with each combination and change in range and activity. There are even extreme situations where silence affects texture; the need for sound or resolution of tension can make silence intense and uncomfortable.

monophony
a single melody with no other musical accompaniment; for example, a Gregorian chant.

polyphony
the performance of two or more melodic parts that are independent and relatively equal in melodic content.

homophony
a single melody supported by chords rather than by additional melodies.

Three easily identifiable textures that parallel the development of music since A.D. 900 are monophony, polyphony, and homophony. **Monophony** is a single melodic idea being sung or played with no accompaniment at all. Even if several performers play the same melody, it is still monophonic. **Polyphony** (or counterpoint) is two or more independent melodic lines performed simultaneously. Polyphonic music focuses attention equally on each melody; each part has melodic integrity and also acts as a supporting accompaniment to the others. The song "Row, Row, Row Your Boat" sung as a round is polyphonic. **Homophony** sets a single melody above the other parts that, in turn, work

Max Ernst, *The Eye of Silence* (1943-44). Oil on canvas. 42¼ × 55½".
Texture is the combination of activities and intensity. In this twentieth-century painting
many shapes melt into one another. This unreal landscape is organic, with smooth shapes
in juxtaposition with ragged rocklike formations. The texture is very busy but does not
represent realistic shapes or objects. This imaginary landscape suggests both fantasy and
mystery. Observing or listening to complex textures requires increased attention; otherwise
perceptions become clouded and confused. (Washington University Gallery of Art, St. Louis.)

together providing chords in accompaniment. A voice accompanied by a
guitar is homophonic. Composers often combine these three textures
into a single work to create interesting textural variety.

Symbols: Traditional and Nontraditional Notation

Musical notation has changed dramatically over the early years of music
and is still subject to change in contemporary compositions. Following
are a few examples of music notations throughout history. Notice the
gradual move to the universally accepted notation of the seventeenth
century.

Like any language, symbols change as new sounds are discovered
and the need to communicate musical ideas grows. The earliest music
was transmitted orally. Musicians sang and played for each other and
imitated sound, posture, and technique. As more and more musicians

Medieval, Renaissance, and Modern forms of musical notation

Figure 3-4

performed together the need for organization became paramount. A highly developed symbol set was slowly adopted to organize the performance of orchestras and choirs. Notation has become so specific today that musicians can produce an amazingly close facsimile of the composer's original ideas without previously hearing the work.

Figure 3-4 shows a staff of lines and spaces that define exact pitches for musicians. The letter names from A to G make up the musical alphabet.

Pitches between these letter names require a ♯ **(sharp)** or a ♭ **(flat)** to move the sound up or down by a small musical distance, a **half step.** Therefore the pitch A can be moved up to A♯ or moved down to A♭. (See Figure 3-5.) These alterations are called **accidentals,** although they are not accidents at all. The Western European musical system is built on a foundation of half steps. The distance between any two notes **(interval)** in a melody or chord is described by the number of half steps that separate them. Large intervals, of course, have several half steps between notes and small intervals have very few.

Another visual pattern familiar to most schooled musicians is the piano **keyboard.** Because it is arranged in a way that shows half and whole steps clearly, the keyboard can be helpful for visualizing intervals and scales. The keyboard has become the musical calculator for composers and arrangers. Study the keyboard with the names of the notes superimposed on the keys in Figure 3-6. Notice on the keyboard how the notes repeat, starting with A once the note G is reached. When

sharp
to raise the pitch of a note by half a step. The symbol is ♯.

flat
to lower the pitch of a note by half a step. The symbol is ♭.

half step
the smallest distance or interval between two notes in Western European music.

accidentals
symbols placed in front of a note to move the pitch up or down by a half step. A sharp moves the pitch up, a flat moves the pitch down, and a natural sign removes the flat or sharp.

interval
the distance between two notes.

keyboard
(visual) the arrangement of keys on a piano or synthesizer.

Figure 3-5

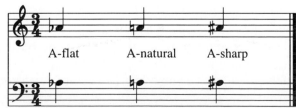

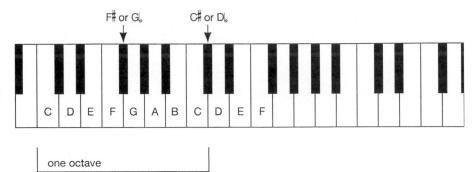

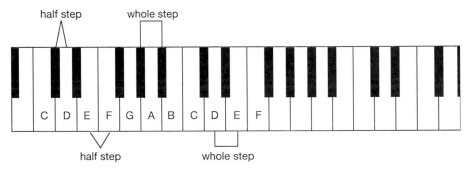

Figure 3-6

octave
the distance (in terms of pitch) between two notes with the same letter name. For example, from the note C up to the next note named C is one octave.

scale
any of several sequences of pitches dividing an octave into whole steps and half steps. The octave has twelve half steps, which is the **chomatic scale**. Major and minor scales are built by using a combination of whole steps and half steps.

mode, modal
A scale of whole steps and half steps. There are seven common modes, including the major and minor scales.

major
a mode based on a scale. This mode is the most familiar mode in our culture today. When compared with the minor mode it seems bright and lively.

minor
another mode based on a scale. It sounds darker than the common major mode.

key, tonal area
One note is more stable than any other, and the key is defined by this note. All other notes in the same key are less stable and eventually lead back to the primary note. The key area establishes a **tonality** where all notes and chords are related to the tonal area or single note.

the starting letter name reappears it is one **octave** away from the starting point. Patterns of seven notes within one octave are used to build **scales** on which compositions are centered. Each scale contains every letter name and progresses up the octave in a pattern of whole steps and half steps. The location of the half steps determine the **mode** and resulting tone color of the music. The most common modes are the **major** and the darker **minor** sonority.

Tonality and Atonality

Once whole steps and half steps are in place to build scales, a single note appears as the most stable sound when compared to the other notes in the scale. This primary note is called the tonal center. The tonal center gives the scale its name. For example, in the **key** of C we should expect the note C to be the position of rest and stability. **Tonality** is this sense of hierarchical pitch relationship. All notes in a scale have a feeling of tension, with the primary note of the key area being the most stable. In large works such as Mozart's Symphony in G minor we know from its title that the most stable key area for the work is G and that the sonority or mode is the darker minor. In addition, when the music moves to other tonal areas or keys, a return to G minor should be expected, making the return to that key a rewarding experience. This single element of establishing a key area, moving away from it, and then returning is fundamental to many of the large and small forms we will study.

The process of moving from one tonality to another is called **modulation.** The introduction of notes from a new key area will move the tonal center to a new note; that is, the half steps in the original scale have been moved. The feeling of modulation is one of instability.

modulation
the movement from one key area to another.

 Tonic and Dominant

Because there are seven notes in a tonal scale and each has a different feeling of stability, chords built on each of these notes must also have various levels of stability. For instance, the chord using the fundamental note C in the key of C is understandably the most stable. The importance of this chord is soon recognized as home, our ultimate destination. Each of the seven chords in a key area is given a Roman numeral corresponding to the number of the scale upon which it was built. (See Figure 3-7).

The most stable chord is **I,** called the **tonic.** The next most important chord is **V,** or the **dominant.** Its function in tonal music is to announce the imminent arrival of the tonic. The dominant to tonic motion provides a sense of completion and rest that is called a **cadence** and ends phrases. An extended cadence to end a movement or work is called a **coda,** again using the tonic and dominant chords.

Other chords exhibit a similar sense of resolution; however, none are as powerful as the tonic-dominant relationship. Throughout our study, the motion from the tonic to the dominant and the subsequent return will provide much of the architectural foundation for the larger works.

tonic (I)
the chord built on the first degree of the scale. It has a feeling of rest and completion.

dominant (V)
the chord built on the fifth degree of the scale. It requires resolution to the tonic chord.

cadence
the end of a musical idea. It can be the end of a phrase, theme group, or movement.

coda
the musical extension at the end of a movement or performance. It can be very short or quite long and developmental.

Figure 3-7

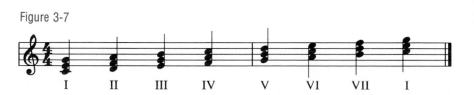

The Move from Tonality to Atonality

A move away from tonality occurred in the late nineteenth century. The technique required composers to avoid any tonal center, and composers began to seek ways of avoiding a sense of key or tonal center. This was accomplished by using all the twelve notes in the octave instead of just seven. No tonal center can evolve because all twelve notes are used and no single note is emphasized more than another. This technique required the elimination of whole steps in scales. The resulting scale of only half steps is called the **chromatic scale.** Tonal works are described as being chromatic when melodic and harmonic motions use series of half steps moving from key to key. An entire movement or work that is based on pure chromatic relationships using all twelve notes of the octave is **atonal.** Compare the sound of the tonal melody (Figure 3-8) to that of the atonal melody (Figure 3-9).

chromatic
the use of half steps in melodies and chords suggesting movement from one key to another.

atonal, atonality
music associated with the twentieth century where the tonality or key area is avoided.

Figure 3-8   **Tonal Melody**

Figure 3-9   **Atonal Melody**

Chapter 4

MUSICAL ARCHITECTURE

 The Need for Structure

Musical compositions present a variety of sounds, ranging from beautiful, calm sounds to aggressive, dissonant sounds. The spectrum from consonance to dissonance can be found in a single composition. Compositions must be structured to allow for such diversity of sound and, at the same time, give a feeling of unity. A successful musical experience is similar in structure to the three stages of taking a vacation. First, there is the excitement of going to a new place. Second, while away, you find yourself experiencing new and often surprising environments. Finally, there is great joy in returning home to familiarity and predictability. Musical forms, both large and small, share some element of such a journey.

 Small Forms

Repetition and **contrast** make musical journeys interesting and rewarding. Repetition gives listeners time to become familiar with melodies. Contrast, on the other hand, brings new musical ideas to bear

repetition
repeating melodies to build familiarity and stability. Composers use repetition and contrast to build large formal musical structures.

contrast
one of the primary techniques used to construct binary and ternary forms. Contrasting themes or melodies add interest and spur a sense of return when the original melody reappears.

■ *45*

A	(usually repeated)		B	(usually repeated)	
Tonic		new key or dominant			return to tonic

A	(may be repeated)		B			A		
Tonic		cadence	Dominant or new key		cadence	Tonic		final cadence

Figure 4-1 Binary and Ternary Forms

ternary form
a three-part formal structure using contrast and repetition of themes (A B A or A A B A).

binary form
a formal structure using theme repetition and contrast (A B or A A B B).

bridge (B)
the contrasting section in a song form (A A′ **B** A). This contrasting section has a different chord progression and melody.

song, song cycles
art songs from the nineteenth century. Cycles were a series of poems set to music that related some common story.

on the now familiar melody. Without contrast there could be no sense of returning to the familiar melodies. To study the structure or form of a piece we use letters to designate the thematic areas. The vacation trip would be a **ternary form;** that is, **A, B,** and a return to **A.** The **binary form** has two contrasting melodic areas, **A** and **B.** Repetition is a vital part of this form expanding the final form to **A A B B.** See Figure 4-1.

Most songs rely on the ternary form. It is common to have an opening melody that repeats with new words (A + A′), and, for contrast, a middle section with a new melody and chords called the **bridge** (B). The first melody and chords eventually return, completing the form of **A A′ B A.** This formula for **song** writing has been used throughout history and is still very popular today in commercial song writing.

Wayne Thiebaud, *Pie Counter* (1963). Oil 30 × 36″. Simple repetition and contrast create structure and balance. This painting relies on the viewer's immediate organizational impulses to group and separate. There are rows of similar desserts; none are out of place. Such organization gives comfort and solidarity to the painting. Any modification would add tension; for example, if one piece of pie were in a row of cakes, it would disturb the balance between repetition and contrast. There would be a need to put it back in its ''proper place.'' Placement of melodies and melodic sections can create similar feelings of stability or tension. (Collection of Whitney Museum of American Art, N.Y. Larry Alfrich Foundation Fund.)

Large Forms and Multimovement Works

Musicians analyze large works by tracing melodic and harmonic structures. A large work such as a symphony is composed of several smaller related sections called **movements** that are in some way tied together. Each movement itself is a complete musical structure and is structured using repetition and contrast of thematic material. The length of individual movements varies considerably.

movement
a self-contained structure that is only part of a larger work. For example, a symphony has four separate movements.

Standard Large Structures

Following is a list of the most common large structures we will study. Notice the placement and contrasting tempos of the major sections or movements.

Symphony: (developed in the 1700s) Usually in four movements whose tempos are usually fast, slow, minuet or scherzo (triple meter), fast.

Suite: (most active in the 1600s-1700s) Overture or prelude followed by several movements based on dance forms. The movements are not related by theme or motive, and the last dance form usually has a very fast tempo.

Sonata: Music that is played (instrumental). The form developed into a larger work with three movements; tempos are usually fast, slow, fast. (Later, a four-movement structure was standard to Beethoven.) Sonatas may be for a solo instrument or for two to four instruments (duo or trio sonatas).

Cantata: (most active in the 1600s-1700s) Music that is sung; small-scale instrumental movements, recitatives, arias, choruses, accompanied by harpsichord, organ, or small orchestra. Cantatas focus on sacred topics.

Concerto: (first appeared in the late 1600s) Three movements; tempos are usually fast, slow, fast. First performed by orchestra and a group of soloists (concerto grosso). The form evolved in the classical period (late 1700s) to a single instrumental soloist accompanied by a full orchestra.

Oratorio: This form, along with opera, originated in Italy in the 1600s, a choral work similar to an opera but with no staging or costumes. The subject of the drama is based on biblical themes. The work includes small instrumental preludes and interludes with choral recitatives, arias, and choruses, performed in a concert setting.

Opera: (began in the early 1600s) A staged music drama with a fully developed text called a **libretto,** character development, and descriptive music. Some include extensive orchestral preludes and interludes and choral recitatives, arias, ensembles, and choruses.

Liturgical Mass: (after 1600) Orchestra and chorus with soloists. Movements are based on the text of the traditional Catholic liturgy. These works also incorporate arias, recitatives, and choruses.

Passion: (1700s) Similar to the oratorio in structure and use of orchestra, recitatives, arias, and choruses. These works are based on the events of Holy Week.

Large movements, like small forms, require contrast and repetition to glue the ideas together; however, each movement may itself be larger in scope than an entire smaller form. Large movements generally present more melodic repetitions with several new areas for contrasting themes. The transitions between major musical sections may introduce small themes merely to carry the listener from a large (A) section to an equally large (B) section. The diagrams for the larger forms will point out where these **transitional themes** are likely to appear. Because of the tremendous momentum these large works develop, cadences and endings are often extended to allow the work to unwind and come to rest.

Following are diagrams of the most commonly used structures we will encounter in this study. Refer to these diagrams when listening to

transitional themes
short melodic sequences or motives that provide melodic progression between larger thematic areas.

Christo, *Running Fence* (1972-76).
Large structures expressing singular concepts have consumed creative individuals in all areas of the arts. This fence, made of 165,000 yards of white nylon, was 18 feet tall and 24½ miles long and ran from Bodega Bay across the California hills of Marin and Sonoma counties. As you can see, it wandered across the land enhancing its shape and curvatures. Because the material was a shimmering white, it reflected different colors throughout the day and evening, from blues and purples to yellows and browns, and its flexibility in the wind gave the fence an animated quality. The fence stood for two weeks before it was dismantled. Unless the viewer is in a plane, only small sections of the fence can be seen at a time; the entire structure can only be imagined. The flow of fabric is the unifying aspect of this enormous work of art.

similar structures. Remember, just as great cathedrals built in the same historical period are similar in many respects, they also differ, making each unique. Significant variances from the standard forms shown here should be expected. It is the change from what is expected that makes many of history's great works interesting and enduring.

The diagrams use letters to show contrasting musical areas and Roman numerals to show where the tonic-dominant relationship is important to the overall structure.

Theme and variations (Figure 4-2) is perhaps the most fundamental and familiar form. Every time someone sings a melody over and over, changes vary the original melody. If the process is continued, the melody may eventually become so transformed that it is no longer recognizable. The composer uses a similar process to develop a musical idea. The final statement of the theme is usually very similar to the first statement, creating a sense of return. The scope and diversity of the variations depend on how organic the original theme and how skillful and imaginative the composer is. The harmonic structure generally remains constant from variation to variation.

Rondo (Figure 4-3) is a form built on the repetition of a single theme and separated by new and contrasting themes. An original theme is presented first, followed by a contrasting theme. The first theme is repeated followed by another contrasting theme. The contrasting themes act as bridges between the repeating first theme and are interesting and important in their own right. **(A B A C A D A)**. The return to one of the contrasting themes is common, combining rondo and ternary structures.

The **sonata-allegro** or **sonata** form (Figure 4-4) uses a large-scale ternary form as its overall structure. Each part of the large form (A B A′) has specific names. The first (A) is the **exposition** and has two themes or theme groups. The term **theme group** is given related material in the

theme and variations
a formal structure of a single work or movement of a larger work. Once a theme is stated, it is varied to the point of obscurity and is usually restated at the end of the selection.

rondo
a formal structure in which the first theme is restated between a series of new themes (A B A C A D A).

sonata-allegro form
the large structure used for the first movement of a symphony. Themes are exposed, developed, and recapitulated.

exposition
the first section of the sonata-allegro form in which two themes (or theme groups) are presented, the first in the tonic and the second in the dominant or relative minor.

theme group
a tonal area that takes the place of a theme in a sonata-allegro form.

Figure 4-2 Theme and Variations

A	A^1	A^2	A^3	
Theme is stated	First variation of theme	Second variation of theme	Third variation of theme	etc.

Figure 4-3 Rondo (in combination with ternary form)

A	B	A	C	A	B	A
Original theme	New theme	Repeat of original theme	New theme	Original theme	Repeat of second theme	Final statement of original theme

A			B	A		

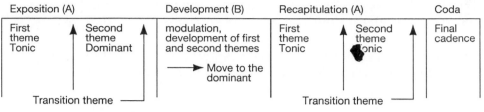

Figure 4-4 Sonata-allegro Form

same key, especially if more than one idea is presented. The first group is stated in the tonic key area, and the second group is stated in the dominant or relative major. The middle section or (B) is the **development,** where material from either or both theme groups is broken down and reworked in an environment of modulation and rhythmic diversity. This section is more unstable than the exposition and drives the movement to the dominant and eventually to the last section called the **recapitulation**. The recapitulation states both theme groups again; this time both remain in the tonic key. Between each large section are transitional themes connecting theme groups or modulating to new keys. As this form developed in the nineteenth century, the final cadence was often extended, creating a long and dramatic coda.

The **minuet and trio** form (Figure 4-5) is based on an early dance form characterized by its triple meter of ¾. The first section, **minuet,** and second section, **trio,** were originally two separate dances. The order of the dances, minuet-trio-minuet, builds a ternary form (A B A). The minuet form and the trio form by themselves are binary forms. The repeats typical of the binary form exist in both the minuet and the trio; however, the repeats are not observed when the minuet returns. The minuet and trio contrast in several ways. The minuet is in the tonic key and the trio is in a related key, usually the dominant. The trio is traditionally quieter with a more flowing melody. When the name changed in the 1800s to **scherzo and trio,** the form of the minuet and trio remained the same; however, the tempo increased. This form, a combination of binary and ternary, yields an interesting sense of repetition and contrast.

development
the middle section of a sonata-allegro form. Thematic material is modulated, broken down into smaller units, and changed and developed.

recapitulation
the last section of a sonata-allegro form in which the two primary themes (theme groups) are restated in the tonic key after the development.

minuet and trio
a dance form derived from earlier suites. This three-part form (A B A) remained a part (the third movement) of the symphony and string quartet until it was modified and replaced by the scherzo and trio form.

scherzo and trio
a musical form designed after the minuet form. Scherzos are usually followed by a trio that returns to the scherzo themes.

Figure 4-5 Minuet and Trio

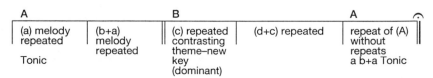

A		B		A	
(a) melody repeated	(b+a) melody repeated	(c) repeated contrasting theme–new key (dominant)	(d+c) repeated	repeat of (A) without repeats	
Tonic				a b+a Tonic	

Contrapuntal or Polyphonic Forms

Counterpoint is the technique of writing multiple melodies that accompany one another but that retain a level of independence. There are two forms of contrapuntal writing, imitative and nonimitative. Nonimitative counterpoint has multiple parts that do not imitate melodic ideas in each part; the different melodic parts accompany one another but do not have to share melodic material.

The most common imitative contrapuntal form is the **canon.** The simple overlapping of the same melody, without change, constitutes a canon. "Row, Row, Row Your Boat" is a true canon. One part begins alone and the other two parts wait and enter consecutively on the next two phrases. As one part finishes the melody, it stops while the others continue until the last part finishes alone.

The **passacaglia** (Figure 4-6) is one of several forms based on the repetition of a **ground bass.** This form uses repetition rather than imitation. The movement is based on the repetition of a melodic idea in the bass above which other melodies are created. The number of repetitions is entirely up to the composer. In the strictest ground bass compositions, there are very few changes, if any, in the repetitions of the passacaglia statement.

The single movement **fugue** (Figure 4-7) weaves a dense musical fabric. This form uses both imitative and nonimitative techniques. The

canon, canonic
a musical form in which a melody is followed by and overlaps the same melody; also called a "round." A familiar canon is "Row, Row, Row Your Boat."

passacaglia
a contrapuntal style. Variations are written over a repeating bass line (ostinato).

ground bass
a repeated melody in the bass (passacaglia) that supports melodies above; also called basso ostinato.

fugue
a musical form that uses subjects, answers, and countersubjects in an overlapping manner. It is related to a very complicated round or canon.

Figure 4-6 **Passacaglia**

Melodic material above is free from repetition

Ground bass	Ground bass first repeat	Ground bass second repeat	Ground bass third repeat	etc.

Figure 4-7 **Fugue**

soprano voice
subject	counter	free material – – – – – – – – – – – – – – – – –
	subject	

alto voice | answer | counter | free material – – – – – – – – – – |

tenor voice | subject | counter | free material – – – – – –

bass voice | answer | counter | free material

subject
the first statement in a fugue. Once answered by another part, it enters again in a third part.

answer
the statement in a fugue that overlaps the original subject. It follows and overlaps each statement of the subject.

countersubject
a melodic statement performed in a duet fashion with the answer in a fugue. It is a complimentary melody and supplies motives and complexity to the texture.

fugue begins with a single part or voice stating a **subject;** a second voice follows with a similar but slightly different **answer.** The third voice repeats the subject again, and the fourth voice repeats the answer. After each part states its required subject or answer, the fugue commonly proceeds to a **countersubject.** Following the countersubject, each part continues with free material derived from the subject or answer. After this freer section, there is usually an abbreviated return to the subjects, answers, and countersubjects.

Benjamin Britten composed a work specifically to introduce the instrumental families of the orchestra. *The Young Person's Guide to the Orchestra* introduces two of the forms discussed above, theme and variations and fugue. Despite its title the work is not childlike; it is a twentieth-century composition based on a theme written by Henry Purcell nearly 200 years earlier. Listen to it as many times as you need to learn the sounds of each instrument and section.

Listening Notes

Benjamin Britten, *The Young Person's Guide to the Orchestra,* op. 34 (1946).

The two structures used in this work, theme and variations and fugue, offer an exciting introduction to the orchestra. The theme is played, in turn, by each family in the orchestra.

0:00 The work begins with a unison statement of the theme by the entire orchestra. Notice the percussion instruments and xylophone.

0:28 First the woodwinds state the theme.

0:53 Next the brass, with the lower brass instruments entering first.

1:14 The strings take their turn.

1:34 The last section is the percussion. Notice that the timpani are tuned to the first three notes of the theme.

1:49 The theme is stated a fifth time by the entire orchestra. The variations, featuring sections and solo instruments, follow. See if you can identify each instrument with every new variation. Notice the many colors available in the percussion section.

2:09 Variation 1—flutes and piccolo play a very active melody while the harp supplies low notes.

2:40   Variation 2—oboes play a slower melodic line; strings accompany.

3:30   Variation 3—clarinets play a melody build on arpeggios; bass notes from the tuba create a marchlike texture.

4:16   Variation 4—bassoons enter, with aggressive chords supplied by the string section.

5:12   Variation 5—violins, brass accompany. This variation ends with the violins plucking the strings (pizzicato).

5:49   Variation 6—violas play a slower melody, bassoons help feed the texture.

6:50   Variation 7—cellos; soft clarinet and harp accompaniment.

7:57   Variation 8—string basses; shaker bells and woodwinds accompany.

8:55   Variation 9—harp; strings repeatedly bow the same note, creating an intense but soft accompaniment.

9:47   Variation 10—French horns enter in chords echoed by the orchestra; they separate melodically in a brief overlapping idea.

10:40   Variation 11—trumpets; snare drum plays a cadence, giving the theme a galloping sound.

11:09   Variation 12—trombones and tuba play a slow rich melody; bassoons end the variation.

12:06   Variation 13—percussion instruments conclude the section of variations.

The fugue follows; each instrument enters again, this time playing the subject. The instruments appear in the same order as heard in the variations.

13:55   The subject of the fugue is first stated by the piccolo.

14:03   Next by the flutes and overlap the piccolo.

14:10   The oboes.

14:16   The clarinets.

14:26   The bassoons. The texture thickens as all the woodwinds continue to play.

14:37   The first violins enter and are followed immediately by the second violins.

14:45   The violas enter and are soon followed by the cellos and finally by the string basses.

15:07   The harp plays the subject.

15:19 The French horns are the first bass instruments to state the subject of the fugue.

15:24 The trumpets are next.

15:32 The low brass; first the trombones then the tubas follow.

15:38 The percussion section makes the last statement of the subject.

Following the percussion section, the theme by Purcell is played by the entire orchestra, climaxed by the return of the percussion.

15:48 The theme is played slowly by the brass section while the strings and woodwinds continue to spin out material from the fugue subject.

16:18 The percussion instruments enter forcefully.

16:33 A final chord ends the work. On subsequent listenings notice the various combinations of the instruments and how they interact to build interesting textures.

 Visual Elements in Musical Performance

Many visual aspects of music help to organize and structure musical events, and not all are compositional. The most common visual tool for the listener is the conductor. By watching the **conductor** listeners are informed of the importance of melodies and rhythms. By using traditional conducting patterns conductors shape music by varying tempos and dynamics while dictating the tempo and beat. Figure 4-8 illustrates the patterns for the most common meter groupings.

Dance offers another visual aspect of musical performance. From folk dances to the most developed forms of ballet, music supplies rhythmic accents and flowing melodies that suggest movement. Dances

conductor
the musician in front of an orchestra or choir who uses hand, arm, and body motions to direct the interpretation of the music.
dance
repeated rhythms that support or suggest movement.

Figure 4-8 Conducting Patterns

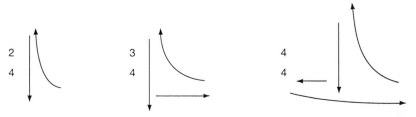

The Negro Ballet performs with the first all-African-American symphony orchestra under the direction of Wen Talbert

such as the mazurka, sarabande, gigue, or waltz all require specific rhythms. Specific rhythms are associated with more contemporary dances such as the fox trot and the twist and with dance style such as reggae, disco, break dancing, and rap. The relationship between music and dance is twofold, with music accompanying movement and movement accompanying music.

Opera and **musical theater** require a blend of sight and sound. Meaning drawn from a story line helps to organize and unify themes and motives. In turn the interpretive powers of music enrich feelings and help define emotion. The film industry provides a prime example of music's ability to manipulate and develop emotion.

Music videos have developed over the last few years, accompanying music with a vast array of visuals. Everything from concerts to abstract scenes with visual effects are seen in this medium. Music videos have become a creative outlet for combining music, dance, and stagecraft with specialized musical and visual effects. In fact, the very meaning of some music videos comes from the visual aspects of the performance. Most songs stand alone without the accompanying video; however, the link between sight and sound often determines a song's success in today's market.

musical theater
a dramatic production based on everyday themes featuring vocal and instrumental sounds that relate to traditional musical styles.

music video
a video production that accompanies or interprets a song.

Part II

STYLISTIC PERIODS IN MUSIC

Chapter 5

THE MEDIEVAL/ GOTHIC PERIOD:
Extant to 1450

Music Outline of the Medieval/Gothic Period

1. The earliest notated music, **chant,** was monophonic.

2. Sacred music was notated, collected, and preserved; secular music before 1200 was passed down through the oral tradition.

3. The move toward **polyphony** began with a technique called **organum.**

4. Polyphony began to flourish around 1150 in the writings of Leonin and Perotin, who were associated with the **School of Notre Dame. Measured rhythm** solidified a metric feeling.

5. Composition after organum continued to be based on chant through a technique known as *cantus firmus*.

6. An essay entitled *Ars Nova* (early 1300s) heralded a new approach to and a wider appreciation of music.

Preliterate Music and Its Function

We do not know when people began to distinguish that "serious" music was different from "popular" music; a great deal of music has been classified as high art today merely because it is old. At the same time, much music in many forms has been lost altogether. In ancient times all art practices were passed from generation to generation through folklore. History was communicated through song and chant. By remembering a melody, the words associated with it were remembered. This oral tradition provided a record of historical events, entertainment, and a sense of family (or national) pride.

Music is found to varying degrees in all societies. In very early cultures most ritualistic activity was organized and accompanied by music, and music was a major part of all group activities. Individuals, families, and villages drew strength and identity from singing and dancing. Participation and sharing were primary concerns. The concept of a performer and audience was not highly developed. In this photo, Kundu drummers perform their traditional dance at a festival in Papua, New Guinea.

Tribal music is still found in different parts of the world. By studying aborigines in Australia, India, and Africa we have learned that music was used to bond tribes and clans together, to communicate heritage, and for play and dance. Obviously the music could not be recorded or preserved, and without the sound to guide us, we can only guess as to its nature. Assuredly, musical substance and style has shifted over millions of years; however, music remains a vital part of today's society. We continue to use music today to tell stories, dance, play, and bond relationships. Clubs, churches, schools, and families lean heavily on the gift of shared music.

Because no system of notation existed in ancient times, music has the shortest documented history of the fine arts. Historians surmise the nature of musical activities before A.D. 500 from a variety of sources such as pictures, drawings in wall sketches, statues, ancient urns, and writings. Much is left to our imagination. The earliest notated music is from approximately A.D. 500. A more precise notation appeared around A.D. 900 when sacred music was successfully collected and preserved. The secular music of that time was not written down and has been lost.

Medieval Music: Early Sacred Music

Gregorian chant is a single melody with a Latin text. The music was used to accompany parts of a religious service. The chants collected by Pope Gregory I were credited to him through legend, but many of them existed long before his lifetime. These chant melodies and other collections such as the **Byzantine** and **Ambrosian** chant are important for two reasons. First, they represent an unparalleled concern for melodic construction in music history, and second, they supplied musical material for other original compositions for hundreds of years.

During the Medieval period (approximately A.D. 900–1100) a notational system was developing for these unaccompanied melodies. The melodic notation was very ornate and represented the detailed melodies in early church chant. This musical notation was specific, but it did not include the free ornamentations that were surely added in performance. Chant could not be notated with rigidity. The rhythm is flexible and fluid; chant possesses a unique expressive freedom brought to life by the performer. Although the stylistic elements can never be exactly determined, the complex melodic flow represented by the notation must have had a highly developed sound. Performances today are a product of research and are probably quite accurate.

Gregorian chant
a form of medieval chant (monophony). There are several collections of chant, and Pope Gregory I assembled this collection. Other collections are named after the individual who collected them or after the location where they were collected, for example, **Ambrosian** and **Byzantine** chants.

Early music notation itself was often a work of art. Monks spent many hours copying manuscripts, and the process was naturally very slow. The first letter on the page could be elaborated by using brilliant colors and gold leaf. Choir books were copied in a very large format so that several singers could share one copy. It would have taxed the patience of even the most dedicated monk to provide a copy for each choir member.

mode
a scale of whole steps and half steps. Each mode is defined by where the half steps are placed in the scale. Each chant is based on a specific mode.

The melodies in individual chants were based on early church **modes** or scales. To our ears these scale constructions sound distant and otherwordly, although we are familiar with similar sounds from movies depicting the Middle Ages or Renaissance. Two of these church modes gave birth to the major and minor sonorities common today in western folk music.

Listening Notes

Introit, *Gaudeamus.*

Pay particular attention to the cadences of each melodic phrase. At each phrase ending, ornaments were used to close the musical thought. There is usually a particular pitch around which the chant is centered. The pitch and range of the melodic line determined the mode of the chant. The resonance you hear in this recording is typical of the church settings in which chant was sung. The echo gives the music a lofty and serious tone. Notice the intricate melodic passages where the melody has several notes for one syllable of text (**melisma**).

melisma
singing several notes per syllable. Some melismas are very long with many notes sung using one syllable of text.

0:00	Unison melodic line, male choir, melismatic setting.
0:16	Second phrase, still two or more notes per syllable; phrase seems to extend beyond the predictable cadence.
0:38	End of long phrase and the beginning of a new one.
0:59	New phrase, still melismatic.
1:17	New section; a more declamatory setting, one or two notes per syllable.
2:00	Strong cadence, "Amen."
2:07	Return to melismatic setting, "Gaudeamus."
2:31	New phrase.
2:38	Extension to phrase.
3:04	Cadence, new phrase.
3:22	Final cadence.

Palatine Chapel of Charlemagne, Aachen (A.D. 792–805).

As well as being an artistic expression, chant served a very important function. It was a vehicle for talking to large congregations. Many of the chants used by priests and soloists were centered around a particular pitch. In a cathedral, as in any large room or hall, particular resonating pitches would naturally amplify when sounded by a voice. For large congregations to hear the recited parts of the Mass the pitch of the room needed to correspond with the primary pitch of the chant. This was a successful form of amplification. Gifted performers and priests were undoubtedly aware of this "divine phenomenon" and, without the knowledge of music physics, would find the pitch and chant not knowing the reasons for its effectiveness. Whether chant was written to correspond with the resonating nature of cathedrals or whether cathedrals were constructed to enhance the beauty of the spoken and sung voice is an interesting question.

Chant remains the oldest known music that has a notational system specific enough to be performed today. The sound of chant, although very old, is not a surprisingly new sound to us today as it has never really left our culture. The Catholic church used Latin chant until the 1960s. Greek Orthodox and high Lutheran churches still use chant formulae to recite their liturgy. As a result of its persistence in the sacred world, chant has enjoyed the longest traditional existence of any musical style.

The Move to Polyphony

The dramatic move to polyphony developed slowly, expanding the monophonic texture into a polyphonic texture. The first step was perhaps unconscious. As women were not allowed to sing in the early church, men's and boys' voices dominated the chant performance. Because their voices had not yet changed the boys sang one octave higher than the men. The upper melody was the same as the lower melody and moved in parallel octaves.

The next step toward polyphony was to sing parallel melodies using another, very consonant, interval. The distance of four or five notes was the natural choice; they are the next two notes in the overtone series (see Chapter 1). This process, called **parallel organum** (see Figure 5-1), was simple. All singers began on the same note, then one part of the group would sing up the scale four or five notes. Once the desired interval was obtained, the two parts would sing in parallel motion until a cadence, at which time the interval would be closed the same way it was opened. The new melody added above the original chant was probably improvised at first, especially when there were only two singers instead of a choir; however, the notated organum part appeared very precise and maintained a strict interval throughout the performance.

In parallel organum the two parts moved as one; this was the first dramatic step toward independent melodic parts. Independence slowly infiltrated the two parts, first through ornamentation and eventually

organum
a two-part form of early polyphony. Each part is sung in parallel either at a fourth, fifth, or octave apart. There are three forms of organum: **parallel**, **free**, and **melismatic**.

Figure 5-1 Parallel Organum

Figure 5-2 Free Organum

through composition, leading to a form called **free organum** (see Figure 5-2). Instead of both parts moving in the same direction they could now move in both opposite and parallel directions; in free organum and parallel organum both parts changed notes at the same time.

Melismatic organum (see Figure 5-3) was the next stylistic development toward independence of parts. The upper part would freely add several notes above each syllable of text in the lower part. The lower part usually had one long note per syllable waiting for the **melisma,** several notes per syllable, above to finish. It was not long before the independence of the two parts moved from free and melismatic organum to a more equal and independent relationship between parts.

The transitional period between monophonic and polyphonic music was radical and not without argument. The church was skeptical of the increased dissonance and took issue with the inclusion of secular melodies. The conflict was probably similar to the impact rock 'n' roll instruments and compositions had on contemporary worship services.

The importance of chant did not diminish with the advent of polyphony. Beginning in the early twelfth century chant was borrowed as a basis for new composition. A preexisting chant or part of a chant was selected as a ***cantus firmus,*** above which new melodies would be written. At first the *cantus firmus* was slowed to a drone, and the new melodies danced above it in striking contrast. Later the *cantus firmus* was altered by the composer, minimizing the contrast and making the

cantus firmus
a melody, most often a Gregorian chant, used as the lowest part, the tenor. Other parts were written above, creating a form of polyphonic music.

Figure 5-3 Melismatic Organum

Cathedral of Notre Dame, Paris (1163–1250).
This Gothic cathedral took nearly 100 years to construct. During its construction
modifications were made which give it a unique blend of early and late Gothic styles. The
famous "flying buttresses" that support the nave walls represent a developing high Gothic
style and give the building an airy appearance. Located on the banks of the Seine, it was
the home of the musical style known as the School of Notre Dame.

School of Notre Dame
a twelfth-century musical style
that devised a clear form of
measured rhythm similar to
the metered music of today.

measured rhythm
a notational system associated
with the School of Notre
Dame that established a more
precise form of metered
rhythm.

relationship between parts nearly equal. It was not long before three or four parts shared equally in the melodic flow of the composition.

The center of activity for this newly developing polyphonic music was the Cathedral of Notre Dame in Paris around 1150. Leonin and later Perotin were choirmasters there and are now associated with the **School of Notre Dame.** Polyphony, representative of this school and exhibiting a new **measured rhythm,** spread throughout Europe. The music took on attributes similar to present-day metered music. Because each beat was divided into three parts symbolizing the Trinity the music had a swinging feeling, and this rhythmic precision gave new momentum to the musical flow.

Listening Notes

Leonin, *Alleluia Dies Sanctificatus* (excerpt) (1160–70?).

The lower part, the **tenor,** moves slowly as the upper part, the **duplum,** is much more active. The texture of this selection moves from the melismatic organum heard at the beginning to interludes of unison singing. Notice how the texture moves back and forth between these two textures. The organ is in unison with the tenor part; instruments, when used, were played in unison with the tenor part. The rhythmic activity of the upper part is based on three notes to a beat. This is representative of the new development of measured rhythm typical of the School of Notre Dame. The tenor part is taken from an earlier chant *(cantus firmus)* and slowed to a drone, and the upper part takes on the melodic activity reminiscent of monophonic chant.

tenor
the lower part *(cantus firmus)* in early polyphony.
duplum
the part written above the tenor or *cantus firmus* in early polyphony.

0:00	The upper part begins a long melisma on the word *Alleluia. Cantus firmus* begins (tenor part) holding a long note, sounding like a drone.
0:20	The upper part continues on the syllable ''lu'' of *Alleluia.*
0:34	The word *Alleluia* is finally completed. Notice the dissonance on the syllable ''ia'' at the end of the phrase.
0:37	A unison line (monophony) contrasts the opening organum.
0:53	End.

Ars Nova

Music from the fourteenth century, especially French and Italian music, reflected several social factors. Because of long wars, the devastating bubonic plague, and confusion in the leadership of the Catholic church, secular music combined with sacred music composition for the first time. Emphasis was on realism and secular emotions. The slowed chants that were the basis of much music of this time were replaced with songs from village life. Much of the music used as the underlying *cantus firmus* was banal, characterizing animal sounds and drinking songs. The text of the *cantus firmus* was in French or Italian, replacing the traditional Latin

ars nova
"new art." This fourteenth-century style is typified by a popular polyphonic motet style using stories of village life and texts in the vernacular.

syncopation
placing an accent on a normally unaccented part of the beat or measure. For example, a Viennese waltz is counted "ONE, two three," but a syncopated jazz waltz sounds like "go-PARK-the-car."

Ordinary
the part of the liturgical Mass that is performed every service.

of chant. ***Ars nova*** or "new art" became the term used to describe this new and extremely popular polyphonic style.

One very important change that eventually shaped the way music was conceived and composed came from an even more precise manner of notation. The triple rhythms of Leonin and Perotin could now be contrasted by beats divided into twos. With this improved notation, **syncopation,** a technique that placed accents in between the beats, became commonplace.

Machaut, a famous musician and poet, was the first known composer to write a complete polyphonic setting of the **Ordinary** from the Mass. The Ordinary is that part of a **liturgical Mass** that remains the same throughout the year, unchanged by the liturgical calendar. Because of its repetitive function in the liturgy the Ordinary remained rather severe, with little ornate melodic motion. The other major part of the

Guillaume de Machaut
(1300–77)

DATELINE	BIOGRAPHY
1300	This French poet and composer was born in the Diocese of Rheims in northern France.
1323	Machaut became secretary to John of Luxembourg, king of Bohemia, after studying theology and taking holy orders.
1323–40	He traveled with King John as cleric during military campaigns to Poland, Lithuania, and Italy, writing songs and poems dealing with sacred and secular themes such as love, praise of women, chivalry, and morality.
1349–57	Machaut served as cleric, poet, and musician to Charles, king of Navarre, who was later imprisoned for political views against France.
1357–77	He served the king of France and Duc de Berry, sharing the adventures of military life as well as the comforts of royal court life, and consequently became a canon of Rheims.
1364	Machaut composed the *Messe de Notre Dame,* the first significant polyphonic setting of the Ordinary.
1377	After living most of his life as friend and advisor to kings and princes, Machaut died in Rheims; he was the most famous writer and composer of the fourteenth century.

mass, the **Proper,** was specific to liturgical seasons such as Easter and Christmas and commonly displayed expressive musical settings. *Agnus Dei* is one of the five parts that make up the Ordinary, and this setting by Machaut is a beautiful example of fourteenth-century polyphony.

Proper
the part of the liturgical Mass that represents the various religious seasons, as opposed to the Ordinary, which remains the same throughout the year.

Listening Notes

Guillaume de Machaut, Agnus Dei I from the *Messe de Notre Dame* (1364?).

This selection is based on a Gregorian chant that has been altered rhythmically to help blend it with the other three voices. The *cantus firmus* is found in a lower part called the tenor. The overall musical structure of this movement is **A** (Agnus Dei I), **B** (Agnus Dei II), **A** (Agnus Dei III).

The text is the same for each of the larger sections except for the final phrase, and the texture is similar in each part. In our example, Agnus Dei I, notice the fullness established through the melodic equality of all parts and the sonority of the cadences that end on consonant hollow intervals of unisons and fifths.

0:00	All parts begin together. A reed instrument plays the lowest part.
0:06	A very light cadence is followed by another short statement. The upper voices continue to move faster than the two lower parts.
0:15	The next phrase begins. Following a full cadence by all the parts, the voices become more independent melodically.
0:29	Second half of the new phrase; the phrase is extended.
0:37	A near cadence develops but is extended by overlapping of voices. There will not be a full cadence again until the very end of this part.
0:42	Another near cadence.
1:00	Final full cadence with all parts singing unisons or fifths.

Chapter 6

THE RENAISSANCE PERIOD:
1450 to 1600

Music Outline of the Renaissance Period

1. The sacred, polyphonic **motet** was the dominant musical form.

2. **Imitation** was the favored compositional technique used in choral music.

3. Italian and English secular **madrigals** established a highly expressive vocal style with a new emphasis on **word painting.**

4. Music in the Catholic church turned to a more conservative polyphonic style in response to the Council of Trent.

5. Popular instrumental music ensembles, or **consorts,** used instruments of the same timbral family.

6. In the late Renaissance, **polychoral motets** developed in Venice using two or more choirs of voices or instruments.

7. Greater emphasis on instrumental sections within Venetian motets, especially polychoral motets, heralded the transition from the Renaissance to the Baroque era.

The Motet

The polyphonic music of the fourteenth century had matured considerably by 1450 when the independence of the melodic parts was fully achieved. The newest technique to dominate composers' thinking was **imitation.** When melodies imitate each other strictly, as in the canon "Row, Row, Row Your Boat," there is no freedom to change or modify the melody. All the parts must sing the entire melody. Imitative polyphony did not use such strict repetition. In this new polyphony, each part was still obligated to sing, in turn, each phrase of the text, but the music had more freedom. As each phrase of text began, called the **point of imitation,** all the parts would enter in turn, imitating and overlapping the text with similar melodic lines. This imitative technique unified each phrase, allowing the text to be repeated several times. Greatest melodic freedom appeared at the cadences where the voices aligned with each other rhythmically, creating a brief homophonic texture. Composers

imitation
repeating a melodic idea or entire melody immediately in another part; for example, a round. Imitation was used extensively in the Renaissance.

point of imitation
the beginning moment of a phrase when each part enters using the same melodic idea. The entrances are staggered, creating a polyphonic style.

Josquin Desprez
(1450?–1521)

IOSQVINVS PRATENSIS.

DATELINE	BIOGRAPHY
1450?	This Flemish composer was born in Hainaut Province near the border of France and Belgium.
1450–70	Josquin received his early musical training as a choirboy at the collegiate church of Saint Quentin and later studied with Okeghem.
1474–79	He was a member of the ducal choir of Duke Galeazza Sforza in Milan and then spent time composing for several Italian ducal courts.
1486–94	Josquin served at the Sistine Chapel in Rome; thereafter he returned to France.
1495–99	He served as choirmaster of the Cambral cathedral and subsequently entered the service of King Louis XII of France.
1502–16	Josquin composed three books of masses, along with several motets and chansons (secular songs).
1516	He became canon at the collegiate church of Conde and remained there until his death in 1521.

motet
polyphonic vocal work sung in Latin. An essential part of Renaissance music, it is sacred choral work but is not part of the Mass.

favored the **motet,** a polyphonic choral work with a Latin text. Although motets are sacred works, they are not based on sections of the Mass. Motets best display the increasing focus of Renaissance composers on imitation and polyphony.

The melodic grace of Josquin has set him apart from other early motet composers. One of his most famous and frequently performed motets is *Ave Maria, gratia plena.* The imitation floats along effortlessly, and each part rhythmically complements the others so that no part is lost in the texture.

Listening Notes

Josquin Desprez, *Ave Christie Immolate* (early 1500s).

a cappella
choral music performed without accompaniment

contrapuntal
a polyphonic writing technique. Melodic parts are overlapped with different rhythms so that each maintains a unique identity.

This setting of the "Hail the sacrificed Christ," an **a cappella** (no instrumental accompaniment) motet, is representative of the highly developed polyphonic style of the early Renaissance. Notice the entrance of each voice and how clearly it can be followed. The clarity of Josquin's writing was recognized by his peers to be the most refined of the day. Listen for the points of imitation, those moments where a new phrase with a new text is begun. Notice how each vocal part changes notes at different times. This **contrapuntal** style allows each voice to be heard clearly and gives each part its own identity. The parts weave together into an elegant polyphonic fabric. Notice the contrasting homophonic section near the end where all voices sing nearly the same rhythm.

0:00	This selection begins with an overlapping duet between the soprano and alto. The two parts are imitative but not exactly the same.
0:10	Tenor and Bass answer with a duet similar in texture.
0:36	Cadence
0:38	Point of imitation starts with the soprano and followed by the alto, tenor and bass respectively.
0:58	Another point of imitation, this time the tenor starts.
1:15	Unison cadence

1:18	Homophonic setting, all four parts move in the same rhythm.
1:36	Point of imitation, first the soprano and alto enter, and, after a delay, the bass and tenor enter.
2:00	Freer polyphonic setting
2:27	Cadence, ending of excerpt.

Renaissance Consort.

Instruments are often grouped by musical family. Instruments from the same family have a natural timbral blend; in this case, the players are using wind instruments that later developed into modern brass instruments. Typical of most consorts, this ensemble is composed of instruments of varying size offering a large range of notes. The four instruments here parallel the vocal ranges in a choir: soprano, alto, tenor, and bass.

consort
a small ensemble of musicians playing instruments from the same family.

Giovanni Pierluigi da Palestrina
(1525–94)

DATELINE	BIOGRAPHY
1525	This Italian composer was born in the small town of Palestrina near Rome, from which he took his name.
1544	He became organist and choirmaster at the cathedral in Palestrina.
1551	Palestrina composed a Mass in honor of Pope Julius III, after which the Pope placed him in the pontifical choir without audition.
1554–65	These years were spent working in several Roman basilicas, including St. Peter's, St. John Lateran, and Santa Maria Maggiore. He continued writing masses, motets, and both spiritual and secular madrigals.
1555	In response to the Council of Trent and inspired by Pope Marcellus, Palestrina composed a Mass that contained only pure, clear, strictly liturgical polyphonic music, with no secular references.
1572–80	Palestrina lost his wife, two brothers, and two sons in an epidemic that swept through Rome and almost killed him.
1578	He became Master of the Music at the Vatican Basilica.
1588	He helped establish the first association of professional musicians, which provided for burials of members and publication of their music.
1594	Palestrina was honored upon his death by a huge funeral at St. Peter's Basilica in Rome.

Later in the Renaissance period choral music in the Catholic church was challenged by the Council of Trent, a group of cardinals and bishops, as being too "theatrical" and not representative of the seriousness of the liturgy. For this reason church composers were encouraged to return to Gregorian chant and *cantus firmus* techniques. One composer in particular, Palestrina, helped shape a new, more conservative, polyphonic texture. He demonstrated that polyphonic music could present the text clearly and still be compatible with devotion.

Changing Styles of Art

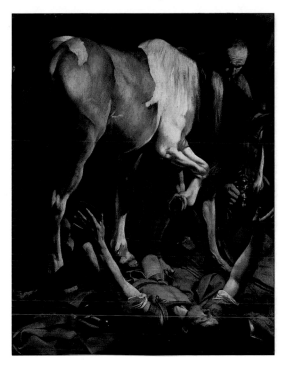

Carravagio, *The Conversion of St. Paul* (1600-1601). Oil on canvas. 90 x 69".

This painting is a powerful statement of Baroque art. The heavenly light that blinded Saul highlights the strength of the horse and the helplessness of Saul. The shadows throw much of the background into darkness. The suspended action creates an intense dramatic moment. The painting is large, 7 1/2 feet tall and over 5 1/2 feet wide. The drama and religious strength of this painting is typical of the baroque mind. Interestingly, Carravagio led a life of violence, ranging from assault to murder. This painting, however, presents quite a different expression. At this instant, Saul becomes St. Paul, moving from a life of violence to a life of dedication to God.

(Santa Maria del Popolo, Rome. Scala/Art Resource.)

Eugéne Delacroix, *The Death of Sarandapalus* (1826). Oil on canvas. 12' 11 1/2" x 16' 3".

Art styles of the Romantic period moved in several different directions. Both the restraint of the Neoclassical style and the passion of the Baroque style continued into the nineteeth century. One of the most influential changes came with the portrayal of extreme emotions. This enormous painting is based on a theme from a tragedy by Byron. The scene captures many emotions. Rather than surrender, an Assyrian king heaps all his possesions on his huge bed and commits murder and suicide. Notice the wide range of color and brightness and the extraordinary contrasts. The passive and soft forms of the women contrast with the stength and active forms of the men and horse. Among the agony and pain is the reclining king and his servant observing the violence.

(The Louvre, Paris. Erich Lessing/Art Resource.)

Claude Monet, *Impression: Sunrise* (1872). Oil on canvas. 19 1/2 x 25 1/2". The inner ear of a musician recalls what has been heard and projects what can be written. It is safe to say that an artist must have an "inner eye," much like a musician must have an "inner ear." Monet believed that an artist should see a picture in his or her head before painting. With Impression: Sunrise, he was instrumental in giving definition to impressionism. Notice the distant port, the thick atmosphere, and the solitary fisherman. There are no precisely defined shapes; nothing is outlined with smooth edges. Impressionism uses small, short brush strokes, often of bold colors that blend and mix with one another when the painting is viewed from a distance. The result is not a true representation or mirror of reality but an impression of reality. (Musee Marmottan, Paris.)

Edvard Munch, *The Scream* (1893). Casein on paper. 35 1/2 x 28 2/3".
This expressionistic work typifies the growing preoccupation with fear, sorrow, and death. The desperate figure in the foreground screams in terror as two figures walk away without noticing. The terrified figure and the landscape swirl in distortion, expressing anguish and anxiety. The loneliness expressed in this work is frightening. Industrialization, dehumanization, and obsession were common themes in expressionistic paintings. (National Gallery, Oslo.)

Pablo Picasso, *Les Demoiselles d'Avignon* (1907). Oil on canvas. 8' x 7'8".
Picasso combines elements of primitivism and early elements of cubism in this
painting. Notice the primitive masks on three of the women. The other two faces
have all of the expected features but are combined into a profile and frontal
view. Notice how the sectioned parts of the body share characteristics with the
drape-like background. Cubism reassembles parts of an object or individual in
contrasting and dramatic ways, presenting new and physically impossible views.
This painting comes from Picasso's rose period, a time when he chose to use
predominantly pink tones. His first or blue period used a blue "tonality." Using
favorite colors or hues is similar to a composer having favorite key areas or
tonalities; for instance, Mozart seemed to favor G minor for his more profound
and expressive works.
(Collection, The Museum of Modern Art, N.Y. Acquired through the Lillie P. Bliss Bequest.)

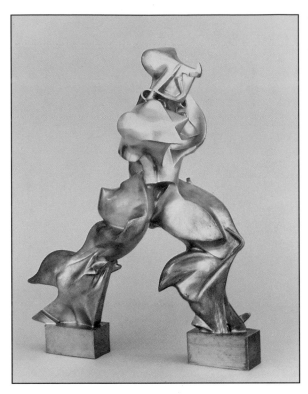

Umberto Boccioni, *Unique Forms of Continuity in Space* (1913). Bronze, cast 1931. 43 7/8 x 34 7/8".
This interesting bronze sculpture represents futurism by using a dynamic sense of motion. Futurists sought ways to portray energy and force devoid of specifics. This sculpture represents the blur of combined motions. Representational detail is purposely avoided so that a sense of perpetual motion remains. This level of abstraction broke ties with traditional senses of harmony and imitation. Futuristic art expresses life and motion unencumbered by images of traditional form.
(Collection, The Musuem of Modern Art, N.Y. Acquired through the Lillie P. Bliss Bequest.)

Andy Warhol, *Green Coca-Cola Bottles* (1962). Oil on canvas. 82 1/2 x 57".
Images of "popular culture" or pop art are based on common, mundane, and even boring subjects. This painting elicited responses of disgust and contempt. There is little of the symbolism, distorted expressionism, or impression found in the works of other contemporary artists. The simplicity of this work is similar to other Warhol subjects, such as his soup cans and Brillo boxes. Pop art is often concerned with industrial themes and images of everyday common objects.
(Collection of Whitney Musuem of American Art, N.Y.)

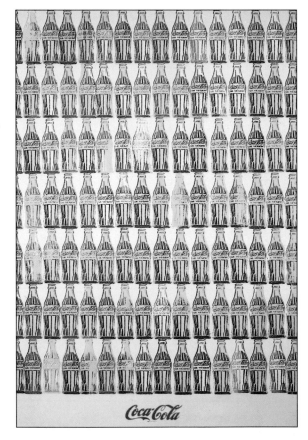

Listening Notes

Giovanni Pierluigi da Palestrina, *Pope Marcellus Mass—Kyrie eleison* (1567).

Notice the fluid lines that are reminiscent of the flowing, serious melodies of Gregorian chant. This particular movement is in an A B A form following the liturgical structure of a *Kyrie eleison.* The three larger sections and the text repetitions of three are symbolic of the Trinity: **A** *Kyrie eleison* (repeated three times), **B** *Christe eleison* (repeated three times), **A** *Kyrie eleison* (repeated three times).

The cadences of each large section are identified by the moments when all of the parts come to rest together. The texture is very full, using six voices instead of the more common four. The specific setting of individual words that concerned secular madrigal composers of the time was forsaken for the development of long melodic lines expressing the general mood of the text and its sacred intent.

0:00   A very delicate beginning in the upper voices. Individual parts phrase; however, no combined cadence is established until the end of the first section.

1:02   Cadence of first section. "Kyrie eleison" has been sung many times by each part but grouped musically into three parts.

1:05   Middle section. This time the imitative texture is less dense at first with more duet pairing.

2:00   Cadence of second section. "Christe eleison" has been presented three times.

2:06   Last section, a more aggressive melodic structure with a wider range in all parts. This time the lower voices begin the section.

3:05   Final cadence. "Kyrie eleison" has been presented again three times.

Palestrina's writing is perhaps the most fluid expression of late Renaissance Mass compositions. To modern ears, the music sounds nearly tonal, with only a few surprising twists in melodic and harmonic direction.

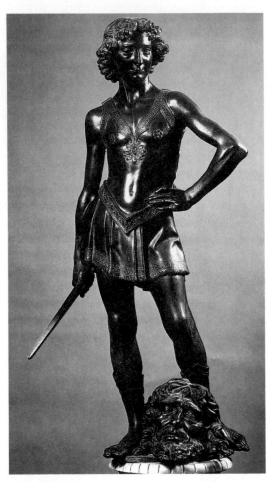

Donatello, *David* (1408). Bronze. Height 5'2. These four sculptures cover a 200-year period and show striking differences. All four are representations of the biblical David who slew Goliath, the Philistine giant, with a stone and sling. Donatello portrays David as an adolescent with a large sword. The smooth Classical features show a boy without superior strength but with the intellect to complete the task. The belief that one could control one's own life was strong in the Renaissance. (Bargello, Florence. Scala/Art Resource.)

Andrea Del Verrocchio, *David* (c. 1470). Bronze. Height $49\frac{5}{8}''$. Verrocchio also portrays David as an adolescent; however, this time he stands with an inner self-confidence. The youth appears a little older and more developed. There is a greater sense of realism in this work. (Bargello, Florence. Scala/Art Resource.)

The varying techniques of the four artists represented here account for some of the differences seen here; however, the changing concept of the subject over time accounts for the major stylistic changes. The arts offer clear pictures of changing attitudes and philosophies. As concepts change, expressions change. When single subjects or structures are followed throughout history, these changes are most evident.

Michelangelo, *David* (1501-4). Marble. Height 13½′.

The Michelangelo *David* stands 13½ feet tall, a giant in his own right. This David looks capable of killing a giant. There is determination in his face with a potential for both intellectual and physical expression. Michelangelo's David is not the victor standing over his victim, but a man who promises great things. (Academy, Florence. Art Resource, N.Y.)

Gianlorenzo Bernini, *David* (1623). Marble. Height 6′7″.

Bernini's *David* shows the drama of Baroque art. There is an implied sense of motion as David coils in the act of fighting. (Borghese Gallery, Rome. Scala/Art Resource.)

 *The Madrigal*

madrigal
a secular poem about love, popular in the Renaissance, set in a polyphonic texture with contrasting homophonic sections. Word painting was prevalent.

Although very similar in sound to the motet, the **madrigal** has striking differences. The compositional differences and similarities between motets and madrigals are compared as follows:

MOTETS

1. Latin text.
2. Sacred topics, performed in worship services.
3. Flowing melodic lines without much accent or **word painting.** Refined expression, smooth and predictable harmony.
4. Polyphonic and homophonic textures.
5. Imitation techniques.

word painting
a word stressed musically to make it stand out from the words before and after it. The emphasis is made to interpret the special meaning of the word.

MADRIGALS

1. Text in the vernacular (French, Italian, or English).
2. Secular topics—love, humor, scenery, affairs—performed at home and at social gatherings.
3. Word painting and **madrigalisms** used to emphasis specific words and feelings. Highly expressive techniques with surprising dissonances and harmonies.
4. Polyphonic and homophonic textures.
5. Imitation techniques.

madrigalisms
specific words or feelings emphasized musically. Associated with word painting.

Italian madrigals generally had a more serious polyphonic texture than English madrigals. Both forms employed polyphonic and homophonic textures. The contrast between these two textures is most striking in the English **ballett** madrigal in which homophonic verses are followed by complex polyphonic settings of fa-la-la. Thomas Morley's *Now Is the Month of Maying* is a well-known example of this lively and dancelike musical style.

ballett (fa-la-la)
a popular English madrigal style in the Renaissance. The homophonic verse is followed by a polyphonic refrain of fa-la-la.

Perhaps the most colorful Italian madrigalist was Carlo Gesualdo who, after finding his wife and her lover in bed, had them killed. His music is perhaps the most extreme example of word painting, and his

Listening Notes

Thomas Morley, *Now Is the Month of Maying* (1595).

This ballett madrigal is a setting of three homophonic verses, each composed of two repeated phrases (aa bb). Each phrase concludes with a contrasting refrain of fa-la. Notice the polyphonic nature of the fa-la. All five parts imitate and overlap, quickly building to a solid cadence. The text is playful, describing springtime games and flirtations.

0:00 First verse begins a homophonic setting of the text.

0:04 First fa-la is sung.

0:08 The same music is repeated softly.

0:16 The second part of the verse begins with another homophonic setting.

0:20 A more complicated fa-la concludes the phrase.

0:25 The second part is repeated, completing the form for each verse (aa bb).

0:33 Second verse begins.

0:43 Repeat of (a), soft.

0:51 (bb), first soft and then loud.

1:10 Third verse begins (aa), first loud and then soft.

1:27 (bb), first soft and then loud.

1:45 Final cadence.

The mood of this madrigal is strikingly different from the more severe sacred motets of the same period. Word painting does not play a major role in this quickly paced madrigal. An example of clever word painting can be found in a discussion of *Song of the Birds* by the French chanson composer Jannequin (Topic 3).

madrigals lend themselves to very dramatic interpretation. Listen to any of his chromatic madrigals, especially *Io pur respiro*. His works display both the style of the period and his strong emotional tendencies.

The French derivative of the motet style was called the **chanson.** The chanson was very repetitive and used strong rhythmic accents. The chansons and sacred works of Guillaume Dufay best represent this fifteenth-century French style. In his Mass *Se la face ay pale* he used a

chanson
literally, "a song"; the French equivalent of the German **lied.**

song he had written two decades earlier as the *cantus firmus.* This is an excellent example of how secular and sacred music continued to influence each other.

Germany had a similar style of polyphonic choral music called the **lied,** but it disappeared when many musicians were imported from France and Italy. Germany quickly absorbed the French chanson and Italian madrigal style. The lied would reappear in the nineteenth century but would be significantly different in texture and style.

lied
a German art song. These songs disappeared after the Renaissance but reappeared in the nineteenth century.

Early Performances

During the Renaissance period, concerts as we know them today did not exist. The church was naturally the performance arena of motets; however, there was no such arena for madrigal singing. Madrigals were most often sung by small groups in common social gatherings. Although sung by skilled singers for nobility and for important occasions, they were also enjoyed by nonaristocratic people. Families who had developed music-reading skills would sing madrigals in the evenings, just as we listen to CDs or watch television. There are questionable accounts of family heads who were displeased with their child's choice of a marriage partner because of the vocal part he or she sang. "You really should marry a tenor; the family needs a tenor." Such social pressure may seem absurd today; however, similar absurdities have existed throughout the centuries.

 Instrumental and Polychoral Motets

Renaissance instrumental music was modeled for the most part after vocal styles. Its liberation from vocal music began in earnest in the later Renaissance. At first, instrumental music had been used primarily to accompany vocal music by playing the same melody as the voice, called **doubling;** there was very little independence. Instrumental music by itself was polyphonic with all of the attributes of a motet or madrigal but with no text. The tonal colors of the viols, krummhorns, shawms, and recorders dominated most small ensembles.

The most important shift toward a new instrumental perspective came with the **Venetian School.** A center for developing this style was St. Mark's, a large cathedral with two choir lofts, each with an organ. **Polychoral motets** took full advantage of this church's configuration. Two or more choirs would perform motets using imitation within choirs and echo effects between choirs. The large choirs were often accompanied by instrumental ensembles, adding rich color to the already thick

doubling
two or more voices or instruments playing the same melody at the same time.
Venetian School
composers who wrote and performed music in the late sixteenth century using the polychoral style. The works required multiple choirs of voices or instruments.
polychoral motet
a motet that is performed by more than one choir or group of instruments.

St. Mark's Cathedral

texture. Works for instruments alone were performed for large festive occasions and accompanied ceremonies within the cathedral and out in the square.

The most notable composer for these large works was Giovanni Gabrieli, who grew up in Venice and played organ at St. Mark's. He was equally fluent writing instrumental and choral works, including works for organ and dramatic polychoral motets. Some of the choral works required the vocalists and instrumentalists to divide into as many as six different choirs. The significance of instrumental music could no longer be denied. The transition from Renaissance to Baroque music came with this new perception of the importance of instrumental musical styles.

Giovanni Gabrieli
(c1553-1556–1612)

DATELINE	BIOGRAPHY
c1553-1556	This Italian organist and composer of choral music was born in Venice.
1557-75	Gabrieli grew up under the tutelage of his great uncle, Andrea Gabrieli, whose works were published along with Giovanni's.
1575-79	Gabrieli worked in Munich as musical assistant to Orlando de Lassus in the court chapel and published two madrigals dedicated to the Duke of Bavaria.
1584	Gabrieli was appointed second organist of St. Mark's in Venice, as his uncle was serving as first organist.
1586	Upon his uncle's death, Gabrieli accepted the post of first organist at St. Mark's, a post he held until his death.
1597	Continuing his relationship with Germany and its composers, he dedicated his first book of ''Symphoniae sacrae'' to a Georg Fugger of Augsburg and established a lifelong friendship with Hans Hassler, with whom he later composed and published.
1609-12	Gabrieli's reputation as a great organist spread as he produced many fine students, including Heinrich Schütz, a celebrated German composer.
1612	Gabrieli died in Venice, and the works written late in his life were not published until 1615.

Chapter 7

THE BAROQUE PERIOD:
1600 to 1750

Music Outline of the Baroque Period

1. Opera, a drama sung with orchestral accompaniment, was born in Italy.

2. Tonality based on major and minor scales crystallized, a move away from medieval (church) modes.

3. Tonal relationships built on the tonic and dominant chords became the most powerful harmonic motion in music.

4. Instrumental music attained a popularity equal to vocal music. Trio sonatas, dance suites, and concerti grossi firmly established instrumental music in the courts and in the churches.

5. The keyboard (harpsichord and pipe organ) remained the dominant instrument for the composer.

6. Keyboard accompaniments were systematized, building chords above a written bass line, a system called **basso continuo.**

7. A search for greater emotional impact led to a new solo melodic writing style called **monodic style.**

8. Late in the Baroque period, polyphonic forms remained popular, producing thick, dense textures in both instrumental and vocal music forms.

Detail and Precision

Detail is a primary concern in all the arts. The control of detail gives each work unity. In addition, detail of a well-conceived artistic thought often spawns new but related thoughts. Recently, mathematical theories about chaos and randomness have shown us that the basic elements or details in any organic entity are related to the whole. For example, a Baroque cathedral, in all its grandeur, has carvings of beautiful detail in places difficult, if not impossible, to see, and we wonder why so much time was spent on so much unnecessary detail. The impact of the detail, however, is felt even if it is far away, up on some roof line or out of sight. This emphasis on detail is the essence of the Baroque period. The Baroque style focused on an increased concern for expression of emotion and a love of contrasts.

Detail and precision were the elements needed to build an intensely emotional, musical world. The Baroque attitude did not develop without guidance. Toward the end of the sixteenth century a group of poets and composers in Florence met to construct a new vocal style called **monody.** This new style required the music to free the words from a thick polyphonic texture. This group, the **Camerata,** propelled music in a new direction, perhaps the only time in music history that such an important stylistic change was determined by committee.

Monodic style was subservient to speech. **Recitative,** a single declamatory melody above a prominent bass line, was the essence of this style. Polyphony from the Renaissance was discarded for a new emphasis on a single melody supported by chords and a bass line. Claudio Monteverdi's music provides the best examples of the elevation of the text in this new song style. It was his belief that the music was to be the servant of the text.

To support a single melody, a **thorough bass** line was written accompanied by numbers to indicate specific intervals that were to be

monody, monodic style
a new vocal technique of solo voice and basso continuo developed by the Camerata.

Camerata (Flòrentine)
a group of composers and poets who gathered in 1575 to develop a new dramatic relationship between music and text.

recitative
a declamatory vocal style used to tell of action or to relate a text without repetition. It is accompanied by a basso continuo.

thorough bass
the continuous-sounding bass line that underpins much of the music of the Baroque period; also called **basso continuo.**

played above the bass line. This shorthand notation, called **basso continuo** or **figured bass,** allowed keyboard players to invent an accompaniment enhancing the solo voice.

figured bass
a system of small numbers written above a bass note to indicate the intervals needed to build the desired chord.

Figured Bass as notated:

The bass line became increasingly important in the Baroque era. In Henry Purcell's opera *Dido and Aeneas* (1689) his most famous aria, "Dido's Lament," used a technique of a repeating bass line melody over which a solo melody was written. This **ground bass (basso ostinato)** technique unifies the aria and gives it a sense of inevitability.

Figured Bass as performed:

ground bass
a repeated melody in the bass (passacaglia) that supports melodies above, also called **basso ostinato.**

Music today still relies heavily on the movement of the bass line to give direction tonally and rhythmically. Today's commercial music is especially locked into the clarity provided by a fundamentally scored bass line.

 Opera and Other Related Vocal Forms

Opera blossomed following the development of monody in a new relationship between text, expression, and emotion. The first opera house was operating in Venice in 1637. To write an opera, composers not only had to set text to music, they also needed to write instrumental overtures, interludes, and endings. These **sinfonias** were instrumental sections that added contrast to the vocal sections.

sinfonias
instrumental musical sections in early opera.

Claudio Monteverdi
(1567–1643)

DATELINE	BIOGRAPHY
1567	Claudio Monteverdi was born in Cremona. During the first twenty years of his life he wrote many vocal works demonstrating his early mastery of the Renaissance polyphonic vocal style.
1590	He was appointed to the court of Mantua working as a singer, violist, and finally as music director. This engagement lasted twenty-one years.
1600-1607	He published several books of madrigals in the progressive new solo style where the poetic word was master over the harmony. Recitative and thorough bass (figured bass) were the basis of these works.
1607	Monteverdi's first opera, *La favola d'Orfeo,* was produced.
1613	He was appointed as *maestro di cappella* of St. Mark's in Venice, where he remained to his death.
1642	He composed his last opera, *L'incoronazione di Poppea.*
1643	After serving at St. Mark's for thirty years, writing required sacred music, music for the aristocracy, and operas for Europe's first public opera house, Monteverdi died.

aria
a lyric and often demanding vocal work used in opera, oratorios, and cantatas.

virtuoso
a performer who excels above all the others; a technically superior musician.

bel canto
a vocal style that displayed virtuosic techniques associated with the da capo form. The vocalist improvised complicated ornaments to display vocal prowess.

da capo aria
a form A B A′ for soloists to sing emotionally intense melodies that were commonly ornamented in the A′ section.

Later, as opera developed, the most emotionally charged moments were the arias, where characters would expound on a feeling. The recitative either produced or told of some action while the **aria** was the resulting emotional outpouring. In comparison to the recitative, the aria was scored more fully for orchestra; the recitative was commonly accompanied by a harpsichord and cello executing a figured bass. The aria also provided opportunities for the new **virtuoso** singers to display their extraordinary talents. The Italian term for beautiful singing, **bel canto,** was used to describe arias and operas which emphasized vocal technique and display.

The structure most popular for this display was the **da capo aria.** The last section of this three-part form, A B A′ (see Chapter 4 for a diagram), was often embellished to the point of absurdity by the singer. Vocal abilities were tremendous and included the popular use of

Listening Notes

Claudio Monteverdi, *L'Orfeo* (1607).
Recitative: *Tu se' morta, mia vita, ed io repiro?*
Chorus: *Ahi, caso acerbo.*

Orfeo just learned of the death of Eurydice and sings "you are dead." The setting is a **dry recitative.** Only organ and a bass lute accompany this freely constructed melodic line. The irregularity of phrasing suggests speech, not singing. Here, the text is supreme. Notice the chorus that follows; this more structured section is in place of what would later become an aria. The **chorus** is a release of expression and emotion in response and contrast to the recitative. The wedding of contrasting declamation and melody is the fundamental element in developing dramatic flow in operas.

dry recitative
a vocal form with only continuo accompaniment as opposed to orchestral accompaniment.

chorus
a section in an oratorio, opera, or cantata performed with several singers on each part.

0:00 Sustained organ notes are followed by the solo voice in a declamatory setting. This is a dry recitative, one syllable for every note.

0:27 The vocal part continues to follow the organ chords. Notice the lightly strummed stringed instrument (lute).

0:47 Climactic phrase, words accelerate.

1:02 The setting of the words allows for very little repetition of words. Notice the increased activity of the continuo.

1:37 Final cadence begins. "Farewell earth, farewell sky and sun, farewell."

2:01 End.

Chorus

0:00 The chorus begins with a homophonic texture followed quickly by a simple imitative phrase.

0:13 A faster ascending melodic line contrasts the first texture.

0:27 New homophonic phrase.

0:35 Imitation.

0:44 Another longer, fast tutti melody.

0:53 Imitation returns.

1:07 Final cadence.

1:13 End.

Pietro Domenico Olivero, *Interior of the Royal Theater, Turin* (1740).
The audiences at operas in the Baroque era differ from audiences today. This painting shows a performance of Francesco Feo's opera *Arsace*. Notice the extravagant set and how the hall seems to extend onto the stage. Notice the patrons in the boxes on the side of the opera house; many of them are not even looking at the stage. Those in front of the orchestra are talking to each other, someone in the aisle is serving food, and a soldier in the aisle holds a gun. The orchestra has two harpsichords and two string basses, brass horns on the left, and several other string players. In many opera houses during this time, patrons in the boxes pulled a curtain if they did not want to follow what was happening on stage. Today these actions would be considered disrespectful of the performers. Productions of Baroque opera often presented grandiose scenes to recapture the attention of the rather fickle audience.

castrati
male singers who sang soprano or alto roles in opera because of castration before puberty.

castrati, male singers who, because they were castrated before puberty, were able to sing powerful soprano and alto roles. These men commanded the most prestige and money of all the singers.

The balance between recitative and aria provides contrast and drama to an opera. Musically the two forms are dramatically different in melody, rhythm, and texture. The following table compares the two vocal styles:

RECITATIVE

Melody: descriptive and speechlike. Line is limited to accents for emphasis with short-valued notes in a declamatory style.

Rhythm: free, without strong regular meter. Text sets the flow of notes and governs the activity level.

Texture: thin, solo voice usually with continuo accompaniment only, called dry recitative. When accompanied by the orchestra it is usually more melodic and fuller in texture.

ARIA

Melody: expressive, flowing, displays vocal intensity and emotion. Can be embellished by the singer for increased virtuosic display.

Rhythm: metrically regular, repetitive rhythm, longer-valued notes.

Texture: very full, orchestral accompaniment. Can be more polyphonic; large vocal and instrumental range used to intensify the texture.

Opera was a serious endeavor. From a twentieth-century viewpoint the plots were not necessarily engaging and the dramatic acting was often weak. Elaborate staging and musical grandeur were important features of these performances.

Soon, however, serious opera found competition from a more popular style of music drama that attracted large audiences from the middle class. This new style, **ballad opera,** did not have the scope of traditional opera; in fact, it had little to do with many of the traditions of serious opera. Ballad opera therefore resulted in a loosening of the musical constraints on opera. Popular in England, it made use of familiar, catchy melodies to tell humorous stories. These operas were very popular in the 1720s and dominated traditional opera productions. *The Beggar's Opera* by John Gay was an enormous success in England in 1729 and helped lead to a decline in interest in Italian opera.

ballad opera
a light and often humorous dramatic form of opera performed specifically in England.

Handel, the most significant composer in England during this time, also made a similar move away from Italian opera to the newer English **oratorio,** which was far less expensive to produce and attracted a much greater audience drawn from the middle class.

Oratorios differed from opera in that they were based on religious subjects. Like opera, oratorios used aria and recitative vocal styles.

oratorio
a large vocal and instrumental dramatic work based on a sacred subject. Like opera it has arias and recitatives; however, there is no staging or dramatic acting.

Musically these works are similar in style to opera. The recitatives present a biblical storyline, and the arias portray the emotional response. Generally, the arias are less difficult to sing than arias in the bel canto style. Choruses replaced some of the arias and ensembles found in opera. Rather than an individual solo, a chorus would express noble and

George Frideric Handel
(1685–1759)

DATELINE	BIOGRAPHY
1685	George Frideric Handel was born in Halle, Germany, on February 23. His family was not musical, but Frideric studied as a child and soon became an accomplished organist and harpsichordist. He became familiar with contemporary German and Italian composers by copying their scores.
1702	He was appointed cathedral organist at the University of Halle where he studied.
1703-6	Handel studied in Hamburg, a center of German opera, which led to the composition of his first opera, *Almira,* in 1705. A strong-willed individual, Handel lived through a duel over who should play harpsichord at an opera. Fortunately, his opponent's sword was broken by a button on Handel's coat.
1706-10	He worked in Italy, successfully, writing for patrons in Rome, Florence, Naples, and Venice. He returned to Germany in 1710, but after only one month he returned to London for the triumphant production of his opera *Rinaldo.*
1720-30	Commissioned by a large group of noble and wealthy gentlemen who invested in these productions, Handel produced many Italian operas.
1739	The productions of *Saul* and *Israel in Egypt* established Handel as a leader in English oratorio composition. Oratorios provided a new and popular format for Handel. He wrote twenty-six oratorios over the next twenty years, assuring his popularity. He performed organ concertos at the opera concerts, maintaining a dual image of performer/composer for the rest of his life.
1759	Handel died and was buried in Westminster Abbey in London.

sacred feelings. A chorus has several voices singing several different parts. The texture is usually more polyphonic. Although some costuming and staging were used in its earliest form, the oratorio was eventually performed in a concert format without dramatic enhancement.

Listening Notes

George Frideric Handel, *Messiah* (1742).
Recitative #14: "There were shepherds abiding in the field"
Chorus #15: "Glory to God"
Aria #16: "Rejoice Greatly"
Chorus #39: "Hallelujah"
Chorus #47: "Amen"

Messiah is the most famous of all the many operas and oratorios Handel composed. Compare the vocal style in the recitative and aria to that heard in the Monteverdi selections. The florid lines of Handel are more relaxed than the extended bel canto techniques in late Italian opera; nevertheless, the singers must be well trained.

The "Hallelujah" chorus is the most celebrated selection of Handel's writing. When heard in concert, audiences traditionally stand. The story is that King George II stood at this time because of a stiff leg; therefore everyone stood. The last chorus, "Amen," is perhaps one of the most flawless fugues in vocal literature. It soars with determination and proves a worthy close to the oratorio.

Recitative #14: "There were shepherds abiding in the field"

0:00   Voice accompanied by harpsichord (continuo).

0:14   Accompanied recitative, strings and harpsichord.

0:38   Return to dry recitative, harpsichord only.

0:55   Harpsichord plays a two-chord cadence following a vocal phrase where there is no accompaniment at all.

1:10   Declamatory statement, "Christ the Lord," followed by the two-chord cadence typical of dry recitative.

1:16   Accompanied recitative that acts as a lead-in to the upcoming chorus "Glory to God." The melodic line builds until the chorus enters.

Chorus #15: "Glory to God"

0:00 Chorus begins with a strong declamatory statement, full orchestra.

0:11 A slow, serious answer to the opening statement.

0:23 Repeat of opening statement and answer.

0:42 Polyphonic section begins. Fugal texture.

1:02 Return to the opening idea.

1:20 Return of the fugal idea with an extension.

1:46 Instrumental ending.

Aria #16: "Rejoice Greatly"

0:00 Instrumental introduction: harpsichord, bass, and cello supply the continuo.

0:20 Soprano voice enters.

0:40 First appearance of a long melisma.

0:58 Return to a more declamatory setting.

1:23 Instrumental interlude, same as introduction.

1:42 Middle section (B), slower tempo, contrast in melody and accompaniment, very declamatory, followed by an instrumental statement.

2:25 A dialogue between the voice and strings sets up an atmosphere that slows the tempo and activity.

2:42 Last declamatory statement, which is identical to the previous recitative. Recitative-like break before a return to the original melody.

2:56 Return to the melody and texture of the original melody. Extended melismas expand the original (A) section.

3:35 Dialogue between the vocal line and the strings.

4:00 Climax of the aria, leading into the final cadence.

4:22 Final instrumental statement, ending the aria.

Chorus #39: "Hallelujah"

0:00 Orchestral opening, homophonic setting of the text.

0:51 First polyphonic setting. Voices separate into different activities while the main statement of "Hallelujah" continues.

1:16 Textural change, homophonic and soft.

1:27 A sudden dynamic change (terraced dynamics).

1:36	Fugal entrances.
2:00	Return to homophonic setting with choral call-and-response.
2:43	Return to a polyphonic texture.
2:55	Return to the dialogue texture.
3:10	Final cadence begins.
3:37	Final homophonic statement.

Chorus #47: "Amen" (conclusion to "Worthy is the Lamb")

3:34	Basses enter with the fugue statement.
3:45	Tenors enter.
3:56	Altos enter.
4:07	Sopranos enter.
4:15	Homophonic statement followed by a short instrumental fugue.
4:36	Sudden entrance of the chorus in a polyphonic texture.
4:47	Softer texture, polyphonic, long lines.
5:30	Point of imitation similar to the Renaissance.
5:53	Texture thickens similar to the fugues of the Baroque period.
6:08	The climax of the fugue.
6:13	Final cadence begins.

Although Handel is remembered for his oratorios, Italian opera established Handel as a worthy composer, and Handel was a master of the Italian opera style while living and writing in England.

Another choral form with recitatives, arias, and choruses is the church **cantata.** As the name implies, these pieces are sung rather than played on instruments as in the early **sonata.** Cantatas accompanied liturgical activities in the yearly Lutheran calendar. Cantatas include solo recitatives and arias and polyphonic choruses. A **chorale** is a four-part, homophonic composition much like a church hymn and is usually the last movement of the cantata. Musical ideas in the chorale were often used throughout the short multimovement work. Cantatas were much smaller in scope than an opera or oratorio but similar in style.

Over a period of several years, J. S. Bach wrote cantatas for each Sunday of the year, nearly 300 in all. Very little is said of the secular

cantata
a musical piece that is sung. The church cantata was a short dramatic work with solos and chorus sections.

sonata
an early term used to describe instrumental music. There are two kinds of sonatas: the secular *da camera* and the more serious sacred *da chiesa*. Later in history the term refers to a three-movement solo work, a soloist with piano accompaniment.

chorale
a four-part, homophonic composition; traditionally, a Lutheran hymn sung by a congregation in church.

cantatas of Bach because of the magnitude of his sacred works. Musically they are very similar, so much so that he borrowed some of his own sacred numbers for his secular works.

passion
a dramatic sacred work using arias, recitatives, and choruses as found in oratorios, that characterizes the suffering and death of Christ.

Passions are large-scale sacred vocal works that rival opera in both scope and complexity. They are musical settings of the Gospel accounts of the suffering and death of Christ, and the most well known are by J. S. Bach. The comparison of passions to oratorios is natural in that they both employ recitative, aria, and chorus settings. However, when compared to the English oratorios of Handel, the Germanic style of Bach is much more polyphonic and weighty.

The *St. Matthew Passion* and the *St. John Passion* are as close to opera as Bach journeyed; however, they are not his only large-scale vocal works. His Mass in B minor is equal in size. Regardless of its title, it is not a liturgical work; it was not intended to act as a Mass. It is a very contemplative work with a unique dramatic outline that separates it from the passions and oratorios of other composers.

 Baroque Instrumental Forms

Instrumentalists in the Baroque era commonly obtained their skills from their families. The skills necessary to be a great Baroque trumpet player, for instance, were commonly passed down family lines; secrets of technique were rarely shared, thus creating job security. Aside from a few books for amateur lute and keyboard players, method books and diagrams on how to play an instrument were virtually unknown. The master-student relationship was the primary source of acquiring well-developed skills.

harpsichord
the most dominant keyboard instrument in the Baroque period. Strings are plucked when a key is depressed.

Because of the importance of basso continuo writing in this period the **harpsichord** was essential to vocal and instrumental music. Orchestras were small by today's standards, and there were no conductors in the modern sense. It was, therefore, natural for the harpsichordist to be the musical director of chamber groups, orchestras, and even opera productions. Very often, the composer took this position.

trio sonata
a sonata with three instrumental parts. The two higher melodies are performed by two soloists while the continuo players perform the third part.

The bass line of the continuo part was usually reinforced with a cello to strengthen and help project the line. In the case of **trio sonatas** the harpsichord and cello were considered one part; therefore, the two melodic instruments, for example, violins and/or violas, would play the upper melodies in counterpoint, with the harpsichord and cello performing the third part. As a result, the trio sonata had four players playing three parts.

Another favorite instrumental form was the **suite,** a collection of dance forms each having a distinctive rhythmic feature. Instrumental music and dance have always been closely linked. These pieces were intended for listening and not dancing. Not all the movements of a suite were dance forms, however, and the opening movement was often an introduction or overture to the suite.

One dance, the minuet, is perhaps the most familiar to us today. It has three beats to the measure and short repeated sections, similar to our waltz. All the dance forms in a suite had characteristics derived from the dance steps used at that time. We no longer remember the steps; however, the feeling of each dance has remained, such as the lively *gigue* or the stately *sarabande*. This popular music was written for solo instruments (keyboard), string quartets, and even small orchestras.

Popular instruments were featured in solo roles accompanied by an orchestra. The most common form used was the three-movement **concerto grosso.** In these works a soloist or an ensemble of soloists would be concerted or pitted against the orchestra or **tutti (ritornello)** ensemble. The dialogue between the two groups consisted of themes that were used in common and themes that were specific to one group. Vivaldi was the most prolific concerto grosso composer of the time,

suite
a group of highly styled dance forms. Suites were written for small ensembles, harpsichord, and orchestra.

concerto grosso
a form in which a soloist or ensemble is contrasted against a string orchestra or full orchestra.

tutti
means everyone plays. In the concerto grosso, tutti is another term for **ritornello.**

ritornello
the orchestral section that contrasts the solo sections in a concerto grosso.

An eighteenth-century estate with Baroque garden

Antonio Vivaldi
(1678–1741)

DATELINE	BIOGRAPHY
1678	Antonio Vivaldi was born in Venice. He studied music and when still a young man was ordained as a priest.
1704-40	He taught violin, conducted, and composed at a famous Venetian music school for girls, Conservatorio dell' Ospedale della Pieta. This school had a fine orchestra for which Vivaldi wrote nearly 450 concerti grossi and solo concertos.
1724-35	He traveled abroad to foreign courts; however, there is little verification of what he did and for whom on these journeys.
1738	He wrote two operas, but these, like most of his vocal music, have been mostly forgotten.
1741	Vivaldi died in poverty and, although very famous during his life, remained relatively unknown for 200 years.

concertino group
in a concerto grosso, the solo group, in contrast to the orchestra or ripieno group.

ripieno group
in a concerto grosso, the orchestral or tutti group, in contrast to the solo group (concertino).

terraced dynamics
a technique used in the Baroque era to change dynamics. More players or more stops on the organ were added, resulting in sudden rather than gradual dynamic changes.

stops
the levers or buttons used to open a rank of pipes on an organ so that the air can go through them when a key is depressed.

writing over 400 concertos. Because of his expertise on the violin, he wrote extensively for solo and duet violin.

The concerto grosso is structured around the contrast of two groups. Two or more soloists (an **ensemble**) accompanied by the continuo is called the **concertino group.** The larger and louder orchestra is called the **ripieno group.** The sudden change in dynamic levels between the two groups best typifies the technique of **terraced dynamics.** Nearly 100 years later when conductors became a common occurrence and the process of changing volume could be directed, the concept of gradually increasing volume developed. During the Baroque period more instruments were added or subtracted to make the volume change. On the pipe organ more ranks of pipes were added by pulling out knobs, or **stops,** increasing the volume; hence the term "pull out all the stops" began to mean "give it all you can." The use of solo versus tutti and terraced dynamics is an excellent example of the Baroque love of contrast.

Vivaldi was a masterful violinist and wrote exquisitely for the instrument in solo and duo concerti. His knowledge of Baroque instruments produced lively orchestrations. His instrumental melodies, especially those from slow movements, exhibit the expression and intensity typical of the new melodic construction that dominated the Baroque era.

The Four Seasons, a famous set of four concerti grossi scored for string orchestra and solo violin, is a prime example of Vivaldi's control over the sonorities available in the Baroque orchestra. Although there are only strings with basso continuo, the musical colors created by Vivaldi are exciting. The use of short sonnets that preface each concerto strengthens the interpretive powers of this composition. The link between the words and the performance was a primary concern of Vivaldi; in fact, he wrote words above the music such as "song of the birds" or "murmuring streams" to aid the musician in the interpretation of the music. The picturesque description of the four seasons by Vivaldi has made these his most famous concerti grossi.

Listening Notes

Antonio Vivaldi, *The Four Seasons* (1725).

"Spring," First Movement, *allegro*

"Spring" is the first of the four concerti grossi in this work. In *The Four Seasons* each concerto grosso, "Spring," "Summer," "Autumn," and "Winter," is accompanied by a sonnet giving interpretation to the interacting themes. "Spring" is scored for solo violin and string orchestra. Typical of the concerto grosso form, there are three movements with the standard tempo contrast of fast-slow-fast. In the first movement, the sonnet speaks of birds greeting the arrival of spring, followed by a storm with lightning and thunder. The second movement pictures soft winds in the leaves and grass as a shepherd sleeps. The last movement is a festival with shepherds and nymphs dancing in celebration. As you listen, notice the thematic repeats in the ritornello sections and how the solo violin bridges the ritornello sections with virtuoso displays of technique.

0:00	Tutti beginning (A), full string orchestra.
0:07	Repeat of opening theme but soft, terraced dynamics.
0:14	New thematic material that is also repeated softly.
0:30	Three solo violins in an imitative texture picture the sounds of bird calls.
1:03	Return to tutti (A).
1:11	Extension to the theme, episode.

1:26	New slow theme (B) above active lower strings.
1:35	Return to (A).
1:42	The storm section begins with repeated chords in the lower strings and fast ascending scales in the violins. The texture is soon filled with tremolos in the strings (fast repeated bowing on the same note).
1:50	The tremolo chords are interrupted by cadenzalike statements from the solo violin (lightning).
2:10	Tutti (A).
2:19	Solo violins return to the opening imitative texture.
2:36	Extended episode serves as a transition.
2:40	Solo violin with accompaniment from the other strings.
2:53	Tutti (A).
3:01	Repeat but very soft.
3:10	End.

The continuo accompanies both the solo violin and the ritornelli. In the slow movement the role of the continuo is more evident. The slow movement is much like an instrumental aria. The basso continuo is as important to this instrumental style as it is to the vocal forms.

Johann Sebastian Bach
(1685–1750)

DATELINE	BIOGRAPHY
1685	J. S. Bach was born in Eisenach, Germany, into a large, six-generation musical family. He received his first musical training on stringed instruments and keyboard from his father and a cousin.
1695	Orphaned at the age of ten, Bach went to live with his oldest brother, continuing his keyboard instruction and singing soprano in the church choir in Ohrdruf.
1703	Bach accepted a position as violinist in the orchestra of the ducal court of Weimar, and the same year went on to become organist at a church in Arnstadt. He began composing choir cantatas and clavier pieces.

1707   Bach married his cousin Maria Barbara Bach and took a position at St. Blasius Church in Mülhausen. During this time Bach began to earn a reputation as an improviser of fugues.

1708   He spent the next nine years as court organist at the ducal court of Weimar, continuing to write cantatas and organ works; he also taught organ and composition.

1717-23   While serving as the court conductor at Cöthen, Bach composed secular chamber music for instrumental ensembles and solo instruments; he wrote the famous *Brandenburg* Concertos as well as a number of overtures, concertos, and sonatas.

1721   Bach married Anna Magdalena Wilcken; his first wife had died, leaving him with four small children. This marriage produced thirteen children, only six of whom survived.

1722   Although Bach was not well known outside Germany, he had gained an excellent reputation locally as an organist, harpsichordist, improviser, and master of the fugue; his *Well-Tempered Klavier,* a set of preludes and fugues in each of the twelve major and minor keys, established him as a giant of keyboard composition and technique.

1723   Bach became director of music at St. Thomas Church in Leipzig, taught music at St. Thomas School, and supervised the musical programs in the three other main municipal churches. He wrote prolifically, concentrating on oratorios, masses, cantatas, and passions; church music continued to be the sole focus of his life.

1750   Completely blind, Bach died in Leipzig, oblivious to the potential impact of his music on generations to come.

Arcangelo Corelli (1653–1713) was an excellent violinist who, like Vivaldi, favored that instrument in his compositions. He was one of the first to write concerto grossi specifically for the improved stringed instruments that had greater projection of tone. He wrote for virtuoso players, who improvised ornamentation that thrilled listeners of the time. Corelli wrote both kinds of Baroque sonatas: the **sonata da camera,** similar to the keyboard suites built on dance forms, and the **sonata da chiesa,** written for sacred settings. The styles of both are very similar. The trio sonata, as mentioned earlier, had three parts, two violin parts with a cello and keyboard playing the continuo part. If the church was large enough, the more somber sonata da chiesa was often augmented by adding more players to each part, thereby sounding very similar to orchestral music. The trio sonata from Italy in the style of Corelli was imitated throughout Europe well into the middle of the eighteenth century.

sonata da camera
secular instrumental music.

sonata da chiesa
sacred instrumental music.

fugue
a musical form that uses subjects, answers, and countersubjects in an overlapping manner. It is similar to a very complicated round or canon.
preludes
the opening movements in suites and fugues in Baroque instrumental music. They are most commonly associated with the pipe organ.
toccata
a flamboyant introductory organ piece that precedes a fugue.

J. S. Bach's six *Brandenburg* Concertos display some of the most sparkling ensemble writing of the period. He used several different combinations of soloists. His third concerto grosso includes violin, flute, and harpsichord, while his second features trumpet, flute, oboe, and violin. When the harpsichord was used as a soloist, it had a dual role: as a soloist separate from the tutti ensemble and as continuo for the ritornello sections.

Besides the violin, another important instrument in this period was the pipe organ, located in cathedrals, churches, and courts all over Europe. Bach's fame during his lifetime was as an organist, not a composer. To be the Bach in a town was to be the best organist in that town. Organists working in churches today improvise for services much as Bach did in the Baroque era. Because of the many colors offered through the various pipe selections this instrument continues to be exciting to serious musicians.

A powerful Baroque form available to the organist and composer was the **fugue.** Fugues were often preceded by **preludes** or **toccatas**

A Baroque organ

that set the mood for the upcoming solitary statement of the **subject.** The subject of a fugue, once played, was answered or restated in the other parts. The dramatic texture comes from the overlapping statements of the subject and answer. The texture was often intensified with **countersubjects** that accompanied the subject each time it was stated. See the description of the form in Chapter 4.

Imagine a cathedral with its massive echo and the four overlapping melodies twisting around one another until the sound blurs and folds back into the echo. Listeners were engulfed by a wealth of sound. The final **cadence** required resolution of all this conflict. Often a long, low note in the pedals of the organ **(pedal point)** would sound out, announcing that the final destination, the **tonic,** was near. The other parts provide dissonance above the pedal note and eventually give definition to a dramatic cadence to end the work. The dissonance placed on the **dominant** chord in a fugue is more complex than in any other musical format of the day. The organist, in playing one key on the organ, may in turn open several pipes playing an array of different notes. When four keys were played together there was a dissonance level unknown to any other instrument. This instrument remains an orchestra in itself; it was the synthesizer of the Baroque period.

subject
the first statement in a fugue. Once answered by another part, it enters again in a third part.

countersubject
a melodic statement performed in duet fashion with the answer in a fugue. It is a complementary melody and supplies motives and complexity to the texture.

cadence
the end of a musical idea. It can be the end of a phrase, theme group, or movement.

pedal point
the long sounding of a low note on a pipe organ while melodies move freely above. The most common placement of a pedal point was at the end of large sections or works.

tonic (I)
the chord built on the first degree of the scale. It has the feeling of rest and completion.

dominant (V)
a chord built on the fifth note of the scale. It requires resolution to the tonic chord.

Listening Notes

J. S. Bach, *Fugue in G Minor ("The Little")* (1709).

The four voices of this fugue enter in order from top to bottom. The exposition of the fugue can be diagramed in the following way:

Soprano	subject and countersubject
Alto	answer (modulation) and countersubject
Tenor	subject and countersubject
Bass	answer and countersubject

Notice the delay before the tenor part enters; there is a modulation back to G minor before the subject enters again. As is traditional, the subjects are written in the tonic and the answers are written in the dominant. The balance of the fugue is composed of partial and full statements of the subject. The texture is rich with imitation, another significant element of fugues. Small musical **episodes** bridge the gap between statements of the subject. The material in the episodes is much freer and offers contrasting textures. Notice how the texture of this fugue

episodes
melodically free sections in a fugue.

(and all fugues) starts from a single voice and grows in intensity and thickness. The final cadence is a resolution of the growing tension. In this case the final statement is in the bass voice, adding finality to the work.

0:00   First statement of the subject.

0:17   Second part enters (answer); the first part continues with the counter-subject.

0:32   Brief extension before the next part enters.

0:37   Third part enters (subject); the second part moves on to the countersubject and the first part continues with free material.

0:53   Final part is played on the bass pedals (answer).

1:07   Episode.

1:16   The subject enters in the midrange.

1:21   The bass notes lead into a pedal point.

1:25   Pedal point begins in the bass as the other parts develop the subject.

1:34   Bass moves out of the pedal point.

1:42   Modified statement of the subject; bass voice drops out.

2:06   Dramatic entrance of the lower voice; same modified statement of the subject.

2:13   Trill in the upper part acts as a short ostinato.

2:20   Slow notes in the bass define the harmonic flow while the upper parts become imitative, episode.

2:36   A very thick texture develops.

2:51   Another imitative section, thinner in texture.

3:03   Modulation to related key areas.

3:14   Bass entrance with the subject.

3:28   Final cadence.

chorale prelude
an organ work based on a Lutheran chorale melody.

Another musical form for organists was the **chorale prelude,** a religious composition based on a Lutheran chorale melody. These works became very complicated in the hands of an improviser like Bach. Frequently a product of improvisation preceding the singing of a hymn in church, the chorales were very familiar to the congregation, and when the melody appeared out of the thick texture of the prelude the words would immediately come to their lips. Unfortunately, we are not familiar with the words or melodies of the chorale and therefore the prelude loses much of its impact and drama. In the case of Bach these chorale preludes were quite often dissonant and **chromatic;** this dissonance was tolerated because of the listeners' familiarity with the tune. Like background music today, dissonance seems to disappear when there is something else that is comprehensible and familiar to draw attention away from the dissonance itself.

chromatic
the use of half steps in melodies and chords suggesting movement from one key area to another.

French Baroque Composers

The Baroque era was a diverse musical period. The novelty of the many newly developing forms inspired composers and spawned incredible activity. Although Italy, Austria (and Germany), and England were centers of musical activity, France also produced many great composers; however, it experienced unique growing pains. The opera-ballets of Jean-Baptiste Lully (1632–87) provided a sharp contrast to Italian opera, and his emphasis on instrumental dances for ballet set his music apart from other opera styles. The long operas were popular and established a unique tradition of French eighteenth-century opera. The difference in the sound and articulation of the French language presented problems not encountered by the Italian, English, or German operas, and the lack of percussive sounds in French made it difficult to project a text in the newly developed recitative style.

A more declamatory use of the French language was developed by another French composer, Jean-Philippe Rameau (1683–1764). As a well-known music theoretician and philosopher, he brought to opera an intellectual approach to composition. As a result there was quite an argument between the Lullists and the Ramists. Rameau put to rest his critics with the triumphant comedy-ballet *La Princesse de Navarre*. Despite the differences in dance and text settings, French opera still carried instrumental and vocal similarities which reflected the Italian influence of Baroque vocal styles.

Chapter 8

THE VIENNESE PERIOD: *1750 to 1830*

Music Outline of the Viennese Period

1. The development of the four-movement **symphony** and the three-movement **solo concerto** expanded orchestral writing.

2. The four-movement **string quartet** and the three-movement **sonata** developed similarly in **chamber music.**

3. Musical forms such as the **sonata-allegro, rondo, minuet and trio, scherzo,** and **theme and variations** expressed a new intellectual posture toward instrumental composition.

4. Melodies built from **motives** led to greater musical development in the larger formal structures.

5. The predominant texture of both instrumental and vocal music was **homophony,** which displaced polyphony and the use of basso continuo.

6. The complex and ornate melodies of the Baroque era were replaced by graceful, symmetrical melodies supported by a less active harmonic texture.

7. Terraced dynamics of the Baroque period gave way to the gradual dynamic changes of **crescendo** and **decrescendo.**

8. The orchestra grew in size, articulating a sharper contrast between orchestral and chamber music.

9. Although patronage from aristocracy and the church continued, it began to break down late in the period.

 Musical Expansion and Line

By the middle of the 1700s many composers began to find the organization and regularity of Baroque composition too intense and domineering. Musical texture reached a new height of polyphony and counterpoint. The brief period of Rococo or "galant style" (1715–40) was framed around composers' reaction to the complex polyphony of the late Baroque and a move to thin the texture. Symbolized by light and frivolous compositions and paintings, the Rococo period served as a transition to the dramatic changes that would mark the music of the mature Viennese period.

Vienna became the musical center for the developments commonly referred to in the art world as the Classical period. The visual and literary artists were obsessed with quoting cultural examples of ancient Greece and Rome. For this reason, Greek temples appeared in the natural setting of a garden, in paintings, and even on coins. The elegance of medieval Greece and Rome was injected into all the arts, resulting in a classical attitude toward cultural expressions.

Ancient music had no historically intelligible notation and therefore nothing from which to quote or borrow. The classical composers in Vienna did, however, assume a classical posture. From this came the music known as Viennese classic. Smooth melodic lines, often constructed of smaller organic **motives,** soared elegantly above an accompaniment with a single purpose: to enhance the melody. Motives offered many new possibilities for musical development. Short melodic ideas could be used to structure similar but different melodies. Motives became the building blocks for **themes** and **theme groups.** Motivic development became the principal technique in expanding the symphony; it bred procedures for expansion of musical thought. This symphonic technique of development matured with Haydn and Mozart and reached a pinnacle late in the period with Beethoven, who

motive
a small musical unit made up of a short identifiable rhythm and a few pitches. The most famous motive is the opening of Beethoven's Fifth Symphony.

theme
a unique and identifiable melody. Extended works rely on themes for unification.

theme group
a tonal area that takes the place of a single theme in a sonata-allegro form.

A garden during the Classical period

successfully bridged the gap between classicism and romanticism. (See Topic 2.)

 The Symphony

The development of the symphony sprang out of the instrumental suites and sonatas of the Baroque period. The expansion of instrumental music into larger structures was limited by the dance forms themselves. Binary and ternary forms, which depended on the repetition and contrast of themes, provided little room for musical development. With the introduction of motivic development, new themes were built of smaller melodic ideas, and composers found the freedom to invent new structures that could support extensive development. As a result, the Viennese period gave birth to multimovement works rich with new structural ideas.

symphony
a large, four-movement work for orchestra that developed in the eighteenth century.
string quartet
a musical group comprised of two violins, viola, and cello. String quartets share the same compositional form as symphonies.

 Four-Movement Works

As in the orchestral **symphony** and the chamber music equivalent, the **string quartet,** the most important large structures had four movements. Of the four movements, only the third retained any connection with dance music. The minuet and trio (see Part I) retained the repetition and contrast associated with dance movements. The remaining three movements were often representative of the structures that also developed in this period: **sonata-allegro, rondo,** and **theme and variations.** (Refer to Chapter 4 for diagrams and explanations of these formal structures.)

The symphony had a status unequaled by any other form in the Viennese period. It continued to expand in length and complexity, offering an endless arena for musical development, and over the last two centuries motivic development continues to be a vital procedure in building large movements.

 ## The Sonata-Allegro Form

Large forms were needed to harness and structure the power inherent in the expanding developmental process. No single form could have answered the call better than the sonata-allegro form. The three sections of this form served different dramatic purposes. The first section, the **exposition,** presents two themes or theme groups and provides the material for later development in the second section, appropriately called the **development.** The last section, the **recapitulation,** is the resolution of the unstable development. The dramatic aspects of repetition and contrast offered in this form allowed inventive composers to add structure and unity to long single movements and eventually to combine several movements into an even larger multimovement structure.

Franz Joseph Haydn became the first composer to unleash the significance of the sonata-allegro form. He worked with the budding form in his shorter, dancelike **divertimenti,** a predecessor to his early string quartets. The most interesting part of this growth process can be seen in how the middle section, or development, took on more and more significance. The first appearances of the development section in the early string quartets were short motivic moments that provided contrast to the stability of the exposition and recapitulation. Over the years Haydn expanded the development section until it became an equal in the three-part structure.

Along with the drama of motivic development came a new musical force, tonal stability. The sonata-allegro form identifies each section by key area and theme. The term *theme group* means an area of melodic ideas grouped by key. The exposition has two key areas: first the tonic, followed by the dominant (or if the tonic key is minor, the relative

sonata-allegro form
the primary large structure used for the first movement of a symphony. Themes are expounded, developed, and recapitulated.

rondo
a formal structure in which the first theme is restated between a series of new themes.

theme and variations
a formal structure of a single work or movement of a larger work. Once a theme is stated, it is varied to the point of obscurity and is usually restated at the end of the selection.

exposition
the first section of the sonata-allegro form in which two themes (or theme groups) are presented, the first in the tonic and the second in the dominant or relative minor.

development
the middle section of a sonata-allegro form. Thematic material is modulated, broken down into smaller units, and changed and developed.

recapitulation
the last section of a sonata-allegro form in which the two primary themes (or theme groups) are restated in the tonic key after the development.

divertimenti
a collection of dancelike forms performed by small string ensembles. They were the predecessors to the modern string quartet.

Franz Joseph Haydn
(1732–1809)

DATELINE	BIOGRAPHY
1732	Franz Joseph Haydn was born in the Austrian village of Rohrau. His home life was simple, but loving, and his parents recognized his early musical talent and beautiful voice.
1740	After two years of strict musical training under Johann Franck, a distant relative, Haydn was sent to St. Stephen's in Vienna to sing in the choir and continue his education.
1745	Haydn's voice began to change, and he was dismissed from the choir at St. Stephen's and forced to earn a living on the streets of Vienna. He continued to practice and perform on clavier and violin while studying composition, particularly the works of C. P. E. Bach.
1756-59	By this time Haydn had developed a good reputation as both a performer and teacher and was making a simple living as music director to Count Ferdinand Morzin.
1760	Haydn married Maria Anna Keller after her younger sister (Haydn's first choice) became a nun; it was an unhappy, childless marriage.
1761-90	These thirty years were spent in the employment of the Esterhazys, a rich Hungarian noble family. Haydn lived on a magnificent country estate and composed volumes of music, conducted the orchestra, trained singers, and oversaw all aspects of the daily performances demanded by the royal family.
1772	Haydn composed and conducted the famous *Farewell* Symphony; during the performance, the musicians left the room one by one until only Haydn and one violinist remained. This musical hint convinced the prince to let the musicians return to Vienna for a much deserved reunion with their families.
1781-82	Haydn met Wolfgang Amadeus Mozart, for whom he held the highest musical respect. By this time, Haydn's music was widely acclaimed all over Europe.
1790-95	After the death of Prince Nicholas Esterhazy, Haydn left his post and traveled to London, where he composed twelve symphonies, later named the *London* Symphonies or *Salomon* Symphonies. Haydn was very well received in London and his concerts were extremely successful.

1795-
1801   He returned to Vienna rich and famous, where he continued writing masses for the Esterhazy family, as well as cantatas, sonatas, and concertos. Inspired by Handel's music, he composed two oratorios, *The Creation* (1798) and *The Seasons* (1801).

1802-9   Haydn's last years were spent in ill health; however, many friends and dignitaries came to pay tribute to him and he was continually honored by performances of his works. When he died in 1809, funeral services and concerts were held all over Europe in his honor. Even the French soldiers and officers who occupied Austria at the time paid tribute to his musical genius.

Listening Notes

Franz Joseph Haydn, Symphony no. 94 in G Major *(Surprise)* (1790).

This symphony is the third in the famous series of *Salomon* Symphonies, which Haydn wrote while in London. The four-movement structure is representative of the early symphonies.

   The first movement begins with a slow introduction marked *adagio cantabile* but quickly moves to a fast *vivace assai* for the remainder of the movement. The movement is structured in a sonata-allegro form with an emphasis on the first theme.

0:00   Slow introduction, *adagio*. The woodwind section and the string section echo ideas.

0:34   A melody starts in the lower strings and is imitated by the other strings, crescendo. The texture thins.

1:19   **Exposition.** *Vivace;* first theme is stated in a duet by the first and second violins.

1:42   A softer transitional idea is built on the three-note motive of the first theme but is inverted here, moving up instead of down.

2:26   A soft syncopated rhythm is followed by a fast passage played by the violins.

2:47   The second theme is played by the violins.

3:07   Trills in the woodwinds signal the closing theme of the exposition.

3:20 Cadence of exposition.

3:25 Starting at the *vivace* the exposition is repeated exactly. See above, starting at 1:15.

5:40 **Development** begins using the three-note motive of the first theme.

6:10 Key changes quickly several times; modulation.

6:20 Fast passage in the violins.

6:29 Lower strings state the theme.

6:36 **Recapitulation** begins with the first theme.

7:14 Syncopated rhythm followed by the fast passage in the violins returns as stated in the exposition.

7:30 Bass instruments play the theme.

7:55 Strong cadence.

8:00 A thin, slower texture leads into the second theme.

8:18 Second theme.

8:37 Oboe trill signals the final cadence.

8:58 End.

The second movement displays the humor of Haydn. This movement is marked *andante* and takes its place as the contrasting slow movement. The structure of this movement is theme and variations. The surprise comes after a very soft melody, like a nursery rhyme. The loud chord that suddenly appears after the repeat will, in the words of Haydn, ''Make the ladies jump!'' Notice how the character of the theme changes with each variation. See if you can hear when the theme is played in the minor key and when it returns to the major. Aside from the ''surprise,'' the shift from major to minor and back again is the most dramatic element of this movement.

0:00 The **theme** is begun very softly.

0:16 Repeat of first measures even more softly.

0:31 Surprise.

0:33 Second half of the theme.

1:08 **First variation.** The theme is heard in the lower strings, the first violins play above.

1:41   Second half of the first variation.

2:13   **Second variation.** Minor key and very loud *(ff)* followed by a very soft answer *(pp)*.

2:45   Second half of variation, active rhythmically with fast passages.

3:22   **Third variation.** The oboe plays the theme, followed by a flute and oboe duet.

3:58   Second half of the variation.

4:31   **Fourth variation.** Very loud beginning and an active violin part. A soft response follows.

5:06   Second half of the variation continues the softer texture but ends very full and loud.

5:41   **Coda.**

5:49   A long unstable chord is held without rhythmic progression, *fermata.*

5:50   A very soft ending with surprising harmonies brings the movement to a close.

6:20   End.

The third movement, *Allegro molto,* is a minuet and trio with graceful dancelike melodies presented in a restrained style typical of the eighteenth century. The last movement, *Allegro di molto,* is similar to the first in that it is based primarily on its first very active theme.

major). The development section increases tension by departing even farther from the tonic key area. The recapitulation is the celebration of key area stability by repeating all themes in the tonic. Key area alone became an organizational parameter, and resolution of key area is the musical goal of many large works.

The symphony developed quickly. Haydn was responsible for much of its early development. Mozart seized the symphonic form and took it to new heights. Finally, the classical symphony expanded further with the writings of Beethoven. His skill pushed the symphonic form beyond the scope of the classical period. He was truly a transitional figure. Refer to Part III, Topic 2, for a discussion of his Fifth Symphony. In just twenty-five years, the symphony moved from an exciting new form developed by Haydn to a dominant instrumental form for the early Romantic composers.

Beethoven conducting an orchestra

coda
the musical extension at the end of a movement or performance. It can be very short or quite long and developmental.

transitional sections
appear between themes or theme groups and help introduce new material. They can be developmental in nature, with motivic interplay and modulation.

A list of Beethoven's works is impressive in length and scope. He was an excellent pianoforte performer and like many composers before him had great improvisational skills. Beethoven's well-developed compositional mind allowed him to improvise on a small theme or motive in such a manner that listeners thought he had worked out the development of the ideas in advance.

The difference between his improvisations and his written works can only be speculated; however, his mature compositions are significant because they expanded earlier forms. The time to perform one movement of his Third Symphony alone dwarfed the time to play one of Haydn's symphonies. The greater length was due primarily to the expansion of the process of development within the symphony. Musical ideas begged for expansion and growth in developmental sections, and even in **codas** and **transitional sections.**

From an early age Beethoven not only performed on the piano and organ, he worked with a chapel choir and learned the possibilities of vocal and instrumental combinations. This broad background led to many works for solo piano, piano and orchestra, chorus, voice and pianoforte, and even one work for piano, vocal quartet, chorus, and orchestra.

Ludwig van Beethoven
(1770–1827)

DATELINE	BIOGRAPHY
1770	Ludwig van Beethoven was born December 16 in Bonn, Germany.
1782	He became a court musician in Bonn, assuming duties to replace his teacher Christian Neefe.
1784	He was formally appointed as assistant court organist.
1787	While in Vienna for study, he met and played for Mozart.
1788	Beethoven, still court organist, was hired as a viola player in the revived theater and opera orchestra in Bonn.
1792	Beethoven studied briefly with Haydn in Vienna.
1798	Deafness began to overtake Beethoven.
1803	With deafness ever increasing, Beethoven, with the *Eroica* Symphony, began a series of triumphant compositions heralding his second period.
1804-8	He became a commanding figure in the musical world, giving a regular series of concerts and publishing works with limited exclusive rights in Austria and Britain. During this time he produced his only opera, *Fidelio*.
1809	Beethoven was paid an annuity to remain in Vienna and not leave for a position in Westphalia.
1810	The Napoleonic Wars brought on economically hard times for Beethoven; however, he continued to write, completing his Fifth Piano Concerto, numerous string quartets, and the Seventh Symphony.
1815-20	Beethoven's compositions became fewer during a time of conflict while attempting to gain guardianship of his nephew Karl. A suicide attempt by Karl devastated Beethoven, a time that marked the beginning of Beethoven's third period.
1818-27	Beethoven, now totally deaf, produced his last string quartets, the late piano sonatas, the Ninth Symphony, and the *Missa solemnis*.

Beethoven became a full-time "freelance" composer, perhaps the first. He performed for years and conducted his works well into 1800; however, due to increasing deafness, he had to give up performance. He continued to make a successful living selling his works to publishers and patrons. He was so popular in Vienna that he received an annual salary from two noblemen to guarantee his presence in the city. By this time the musical community had become large enough in Vienna that his concerts and publications provided a comfortable income.

 ## Soloistic Three-Movement Works

The three-movement works that arose from the classical period usually involved soloists. The elimination of the minuet and trio from the large four-movement works is the most common structural difference. The sonata-allegro form still structured the first movement. The second movement provided a slow, strongly melodic contrast to the faster movements that surrounded it.

concerto (solo)
a three-movement work featuring a soloist accompanied by the orchestra.

The **solo concerto** was designed to feature an instrumental soloist with full orchestral accompaniment. With the appearance of the new, more forceful-sounding pianoforte, the number of solo concertos written for piano with orchestra outpaced those being written for any other instrument. The solo concerto became a showcase for technically superior musicians. In these concertos are short sections when the entire orchestra stops while the soloist improvises. These **cadenzas** allowed the performer to improvise on the musical material of the composer. Composers often performed their own works and were able to weave in spontaneous musical ideas with those they had already created. Later in this period and into the nineteenth century, composers took control by providing prewritten cadenzas, thus reducing some of the excitement of improvisation but guaranteeing a more consistent product.

cadenza
an unaccompanied solo that is rhythmically very free in both pulse and meter. Cadenzas are most commonly associated with the concerto form.

sonata
an early term to describe instrumental music. There are two kinds of sonatas: the secular da camera and the more serious sacred da chiesa. Later in history the term refers to a three-movement solo work, a soloist with piano accompaniment.

If the soloist is accompanied by a piano and not an orchestra, the work is called a **sonata.** The term *sonata* became more specific in this period; sonatas are now considered solo works rather than the more generic "played" or instrumental music. Pianists provide their own accompaniment in a sonata and therefore do not require a second musician. On the other hand, a violin sonata requires a piano for accompaniment. The piano becomes an equal with the soloist in the later sonatas of the period.

Vocal Music

Sacred music continued actively in the Viennese period with traditional large works like masses and oratorios. Haydn continued the tradition of oratorio writing established by Handel with two very successful works, *The Creation* and *The Seasons*. These works remain staples in concert literature today. The famous *Requiem* of Mozart, a Mass written for funeral services, shows the serious and weighty writing possible in the classical style. This piece has been recently popularized by the movie *Amadeus*. Sacred compositions large and small appeared throughout the period; however, the greatest change to take place in vocal music in the eighteenth century developed with opera.

Opera

In the Baroque period, serious opera had lost a good deal of its audience to oratorios and ballad opera. In the Viennese period, serious opera got a breath of fresh air with the **reform operas** of Gluck. In France in 1762 Gluck produced *Orfeo ed Euridice,* an opera that would signal a reformation movement to establish more balance between music and drama. With this opera and those that followed there was an attempt to better blend music, drama, and dance into a more theatrical whole. Gluck was partly successful because he softened the contrast between recitative and aria sections, both of which supported dramatic moments and freer expression. His accomplishments were substantial in that he tackled opera reform using a language thought by many to be unsingable, French. He not only successfully produced French **librettos,** but he placed new importance on the opening instrumental section, establishing the **overture** of the opera as an integral part of an opera. He used the orchestra thematically, giving further definition to the importance of instrumental music in this period. Gluck's greatest accomplishment came with the move to simplicity of melody and texture.

Although constructive and long lasting, reform operas found strong competition from the very popular **comic operas** written in England, Italy, and Germany. Each country had a different name for these very light and often farcical works. The French called them ***opéra comique*** and the Germans called theirs ***Singspiel.*** In each case the melodies

reform opera
a form of serious opera where the difference between recitative and aria was softened. It recaptured some of the audience lost to oratorios and ballad opera.

libretto
a text designed specifically to be set to music.

overture
the opening instrumental selection that precedes a music drama or theatrical work.

comic operas
very popular operas written in England, Italy, and Germany. Comic operas were not considered a part of the serious opera tradition.

opéra comique
French comic opera that was based on satire. These operas developed into a more realistic form in the late nineteenth century; they were not equal in scope to grand opera of the same period.

singspiel
a German form of comic opera. It is based on folk topics and songs.

Wolfgang Amadeus Mozart
(1756–91)

DATELINE	BIOGRAPHY
1756	Wolfgang Amadeus Mozart was born in Salzburg, Austria, into a musical family. By the age of six he was already considered a child prodigy, writing and performing his own compositions on harpsichord.
1762-69	Under his father Leopold's strict supervision, Mozart traveled all over Europe, performing in most major cities, including London and Paris. They were well received in all the royal courts, and Mozart's youthful charm and obvious musical genius overwhelmed and delighted his audiences.
1769-71	Mozart and his father toured Italy, where he established his genius by writing down an entire Mass performed by the Sistine Chapel choir after only one hearing. His successful tour of Italy brought several commissions by wealthy patrons, and he continued working on operas, symphonies, and oratorios as well as performing his own keyboard compositions.
1771-77	Mozart returned to Salzburg and spent these years feverishly composing. His popularity as a child performer, however, began to wane, and Mozart became more and more dissatisfied with his life in Salzburg. His total dependence on his father had resulted in a selfish, pampered, and intolerant personality.
1777	With his mother as chaperone, Mozart left Salzburg to seek possible employment in Munich, and later Paris, where his mother died in 1778. He returned to Vienna, which remained his home.
1782	Soon after the success of his first opera, *Die Entführung aus dem Serail,* Mozart married Constanze Weber. Although he continued to write and perform, Mozart had no fixed income and the marriage was plagued by money problems.
1786-87	The operas *Le nozze di Figaro* and *Don Giovanni* were successful, but Mozart's popularity in Vienna began to decline.
1790	Mozart was commissioned to write a **requiem** for an unknown patron; as his health grew worse, he struggled to finish the requiem, believing that it was his own.
1791	Mozart died in Vienna at the age of thirty-five and was buried in a pauper's grave.

requiem
a Mass for the dead.

relied heavily on folk songs and popular music of the day to present romance and comedy. All forms of these comic operas, except the Italian, had spoken parts to elaborate the plots and provide sharp comic moments. The use of the vernacular language drew strong support for these simply produced operas.

Italian composers of serious opera also found the use of comedy increasingly successful and eventually developed **opera buffa,** which placed individuals in socially humorous situations. These works often concluded with an **ensemble finale** where each singer on stage would sing independent words and music, creating a clever and complex polyphony that intrigued listeners. The compositional skills exhibited by Mozart in his brilliant opera buffa *Le nozze di Figaro* not only enraptured the audience but has fascinated musicians for years. He enhanced the drama by cleverly controlling key areas and manipulating thematic material. His symphonic writing skills propelled him ahead of his peers. His operas tease the intellect as much as they do the ear. He built large structures in his operas on a par with the forms being developed in instrumental music at the same time.

opera buffa
opera that was entirely sung (Italian) but was still part of the comic opera tradition. Recitative was used instead of spoken dialogue.

ensemble finale
the final scene of an operatic section where several singers perform at the same time, but sing independent texts and often express different moods; for example, Italian opera.

Cherubino, from Mozart's
Le nozze di Figaro

Listening Notes

Wolfgang Amadeus Mozart, *Le nozze di Figaro* (1786).

The second half of Act I is a brilliant example of Mozart's mastery of key areas and their relationship to the libretto. As the story unfolds, so does a parallel musical drama. This ensemble section has four characters:

1. Susanna (soprano) is the maid to the Countess Almaviva and will eventually marry Figaro.
2. The Count (bass) is in love with Susanna.
3. Cherubino (male part sung by a soprano), a page to the Countess, is just maturing and is in love with any woman he sees. The Count discovered Cherubino having an affair with Barbarina and promises to expel him from the castle.
4. Don Basilio (tenor) is a music master who will aid the Count in discovering Cherubino.

The scene takes place in a room with Susanna and Cherubino. As they talk of love Cherubino sings an aria that will appear later in the scene in a slower or augmented fashion (sung by Basilio).

The Count enters while Cherubino hides behind a chair. The Count pleas for an affair with Susanna. Basilio then enters while the Count hides behind the chair and Cherubino moves, unseen by the Count, into the chair and is covered by a dress. Basilio makes accusations about Cherubino and Susanna. He then sings the augmented melody of Cherubino's aria. He must know that Cherubino and the Count are hiding and is teasing them. The Count jumps out and angrily joins into a trio with Susanna and Basilio about Cherubino's escapades. They share melodic ideas from the augmented melody of Cherubino. As the Count tells of his earlier discovery of Cherubino with Barbarina, he lifts the dress and discovers Cherubino again in another compromising situation.

The scene is visually very funny and the music helps feed the humor and suspense. As the discovery of Cherubino approaches, there is a movement toward the key of B♭. Basilio feeds the Count the dominant key area. Susanna takes the Count to the key of B♭ minor and faints; she wakes up when he comes back to the dominant. The Count discovers Cherubino in a solid statement of B♭.

Mozart did not rely on the story alone to tie his music together. He used every avenue possible to unify the dramatic flow. His mastery of key area parallels the strength offered in other forms such as the sonata-allegro form where juxtaposition of key area is so important. In fact, the trio section takes on a modified sonata-allegro form. See if you can recognize the augmented melody sung by Basilio and finally the Count. Compare it to the aria that starts this listening example.

Cherubino's aria

0:00　A light, frivolous melody. Cherubino sings of his need of love and how he is always thinking of it.

0:21　A new melodic idea contrasting the first. It is more passionate and emotional, and strings accompany.

0:56　Return to the original melody; woodwinds are added to the accompaniment.

1:17　Brief instrumental interlude with short vocal lines floating above.

1:30　Voice takes the lead again.

1:43　Cadence. A new section begins with slow melodic lines and brief moments where the accompaniment almost disappears.

1:57　The aria seems to be unwinding.

2:43　The tempo slows greatly, eventually leading to a sudden final cadence.

3:19　The aria ends.

3:21　A recitative between Susanna and the Count immediately follows while Cherubino hides behind a chair. The Count tries to seduce Susanna, but she avoids all advances. The only accompaniment is the harpsichord.

4:07　Notice the fast fluid setting of the Italian syllables.

4:17　Basilio approaches from offstage.

4:34　The Count hides behind the chair as Cherubino moves into the chair and hides under a dress. The recitative continues with Basilio and Susanna.

4:57　Basilio obviously knows that the Count and Cherubino are hiding and he teases them indirectly by comparing Susanna's feelings toward them.

6:27　The Count comes out of hiding and is angry over Basilio's implications.

Trio between Susanna, the Count, and Basilio

6:33　The trio begins with full orchestra. The Count sings in an angry tone; Basilio maintains a teasing quality.

7:01　Susanna takes the mode from major to minor and pretends to faint.

7:12　The subject moves to Susanna's condition and away from Cherubino.

7:45　Basilio moves the key to the dominant (F); Susanna steps in angrily and moves the key away to G minor while she physically moves away from the chair.

7:58	The Count and Basilio sing together once again, this time in the subdominant. Susanna moves it to the minor but it is destined to reach B♭.
8:58	The Count sings in a more declamatory style (almost like a recitative) to tell how he found Cherubino with Barbarina.
9:32	As the Count lifts the dress in demonstration of his story, Cherubino is discovered again.
9:47	The scene ends with the Count angry, Basilio laughing, and Susanna distraught.
10:45	Coda material to end the trio.

 Patronage and the Working Musician

The classical period was dominated by the genius of three great composers: Haydn, Mozart, and Beethoven. Due to the quality and quantity of their compositions they are remembered today with a certain sense of reverence. The social environment of that period, however, did not see these men in such an elevated light. For nearly thirty years Haydn enjoyed the patronage of the Esterhazy family, an aristocratic family typical of the wealthy class. The aristocracy was capable of hiring composers and orchestras alike. During his long life Haydn slowly became independent of sole patronage. Publishing music became a substantial business, and Haydn was one of the first to make it work for him. Along with publishing, public concerts, increasingly popular with the emerging upper middle class, offered a source of income. With increasing independence, composers moved from being "hired help" for the aristocracy to freelance artists with an improved level of public recognition. It was and still is difficult to compose music without combining patronage with activities of performance and publishing. One sees the humor of Haydn in his *Surprise* and *Farewell* Symphonies; in writing music required of his patrons, he wittingly poked fun at those who hired him while satisfying both his expressive needs and the taste of his patrons.

Mozart was tragically caught between the image of menial skilled labor, which he despised, and that of a new, emerging, self-sufficient artist. He performed and composed desperately to make a living. His move to Vienna barely paid, and he died in poverty. He was a failure at soliciting patrons to subsidize his other activities.

On the other hand, Beethoven broke away from the old image completely. He received his greatest support from the growing demand for music and concerts for the middle class. He did, however, continue to nurture links with the aristocracy who continually lent support to his talent. He demonstrated well-developed skills in balancing patronage, publication, and performance.

History has placed these three individuals outside their common beginnings. Haydn wrote music that served the fancy of those who paid him; Mozart was less willing to compromise and struggled his short adult life; and Beethoven was amazingly successful considering that he rarely compromised his goals. The conditions around each impacted many of their actions. Regardless, each responded to his conditions by producing great music. As music developed after Beethoven, the music industry itself broadened and gave increasing support to struggling composers.

Chapter 9

THE ROMANTIC PERIOD:
1830 to 1900

Music Outline of the Romantic Period

1. A wide variety of musical structures developed, from small intimate works for solo voice and/or piano, called **miniatures,** to grandiose symphonies and operas.

2. The **art song** flourished, focusing on the Romantic desire to be dramatically expressive.

3. **Program music** blossomed as a single-movement instrumental form offering a continuous flow of descriptive musical composition.

4. The symphony increased in length and scope. **Dynamic** and **pitch ranges** expanded and **tempi** varied dramatically within movements.

5. Orchestras increased in size, and the role of the **conductor** in coordinating the changes in tempo and dynamics increased.

6. The composer's goal shifted from displaying musical craft to expressing personal emotions and ideas. Nationalism and exoticism became favorite topics for expression in opera and program music.

7. Techniques of combining instruments, **orchestration,** along with new colorful and dissonant harmonies became expressive tools for composers.

8. Opera expanded with increased instrumental sections and flamboyant plots.

"I feel, therefore I am." These famous words by Jean Jacques Rousseau became the echoing call of the Romantic period. Feeling was taking precedence over thinking. Love and nature pushed against authority. This theme motivated the genius of Beethoven and eventually later Romantic composers. Music expanded to the grandiose, and performances required more musicians playing an extraordinary range of dynamics. The extremes from very soft to very loud widened. Along with the powerful large works were miniature, intimate works that also moved to express powerful, personal feelings.

 The Art Song

Solo compositions in the Romantic period are perhaps the most representative forms of the expressive goals of the artists of this time. Literature provided the emotional content necessary for elaboration by the composer. As seen in the early madrigals of Monteverdi, the sacred music of Palestrina, the recitatives and arias of Handel, and the operas of Mozart, the balance between words and music remained an ever-present concern, but the balance shifted with each period. In the Romantic period, words were given added emotional significance instrumentally. At times in art songs the pianist becomes a soloist of equal importance, balancing the dialogue with the vocalist.

Each country had a form of **art song** or **lied** (German) for singing at home or in other intimate settings. Although the songs cover all topics imaginable, the most common was romance. The pain and joy of

art song
a setting of a poem by an established literary writer. The most common languages for these songs are Italian, French, and German.

lied
a German art song.

romantic love dominated the thoughts of musicians. These songs were miniatures of the phenomenon that was taking place in the entire artistic community. In setting poems to music, composers relied on a long tradition of word painting. Special emotionally laden words would receive dissonance or resolution to help express feelings of yearning, frustration, or sadness.

Composers grouped songs with related themes into cycles filled with a variety of emotions. When viewed as a whole these **song cycles** are really larger works. Structural elements may group two or three songs at a time into a larger section that would, in turn, balance similar groups of songs. The overall structure may be a large binary or ternary form. This technique was especially effective in the Schumann song cycle *Frauen Lieben und Leben* (A Woman's Love and Life) or Schubert's *Winterreise* (Winter's Journey.)

song cycles
art songs from the nineteenth century. Cycles were a series of poems set to music that related a common story.

Franz Schubert
(1797–1828)

DATELINE	BIOGRAPHY
1797	Born in Vienna, the son of a pious schoolmaster, Franz Schubert was surrounded by music and began piano and violin lessons at an early age.
1808	Schubert was admitted to the court chapel choir and subsequently won a scholarship to the Imperial Seminary, a prestigious Viennese boarding school, where he furthered his musical studies and began composing songs and piano works.
1813	He left school, studied elementary education at a teacher training school, and began working at his father's school in 1814, a position he loathed as it hindered his desire to compose constantly.
1814	Schubert continued composing volumes of music, taking the poetry of the great writers of his day such as Goethe and Schiller and converting it to romantic art songs, as in his first great song, ''Gretchen am Spinnrade.''
1815	Schubert wrote 144 songs, including ''Erlkönig,'' a fine example of musical romanticism; he centered most of his songs on themes of nature and unhappy love.

1816-18 He composed 179 works, including piano sonatas, art songs, symphonies, and operas; almost 1,000 works would be completed before his early death.

1818 Schubert quit his teaching job and eked out a living writing and selling his music and teaching music lessons. He surrounded himself with a small circle of poverty-stricken friends, mostly artists, poets, and musicians, and spent his days composing, frequenting small cafes, and performing at parties for middle-class patrons.

1822 At twenty-five years old, Schubert contracted venereal disease; although in ill health and depressed, he continued writing. His *Unfinished Symphony,* written this year, was not performed until forty years after his death.

1823 Schubert composed his first song cycle, *Die Schöne Müllerin,* a collection of art songs that tells a story; his second cycle, *Die Winterreise,* was completed in 1827.

1828 His general health declining rapidly, Schubert contracted typhoid and died in Vienna. His last request was that he be buried near Beethoven, and so he was.

The technique for structuring single songs falls into one of two categories. The most familiar is to set several verses or stanzas of a poem to the same or slightly varied music. This **strophic** technique provided the repetition necessary for audience comprehension. Strophic songs were easily remembered and became favorites. The second category relies on contrast and development to interpret the story. In a **through-composed form** (from the German *durchkomponiert*) the dramatic development is apt to increase as the story unfolds. The music does not rely on strict repetition; as the story unfolds and characters change mood, the music changes, representing and amplifying the changes in the storyline.

The dramatic use of both these techniques can be found in the songs of Franz Schubert. At times he combined the two techniques to reap the benefit of both. At the age of seventeen he composed his musically descriptive song *Gretchen am Spinnrade* (Gretchen at the Spinning Wheel) and at eighteen he wrote in one sitting the dramatic *Erlkönig* (The Erlking). These two songs fully represent the finest products of a musical romantic. Although art songs were not new to the Romantic period, Schubert brought the form to a new level of intensity representative of the romantic temperament.

strophic form
a song that retains the same music through multiple verses.

through-composed form
music without repetitive sections for different verses. Although the text of a song is strophic, the music may be different for each verse.

Listening Notes

Franz Schubert, *Gretchen am Spinnrade* (1814).

The poem by Goethe is an expression of the longing of Gretchen for her lover Faust. Schubert paints a musical picture of the spinning wheel with the repeating pattern in the piano. Notice how the motion in the piano increases as Gretchen becomes more emotionally upset. The end of the middle section provides the only moment of relief from the spinning wheel as she stops spinning to think of ''his kiss.'' After this short break the spinning continues.

Although this song has ten short stanzas, Schubert creates a larger ternary form by grouping the verses into three larger groups. This **modified strophic form** came naturally to most mature songwriters.

modified strophic form two or more verses of an art song set to the same music but additional verses set to new music.

0:00	Introduction on the piano is very short but establishes the spinning motion used throughout the song. The text is divided into three larger sections, each of which begins with the same four lines of text. ''My peace is gone, my heart is heavy.''
0:38	Higher vocal range; short phrase is repeated a little higher. Gretchen's anxiety has increased.
0:49	Second part of the song starts just as the first part with the same four lines of text.
1:21	The text moves to thoughts of her love and the peace it brings her. The music makes slight changes to accommodate the change in mood.
1:35	The music grows in volume and range.
1:48	The climax of the crescendo is her thought of his kiss. The piano briefly stops the spinning motion but builds up momentum again and reestablishes the spinning sound.
2:03	The third part begins as the other parts did, with the same text and melody.
2:25	Another emotional crescendo builds but soon fades.
3:07	The coda uses two lines of the opening text; the piano motion in the piano slowly unwinds.
3:20	End.

Listening Notes

Franz Schubert, *Erlkönig* (1815).

The drama of this through-composed song unfolds above the tension-filled bass melody in the piano. Although there is only one singer performing the song, there are, besides the narrator, three characters in this story by Goethe.

The narrator tells of a father riding late at night in bad weather with his sick child in his arms. The father sings in a low register, trying to comfort his son. The Erlking sings in a higher register with enticing and luring melodies beckoning the child to him. The son sings fearful outcries of ''Mein Vater'' (''My father, my father'') and tries to describe the pleas of the Erlking to his father.

The Erlking is the king of the elves and represents death. In a contrasting vocal range from the father's desperate assurances the Erlking promises games and happiness to the child. The part of the narrator appears twice, starting and ending the song. Notice the differences of melody and range that separate the identities of the father, the Erlking, and the son.

The song ends with the narrator. The father arrived home and ''in his arms, the child was dead.''

0:00   Piano begins with a galloping theme in the bass.

0:23   The narrator tells of the father and son in a hurried journey home.

0:57   The father asks what his son sees.

1:07   The son replies that he sees the Erlking.

1:22   The father says it is only an image in the mist.

1:32   The Erlking invites the son to join him. The melody is light, soothing, and vocal range is higher and floats above the accompaniment.

1:54   The boy yells out in fright. The vocal range is more strained.

2:08   The father tries to comfort the child. A lower vocal range is used.

2:18   The Erlking again tells the boy that they will sing and dance in a wonderful world.

2:35   The son yells again in fright.

2:48	The father again tries to comfort him.
3:00	Brief piano interlude.
3:07	The Erlking continues to call the boy.
3:18	Desperate screams from the boy.
3:34	The narrator enters, telling of the panic of the father.
4:00	"In his arms, the child was dead."
4:15	End.

 ## Solo Piano

pianoforte, piano
the dominant instrument in
music since the nineteenth
century. The instrument is
named for its ability to play
both loudly *(forte)* and softly
(piano).
miniatures
short works in the Romantic
era such as art songs and
single-movement piano
compositions.

With the development of the **pianoforte,** short works or **miniatures** exploded in popularity. In the late 1700s the piano, because of its ability to play dynamics between loud and soft, quickly replaced the harpsichord. For keyboard soloists, the piano offered greater scope of expression than any other instrument except the pipe organ. The expressive needs of Romantic composers found the singing nature of this percussion instrument exciting. As a result, it became the favored instrument for solo composition.

As in art songs, mood development dominated the thinking of composers for the piano. There were many single-movement forms from which Romantic composers could choose. Chopin explored most of them but, except for a few orchestral accompaniments, directed his attention to composing strictly for the piano.

Character Pieces

Chopin used several forms of character pieces, or single-movement works that develop a specific mood. Following are several of the favorite forms of Chopin.

Nocturnes, pieces for night, were slow compositions with rich and lyric melodies. They were generally in a three-part form (A B A). The B section was very different in texture and mood from the A sections.

Études were literally studies designed to develop a student's technique. The specific technique to be developed became the primary thrust of the work. In the hands of great composers, these studies took on musical qualities, making them suitable as concert pieces.

Polonaise and the **mazurka** are both traditional Polish dances characterized by their triple meter. The polonaise retained its stately nature and was traditionally a processional for the nobility.

Impromptus demand a great deal of technique and sound free and reflective, similar to what might be expected during an improvisation. They did not, however, allow for improvisation.

Ballades are musical narratives without words. The music unfolds much like a developing story.

Preludes are a series of short pieces that develop rich moods exploring all the major and minor keys.

Chopin's mastery of the piano as a performer, improviser, and composer gives him a unique place in history. Compositions for piano such as Schumann's character pieces and the intermezzi of Brahms

Frédéric Chopin
(1810–49)

DATELINE	BIOGRAPHY
1810	Frédéric Chopin was born in Warsaw, the son of a French father who taught his native language to children of the Polish nobility.
1818	Chopin gave his first public concert at the age of eight, having studied piano at the Warsaw School of Music. By the age of fifteen he was already a published composer, and by nineteen he was widely known for both composition and performance.
1831	He gave concerts in Paris, where he was immediately accepted by the aristocracy and invited into a circle of well-known artists, writers, and musicians, including Victor Hugo, Alexandre Dumas, Franz Liszt, Hector Berlioz, Robert Schumann, and Eugène Delacroix, who became his closest friend. He decided to make Paris his home.
1836	Chopin met novelist George Sand (Mme. Aurore Dudevant) and began a ten-year relationship; these proved to be his most productive composing years. Writing almost exclusively for the piano, Chopin composed études, preludes, polonaises, nocturnes, waltzes, and ballades.
1847	After his relationship with George Sand ended, Chopin's general health began to fail due to previous bouts with tuberculosis. His desire to compose dwindled dramatically.
1849	After spending the last year of his life in Scotland, Chopin returned to Paris where he died and was buried.

Listening Notes

Frédéric Chopin, Étude in C Minor, op. 10, no. 12 (1831).

This étude was called the *Revolutionary* Étude because of its heroic and aggressive nature. This particular study was designed to develop speed and endurance in the left hand of the pianist. Notice the active and relentless motion in the bass. The heroic nature comes from the strong chordal melody in the treble. Following the opening chords the right hand continues with a powerful melody played in octaves. The ending arises from the single moment where the motion calms; there is a strong, ornate pattern descending the keyboard, concluding in the final loud chords.

Notice the interaction between the left and right hands. Typical of Chopin's performance style, the right hand pulls against the rhythm of the left hand. This feeling of freedom, **rubato,** is a critical element in Chopin's music. The melody is set apart from the accompaniment through rubato, adding strength and tension to the melodic line. This étude surpasses any image of being a mere exercise for a student. It, like most of his others, has become a staple for virtuoso pianists.

rubato
"robbed time." In the piano style of Chopin, the right hand would pull and push against the regular rhythm being played in the left hand, suggesting a sense of rhythmic freedom.

0:00	Introduction; full chord in the right hand followed by a long descending line in the left hand. Fast notes swirl down into the bass range, preparing for the entrance of the theme.
0:16	The theme, a forceful dotted rhythm (long-short), is stated in the right hand. The left hand continues with fast, difficult passages.
0:33	Repeat of the theme, started softer this time but crescendos quickly.
0:47	The middle section has new chords and a new melody.
1:17	The descending, swirling passage returns again, leading into the theme.
1:26	Repeat of the opening theme and texture.
1:56	The texture thins a little with a decrescendo.
2:10	Soft ascending passage begins in the bass and continues up through the range of the piano.
2:17	Cadence, softer but still active.
2:25	Ending.
2:30	Final chords.

explored additional sonorities for the piano. Their works are unique and musically powerful. However, no composer dedicated himself so completely to exploring the rich new harmonies and sonorities within the expressive nature of the piano as Chopin.

🎼 *Program Music*

The emotional outpouring typical of art songs existed in instrumental music as well as piano music. The most popular format was **program music.** Although there is no vocal text, the music depends on poems, stories, ideas, or just a single word to guide and define the developing moods of the composition. Regardless of how short or long the literary idea, program music provided a new dimension to both single-movement and multimovement works. In contrast, instrumental music that had no program was called **absolute music;** the musical elements were supreme with no association with literature.

There are three basic forms of program music: concert overtures, tone poems, and program symphonies.

1. **Concert overtures** are a single-movement works usually in sonata form. Traditionally, overtures preceded a dramatic work such as an opera or play and set the mood for the upcoming drama. The concert overture, however, had no such function; it used the title to define the mood of the unfolding instrumental drama. Concert overtures were for performances where no stage drama was expected to follow. Examples include *Romeo and Juliet Overture* by Peter Ilyich Tchaikovsky and *Hebrides Overture* by Felix Mendelssohn.

2. **Tone poems** or **symphonic poems** are long, single-movement compositions. The sonata-allegro form or rondo was commonly used to structure the musical development. Irregular forms were also designed to respond to a unique developing story. These freer structures provided the same flexibility songwriters had with through-composed forms. In both cases the literary structure holds the work together. Exotic tales were favorite subjects for these flexible symphonic compositions. Examples include *Don Juan* by Richard Strauss, *The Sorcerer's Apprentice* by Paul Dukas, and *Les Preludes* by Franz Liszt.

3. **Program symphonies** are similar to single-movement tone poems but offer an expanded format for organization and development. The program symphony, as the title implies, had a program to unify a multimovement form. Commonly, each movement had a title or phrase

program music
music based on some literary element, either a poem, story, or title. The music is interpretive of the story or mood presented in the program.

absolute music
instrumental music not associated with a poem, story, or title. The music is not meant to be interpretive of any literary element.

concert overture
an overture played on the concert stage. The overture is not the introduction to a literary work or opera.

tone poem, symphonic poem
a single-movement work for orchestra based on a poem, story, or title.

as a program. In the case of Hector Berlioz's *Symphonie Fantastique* (Fantastic Symphony), each movement describes a single event; the movements build a larger program for the entire symphony.

Listening Notes

Hector Berlioz, "March to the Scaffold" from *Symphonie fantastique* (1830).

This symphony is in five instead of the usual four movements, and each movement has a specific program. The overall program for the symphony is long and descriptive; it is also quasi-autobiographical. Berlioz was in love with a Shakespearean actress who was extremely popular in Paris. Although she refused to see him at first, she did attend a concert two years later of his *Symphonie fantastique* and was swept off her feet when she realized that it was about her. Their marriage, however, could not live up to the fantasy and ended after a few years. The program for this symphony depicts his yearning for her love and his depression from her lack of response. Because of his despair, he attempts suicide with opium, but rather than dying he falls into a heavy sleep and dreams.

His love appears in the dreams as a recurring musical motif called **idée fixe** or **fixed idea.** The fixed idea unifies the five movements by its reappearance. The theme is altered each time it appears, taking on dramatically different personalities. In the second movement the fixed idea is an elaborate waltz theme; in the fourth movement it is played by a solo clarinet that is shockingly interrupted. The technique of developing and changing the same theme throughout several movements, called **thematic transformation,** was becoming more prevalent following its use by Beethoven in his Fifth Symphony (discussed in Topic 2).

The titles of the five movements are 1. "Reveries, Passions" 2. "A Ball" 3. "Scene in the Country" 4. "March to the Scaffold" and 5. "Dream of a Witches' Sabbath."

The fourth movement, "March to the Scaffold," is a story of the dreamer as he walks to his execution for murdering his beloved. The fixed idea at the end of the movement is abruptly cut off before it is completed by a loud orchestral chord representing the fall of the guillotine's blade. This movement unleashes some of the most striking orchestrations in the symphony. Notice the enlarged brass and percussion sections.

fixed idea
a recurring theme (specific to Berlioz's *Symphonie fantastique*). It appeared, although transformed, in each movement of this program symphony.
thematic transformation
changing the theme to take on a different character or personality each time it returns in the movement or work.

0:00	Tympani opens the movement, French horns make short statements above.
0:26	Descending melody follows full orchestral chord.
0:42	Repeat of the melody with the addition of a bassoon solo melody.
0:53	Violin takes the melody with activity in the lower strings.
1:05	Sudden brass and percussion shouts; violin and lower string activity continues.
1:20	New texture, pizzicato strings; very active bassoon line accompanies.
1:39	Brass and woodwinds play a powerful march theme. Notice the tympani.
2:05	Trumpet call and low pedal note in the trombone. Phrase completed by a very dissonant chord.
2:11	Return to pizzicato strings.
2:21	March returns.
2:52	Soft strings and woodwinds, crescendo.
3:14	Climax of march theme, cymbal crashes, lower brass.
3:25	Transition.
3:40	Sudden orchestral accent, galloping string activity.
4:16	Solo clarinet playing the fixed idea.
4:26	Loud accented chord interrupts the clarinet solo.
4:30	Drum roll, cymbal crashes, brass chords conclude the movement.

The novelty of the returning theme and the surprising autobiographical program made a strong impression on the Parisians. In addition to these innovations, Berlioz enlarged the orchestra with additional trumpets, trombones, tubas, and percussion. The larger brass and percussion expanded the range of dynamics. He was the first to write dynamic levels greater than *ff* and less than *pp*.

Berlioz was known as a revolutionary because of his new instrumental combinations. His **orchestrations** grouped instruments nontraditionally, producing some of the most exciting tone colors of the period. He was not a pianist; he played flute and guitar. His writing for orchestra was unique in that he used the orchestra as his instrument rather than merely orchestrating what he played on the piano. For this reason, his inability to play piano was very possibly a blessing in disguise.

orchestration
the process of assigning instruments to musical ideas. Orchestration is part of the compositional process, important to the mood and spirit of a work.

Hector Berlioz
(1803–69)

DATELINE	BIOGRAPHY
1803	Hector Berlioz was born in a small town near Grenoble, France. His father, a physician, insisted on early medical training, although his son's great musical interest was obvious.
1821	Berlioz went to Paris to study medicine, but spent many more hours in the opera house and music library. To the horror of his family he abandoned medical school and began composing while studying at the Paris Conservatory.
1830	He won the coveted Prix de Rome, a compositional award that gave him scholarship money to study in Rome for two years; this same year he composed and conducted the *Symphonie fantastique,* dedicated to Harriet Smithson, the Shakespearean actress he had seen perform two years earlier and with whom he had fallen madly in love.
1832	Berlioz married Smithson and had a son; he spent the majority of his time writing and producing his own concerts to publicize his works. This was a costly endeavor because Berlioz's grandiose orchestrations meant hiring hundreds of musicians and vocalists.
1835	To provide enough income for his family, Berlioz took a job as a music critic, writing for local Parisian journals.
1837	Although Berlioz's unconventional music was generally accepted by the public, he had no support from the organized music societies or the Paris opera house directors. The production of his *Requiem* this year involved a huge orchestra, hundreds of voices, and four brass choirs; this and subsequent concerts pushed him further into debt.
1838	The debut of his opera *Benvenuto Cellini* resulted in open audience disapproval; *Romeo and Juliet,* a dramatic symphony based on the Shakespeare play, was performed successfully in 1839, but again without profit.
1840-46	Growing bitter by the lack of his acceptance in Paris, Berlioz traveled all over Europe, composing and conducting major works including the *Damnation of Faust,* based on Goethe's poem.
1869	Berlioz died in Paris, having spent the last years of his life in mental and physical agony, fighting several chronic illnesses that left him almost bedridden.

Opera: Grandeur and Dissonance

Emotion and passion dominated most of the dramatic plots in the nineteenth century. In Romantic opera the love between two individuals was commonly depicted as being so great that if one died the other also died because their love had ended. In the opera *Tristan und Isolde* by Wagner, Tristan is mortally wounded early in the opera; when he finally dies in the last scene Isolde dies, singing her love for him. Emotions were further expanded by using mythology, which offered magic and supernatural suspense for heroes and villains who were larger than life.

To best understand nineteenth-century opera we will look at two powerful composers of the period. Their contrasting compositional styles exhibit a wide scope of operatic possibilities. Verdi in Italy and Wagner in Germany wrote with conviction for what they believed was the function of opera.

Verdi believed that opera must, above all else, be passionate; it should also be interesting and provide entertainment for the mass

Giuseppe Verdi
(1813–1901)

DATELINE	BIOGRAPHY
1813	Giuseppe Verdi was born in the small Italian village of Le Roncole, the son of a tavern keeper.
1823-35	He studied music in the nearby town of Busseto, where he became the municipal music director and married Margherita Barezzi, the daughter of a patron. As a teenager he walked miles barefoot to his job as church organist to save his only pair of boots.
1839	Verdi wrote the first of his twenty-six operas, *Oberto,* which was performed in Milan and led to a contract for three more operas.
1838-40	His wife and two small children died. Verdi quit composing for months and fell into a life of quiet despair.
1841	Inspired by the libretto of *Nabucco,* a biblical story that told of the plight of the Jewish people, he wrote the opera. His own sense of nationalism and patriotism was further fired by the fight for a united Italy, free from Austrian domination.

1851-53	During this time, Verdi composed three famous operas, *Rigoletto, La Traviata,* and *Il Trovatore.*
1859	He married his second wife, Giuseppina Strepponi, with whom he had spent the previous ten years.
1861	Verdi was elected to the first Italian parliament after Italy became a nation.
1871	The opera *Aida* was performed at the Cairo opera house in celebration of the opening of the Suez Canal in 1869.
1887-93	Verdi composed his most famous tragedy, *Otello,* and at the age of seventy-nine he completed his most famous comedy, *Falstaff.*
1901	Verdi died in Milan, several days after suffering a stroke.

public. He wrote in a conventional manner, placing emphasis on melody. Throughout his life his orchestrations became increasingly more descriptive in support of the melody; however, the melodic line and its ability to enhance the text were always supreme. As he matured, the emotionally charged arias and the more descriptive recitatives became more and more similar, especially in his last three operas, *Aida, Otello,* and *Falstaff.*

Verdi's popularity was tremendous and his ability to build strong musical characterizations set him apart from his contemporaries. His operas became the model for Italian opera. A favorite part of many of his operas was the ensemble that ended large sections. In these sections several individuals sing separate melodies with different texts and act as if they do not hear each other. Verdi identified each melody and text with individual emotions for each singer in the ensemble.

Listening Notes

Giuseppe Verdi, *Falstaff,* excerpt from Act III, Scene 2 (1893).

Falstaff, the last opera composed by Verdi, represents his mature ensemble and orchestral writing style. The final scene of the last act finds Falstaff, an overweight comic figure, trying to court two ladies who are well aware of his intentions and are quite uninterested. As is typical of opera buffa, the plot is filled with individuals, all with schemes at work. The schemes of Falstaff and those of the ladies collide with schemes of yet another individual, Ford. In this scene all the schemes intersect and are exposed. The plot is complicated by the use of masks, confusing everyone except the audience. As usual, true love, in this case that of young Fenton and Anne, wins over all the other schemes. While in disguise (disguises that had been switched), they are married in front of everyone while Falstaff, Ford, and Dr. Caius, who all had other plans, watch unknowingly. The successful schemes of the two ladies and the young couple put everyone else in their rightful place. The scene ends with everyone reconciled to the marriage.

The music is a brilliant interplay of several solo voices expressing diametrically opposed emotions ranging from joy to surprise and anger. There are short orchestral statements throughout that help articulate the various moods of the soloists. A chorus of voices appears at the very end and takes on the role of a quasi-narrator expounding on the situation. This chorus is cleverly structured as a fugue. See if you can hear the staggered entrances. Finally, be aware of the quick movement from texture to texture. At times, several voices interact at once; at other times there are short, melodic ideas. Interspersed between all these textures are moments that sound like recitative settings. This contrast of textural colors is evidence of Verdi's compositional control.

0:00	This selection begins with Ford making a recitative statement announcing the end of the ridiculous masquerade and upcoming wedding. No accompaniment.
0:16	Strings enter in accompaniment. The music takes on an air of reverence for the very brief ceremony.
1:00	Fenton and Anne, in disguise, are brought forward to make it a double wedding.
1:28	Both couples are joined in marriage and they unmask.
1:30	To the surprise of Ford, Dr. Caius, and Falstaff it is discovered by all that the young lovers Fenton and Anne were married.
1:47	Dr. Caius is shocked to discover he mistakenly married Bardolph.
2:13	Rapid delivery of single words in disagreement as to who is more the fool.
2:39	Ford reluctantly accepts the outcome. Everyone except Dr. Caius is happy.

3:12 The orchestral and choral fugue begins:

"Hurrah!
The whole world is but a joke,
And man is born a clown.
Within his addled head
His brains are in a churn.
We all are fools! And every man
Laughs at the others' folly.
But he laughs best who sees to it
That the last laugh falls to him."

3:42 First of a series of forte interjections by the chorus and orchestra. The soloists continue in counterpoint.

4:36 Another powerful interjection.

5:27 Sudden stop, then a slower and softer part. "We all are fools."

5:49 Final orchestral cadence.

6:03 End.

music dramas
a self-proclaimed name for Wagner's operas. He considered them larger in scope than other operas.

While Verdi actively wrote opera in Italy, another style of opera was developing in Germany. Wagner believed that he wrote operas larger in scope than traditional opera. His characters were super beings with super problems. He called his works **music dramas** because he felt that they blended all aspects of music and drama. He not only wrote the music; he wrote the librettos that were often derived from legends and myths. He had control over the set designs and all aspects of the visual arts that made up the total experience. He even designed and had built an opera house in Bayreuth worthy of his elaborate music dramas.

In Wagner's operas the musical flow never stops and the demarcation between aria and recitative dissolves. Wagner considered his "unending melody" the thread unifying each act. He removed all traditional places for applause so that there would be no interruption of the musical flow. The audience is engulfed in sound; large instrumental sections, composed symphonically, inject the drama with development similar to the large symphonies of the day.

Wagner's enormous cycle of operas, *Der Ring des Nibelungen* (The Ring of the Nibelung), is made up of four operas. He used myths filled with gods, gold, and magic to portray his philosophical beliefs about society. In this cycle of operas it is common to hear long descriptive discourses sung in unending melody. To some critics, these dialogues seemed long-winded; however, they represent a composer's ability to

A scene from Wagner's opera *Siegfried*

use his craft to express personal ideas and thoughts. It was no longer enough to show off one's craft; composition was now a tool for expression and communication.

The most significant innovation in Wagner's operas is the special use of motives. Motives are melodic and harmonic ideas assigned to each character, object, place, or thought. These **leitmotifs** were handled symphonically; that is, they were developed or transformed as the drama unfolded. Leitmotifs combine and change to the point that they can hardly be recognized. Throughout the four operas these motives have a profound impact on the listener and, with their transformations, express the changing conditions of the plot and characters.

Most of this motivic development is carried by the enlarged orchestra. Wagner's harmonies are rich and chromatic, full of dissonance and tension. The orchestra provides descriptive colors and uses an extremely wide range of dynamics. The orchestra was so large that only the strongest voices could sing over it.

leitmotifs
motives associated with a person, act, or object. Leitmotifs are a unifying feature of Wagnerian opera; they develop and change as the characters change.

Richard Wagner
(1813–83)

DATELINE	BIOGRAPHY
1813	Born in Leipzig, Germany, Richard Wagner was raised in a family engrossed in musical theater; he grew up surrounded by actors and singers and showed an early interest in operas.
1828	Influenced by Beethoven's music, Wagner began studies in harmony and musical composition. He entered Leipzig University in 1831, but spent more time drinking and gambling than studying music.
1833-35	In his early twenties, Wagner began writing operas, and he worked briefly as producer and conductor in several theaters and opera houses. Believing in his own greatness, Wagner grew to be a selfish, arrogant, and ruthless artist.
1836	Wagner married Minna Planer, an actress. The next few years were spent writing and producing unprofitable operas, living off loans from friends and relatives, and constantly moving to escape from creditors.
1842-48	After spending time in London and Paris, Wagner returned to Germany to become the director of the Dresden Opera. Here he wrote *Der fliegende Holländer* (1843), *Tannhäuser* (1845), and *Lohengrin* (1848).
1848-50	To avoid being imprisoned for his revolutionary political position, Wagner fled to Switzerland where he began work on *Der Ring des Nibelungen,* a cycle of four operas based on Nordic mythology that would take him more than a quarter of a century to complete.
1864	Wagner was helped out of debt by King Ludwig II of Bavaria, who financed and supported Wagner's opera productions in the Munich opera house.
1870	For several years while still married, Wagner had been involved in an affair with Cosima von Bülow, daughter of Franz Liszt; they had produced two daughters and after Wagner's wife died in 1866, Cosima left her husband and obtained a divorce after giving birth to Wagner's son, Siegfried.
1876	This year marked the opening of Wagner's theater in Bayreuth, built specifically for performances of Wagner's works. *Der Ring des Nibelungen* was performed in its entirety for the first time.
1883	On vacation in Venice, Wagner suffered a heart attack and died. He was buried in Bayreuth.

Listening Notes

Richard Wagner, *Götterdämmerung,* conclusion to Act III (1874).

This opera is the fourth in the monumental cycle *Der Ring des Nibelungen.* Wagner worked on this cycle for over twenty years (1850-74). During the process he completed two other operas, *Tristan und Isolde* and *Die Meistersinger von Nürnberg. Götterdämmerung* is a very long opera filled with story lines that began in the earlier three operas. The leitmotifs in this cycle were developed and transformed over a very long period. As this scene ends, the hero Siegfried is dead and his wife Brünnhilde is preparing a funeral pyre for him. The gold that had been taken from the Rhinemaidens in the first opera and fashioned into a ring with extraordinary powers is being returned to them now. Forsaken love, greed, power, and ruin were all that remained in its wake. The culmination of this ruin comes in this scene. Brünnhilde takes the ring from the dead hero's finger and returns it to the Rhinemaidens as they ride on a huge wave of the flooding Rhine. She beckons fire for the pyre and for Valhalla, the place of the gods. As the flood subsides, Valhalla, with the gods inside, is seen burning in the sky while Brünnhilde rides into the pyre to join her dead love.

   Notice the unending melody mentioned earlier. The textural changes seen in the opera by Verdi are not a part of Wagner's style. He wrote long melodic ideas that developed free of the familiar structures seen in traditional arias. Brunnhilde's melody in this scene is neither aria nor recitative. The music flows without stopping, and there is no break until the last note of the opera. The orchestra provides strength and support for Brünnhilde's grief. In the orchestral writing that concludes the work are motives associated with the gold ring, Siegfried, Valhalla, and the gods. Their impact can only be fully experienced by following their development throughout the cycle of four operas. This last orchestral statement sums up an extraordinary journey through powerful emotions and events.

   The scope of Wagner's writing is incredible. This is a music drama where emotional development is carried to its extreme. Notice the many colors of his expanded orchestra. To carry over such a large orchestra Brünnhilde's voice has to be enormous. The staging for such a scene surpassed anything seen before. The technical developments of Wagner's productions enhanced the superhuman qualities of his heroes and heroines and the music they sang.

0:00   Orchestral introduction. Notice the lack of cadences.

1:31	Brünnhilde gives an order to begin building the funeral pyre for Siegfried. She sings of her sorrow.
1:50	The melody builds slowly to a climax.
3:11	Full orchestral statement, full brass section. The voice answers. The orchestra continues with a longer statement. The men begin to build the funeral pyre.
4:03	Clarinet solo accompanied by a slow thin texture.
4:17	"Like clear sunshine his light shines upon me." Brünnhilde recounts their love.
5:15	The orchestra dialogues forcefully with Brünnhilde.
5:35	Texture thins considerably.
6:21	Sudden loud statement as she tells how Siegfried was forced to betray her.
6:40	Texture thins again.
9:02	"All things, all now I know."
10:21	"Rest! Rest thou, oh god!"
10:50	She signs to the Vassals to lift Siegfried's body onto the pyre; she draws the ring from his finger and looks at it meditatively.
12:08	The orchestra plays the ring motive.
13:50	"Fly home, ye ravens!" "For the end of the gods is now dawning."
14:26	She hurls the torch onto the pyre. Two ravens fly up and disappear in the background. She turns to her steed and invites it to go with her to join Siegfried.
18:00	She swings herself onto the horse and makes it leap into the burning pyre. The Rhine overflows its bank in a mighty wave bearing the Rhinemaidens on its crest.
19:10	Hagen, standing nearby, shouts "Away from the Ring!" and is pulled into the Rhine.
19:30	Orchestral postlude. The Rhinemaidens joyfully hold up the recovered ring. The firelight grows in the heavens until the flames are seen to seize upon Valhalla and the gods.
20:00	Motives, including those for Valhalla and the ring, soar throughout the symphonic texture.
22:19	End.

Nationalism and the Russian Five

In the nineteenth century an emphasis on nationalism followed in the wake of the French Revolution and the Napoleonic wars. There was a deliberate attempt to reinforce national identity in the arts. Musicians used direct quotes of folk songs or, in larger instrumental compositions, the sound of those songs. When literary topics were available, such as in opera or tone poems, it was easy to adopt patriotic or national subjects. Even titles to overtures and symphonies expressed nationalistic feeling; Dvořák's *Slavonic Dances* or Rimsky-Korsakov's *Russian Easter Overture* are prime examples. Composers became more and more interested in showing the strength of their traditional heritages through their own music.

    Italy, Germany, and France had dominated European music for centuries. Nationalism emerged in Norway with Grieg, in Finland with Sibelius, in Bohemia with Dvořák and Smetana, and in Russia with the **Russian Five.** These five musicians met to create a truly Russian music. In a manner similar to what took place in the Baroque era with the

Russian Five
five composers who worked together in hopes of producing a music style representative of their Russian heritage rather than the music imported from Europe.

The coronation scene from Mussorgsky's opera *Boris Godunov*

Camerata the direction of music was deliberately being designed. Out of the collaboration of Mily Balakirev, César Cui, Alexander Borodin, Nikolai Rimsky-Korsakov, and Modest Mussorgsky emerged a brilliant sense of orchestration and national thought. Except for Balakirev, the five musicians were not traditionally schooled composers; as a result, they sought a new direction for Russian music free from traditional concepts of composition. Much of their music has an exciting sound of roughness and rebellion.

Perhaps the most significant work to rise out of this group was Mussorgsky's opera *Boris Godunov.* The writing is original, with angular rhythms and harmonies, and was first considered unschooled. To a small degree Rimsky-Korsakov had a hand in its orchestration when the work was republished after Mussorgsky's death. The Russian flavor to the music comes from the folklike melodies and rhythms typical of speech patterns inherent in the Russian language.

Modest Mussorgsky
(1839–81)

DATELINE	BIOGRAPHY
1839	Modest Mussorgsky was born in Pskof, Russia, the son of a wealthy aristocratic landowner. His early music education consisted of a few piano lessons from his mother and later from teachers in St. Petersburg; he had no formal training in music theory.
1856	After completing a military education, Mussorgsky became an army officer, a position he soon quit to devote his time to composing. He had already begun suffering from a nervous disorder, possibly epilepsy.
1861	After his family lost most of its wealth as a result of the emancipation of the Russian serfs, Mussorgsky got a job as a government clerk in St. Petersburg, a job he held until his early death.
1867-74	Mussorgsky's major works written during this period include the symphonic poem *A Night on Bald Mountain,* the piano piece *Pictures at an Exhibition,* and the grand opera *Boris Godunov.* Extremely nationalistic, Mussorgsky based his music on the modal sounds of Russian folk songs.
1881	After years of suffering from depression, alcoholism, and epilepsy, Mussorgsky died in a military hospital at the age of forty-two.

Listening Notes

Modest Mussorgsky, *Boris Godunov,* coronation scene (1874).

Using a new sense of rhythmic and block repetition seen later in the writing of Igor Stravinsky, the coronation scene was perhaps the most influential music of Mussorgsky. The scene opens with the sound of bells ringing. Bell ringing is a Russian tradition announcing all important events. The orchestra alternates two contrasting chords that up until the time of Mussorgsky were rarely used in combination because an interval of a diminished fifth separates them. This colorful progression accompanies the march by Boris in his coronation at the Kremlin.

The chorus enters with a hymn of praise, based on a traditional folk song, for Boris. In the last part of the scene Boris invites everyone, both noble and poor, to a feast; he leaves to offer a prayer at the cathedral for the Russian tsars before him. As you listen to the grandeur of the music, picture an ornately dressed Boris among a throng of followers, the chorus. The scene sparkles visually as much as it does in the brilliant orchestration. To Mussorgsky's contemporary listeners the music was startling and powerful. It stands today as a bold statement of nationalism from a country that had formally been musically overshadowed by Western Europe.

0:00	Two low notes precede the entrance of the triangle and the two alternating chords.
0:16	Pizzicato strings enter.
0:36	The pattern repeats and begins to build and accelerate to a solid cadence.
0:57	Chords are played forcefully by the brass along with church bells.
1:27	Music accelerates and stops, leaving the ringing chimes.
1:48	Fanfare, followed by an announcement, ''Long life Tsar Boris Feodorovich!''
2:00	The chorus echoes the call and falls into a hymn, ''Glory to you!''
2:29	Orchestra and chorus become more polyphonic and contrapuntal.
3:02	Echo phrases between high and low voices.
3:35	The nobles join in with ''All hail!''
3:55	A thick overlapping of phrases.
4:23	Forceful tutti statement of the hymn with full orchestral support.

4:46	"Glory, glory."
5:05	Orchestra leads into the solo passage by Boris.
6:51	Cadence and new texture develops.
7:05	Solo passages answered by brass section.
7:30	Chorus enters singing Boris's praises. The bells return with the two dissonant chords. The chorus resumes its hymn.
8:40	The people create a great commotion as the police try to control them.
9:23	The scene ends with the ringing of bells.

Chapter 10

TWENTIETH-CENTURY MUSIC:
1900 to 1960

Music Outline of the Twentieth Century

1. In the early part of the century several artistic movements developed.

2. In France, while poets were concerned with **symbolism,** painters and musicians (Debussy in particular) were interested in a movement in art and music called **impressionism.**

3. Impressionists worked to convey mood, suggestion, impression, a thought, or an experience. They were less interested in being specific or objective.

4. Tonality weakened and was replaced by a juxtaposition of beautiful sonorities.

5. Another movement, called **primitivism,** was represented by the early works of Stravinsky. Music was twisted into angular rhythms and melodies, reflecting basic needs and desires.

6. **Neoclassicism** appeared shortly after World War I. These composers wished to bring back the objectivity and restraint the impressionists were avoiding. They looked back to the music of

the eighteenth century (Baroque and Classical periods) as a model for a refined sense of order.

7. Works by neoclassicists exhibited an interplay between melodic and harmonic ideas borrowed from the Classical period and the sharply contrasting rhythmic complexity and melodic angularity of the twentieth century.

8. **Serialism** was perhaps the most dramatic development in music composition at this time. In Vienna Schoenberg developed an entirely new system of composition using **atonality.**

9. In America jazz was emerging from its folk and blues heritage into an identifiably unique genre. The three styles to develop out of the **blues** in this period were **Dixieland, swing,** and **bebop.**

 New Images and Progressions

Traditional chords based on tonality met a new challenge with the advent of the twentieth century. Major and minor sonorities had been stretched with increasing amounts of dissonance. The extended harmonies introduced by Chopin, Liszt, and Wagner were now being pushed to the point of breaking. When tonal chords and melodies are bombarded by increasing chromaticism and dissonance, the tonal center weakens and eventually breaks down. As a result, the forward motion inherent in tonality weakens and a new means of unity and motion is needed. All the stylistic developments in the first part of the twentieth century played, in some way, a role in the search for and the establishment of new sonorities that did not depend on tonal harmonic progression.

 Impressionism

impressionism
in music, a style at the turn of the twentieth century emphasizing tone color, sonority, and image.

Impressionism led Claude Debussy to change the progression of music harmonically. The goal of impressionism was to ponder reality and live within one's feelings and impressions. Prior to this chords were constructed by stacking notes on top of one another using the interval of a third. Other intervals, fourths and fifths, became the new building blocks for harmonies. The new chords sound similar to traditional chords but are free of traditional concepts of resolution. The need for a dominant chord to resolve to a tonic chord became less important than the quality of the sonority of a chord and how it sounds in relation to the next chord. The relationship of consonance to dissonance changed. By weakening tonality, a chord could now be considered dissonant if it was less consonant than the chords around it.

Claude Debussy was influenced greatly by the symbolist poets in France who sought to express reality by evoking impressions of objects and ideas. Their works became focused less on specifics and more on personal, expressive perceptions. This aesthetic ideal shaped the way that Debussy thought about composing. For example, his opera *Pelléas et Mélisande* has a very loose and vague story line. The dramatic flow is freed to the point that the order of the scenes can be changed without disturbing the plot. The sequence of scenes presents a flow of weakly related impressions and moods. As the orchestra subtly weaves understated colors around the melodies, there is little communication between the characters. This music is at the other end of the emotional spectrum from Wagner.

To further weaken the tonal center, Debussy used Eastern scales he had heard in his travels to Russia. Scales such as the **whole-tone scale** along with sonorities based on fourths and fifths give his music a shimmering quality. His harmonic vocabulary was enriched by these influences, and his ability to create beautiful sonorities has made his works favorites in this genre.

whole-tone scale
a scale without half steps. Major and minor scales both have half steps and whole steps.

Claude Debussy
(1862–1918)

DATELINE	BIOGRAPHY

1862 Claude Debussy was born in St. Germain-en-Laye, near Paris.

1873 He entered the Paris Conservatory at age eleven as a piano student; he studied there for eleven years.

1880 Debussy met Nadezhda von Meck, a patron of Tchaikovsky, who employed him as a pianist for the summers. He traveled with her family to Switzerland, Italy, and Russia, where he was greatly influenced by the Russian school of music.

1884 He won the prestigious Prix de Rome, which allowed him to study in Rome. He missed Paris terribly, however, and returned as soon as the required two years of study were over.

1888–89   Debussy traveled to Bayreuth, Germany, to hear some of Wagner's opera productions. He had mixed reactions to Wagner's music. Debussy rejected the traditional sonata form, the use of thematic development, and the strong musical and visual statements associated with traditional German Romantic music. Instead he sought to create a mood through his music.

1889   He attended the Paris Exposition and was greatly impressed by the sounds of Far Eastern music.

1890   Debussy wrote his most famous piano piece, *Claire de Lune.*

1894   The performance of the orchestral composition *Prelude to the Afternoon of a Faun* helped Debussy gain public notice.

1899   Debussy married Rosalie Texier; she attempted suicide when he left her for another woman, Emma Bardac, in 1904. Although he rarely made public appearances, Debussy went on concert tours of Europe to support his and Emma's high standard of living.

1902   The only opera Debussy completed, *Pelléas et Mélisande,* based on the symbolistic play by Maeterlinck, established him as the most important French composer of his time.

1914   The onset of World War I deeply disturbed Debussy and his sense of French nationalism. Both the war and his fight with cancer contributed to his failure to compose large extended works during his latter years.

1918   Debussy died in his beloved Paris as German bombs shelled the city.

Listening Notes

Claude Debussy, *Prélude á l'après-midi d'un faune* (Prelude to the Afternoon of a Faun) (1894).

This prelude is a miniature tone poem with an exotic story, based on a poem by Mallarmé. Debussy paints a picture of a dreamlike world where a faun (half man and half goat) plays a flute and dreams of carrying off two beautiful nymphs. The faun is confused about whether he actually carried them off or merely dreamed about it.

    The structure of Debussy's tone poem falls loosely into three parts (A B A'). The middle section is more agitated, evoking an impression of confused dancing by the nymphs. The return (A') is a condensed version of the opening section with differences in orchestration. The most striking element in this work is the freedom of rhythm and melody. There is no strong pulse to suggest meter. Phrases seem to float by, never to return. The lonely flute solo that begins the work sets the mood for what follows.

Notice how independent the instruments in the orchestra are. There are many soloistic moments for the woodwinds, creating a very thin but delicate texture. The expanded orchestra of the late nineteenth century has been thinned considerably. There are no trumpets, lower brass, or percussion, and the orchestra is limited to woodwinds and strings. The strings are **muted** most of the time, adding a dark, mysterious quality. The only percussive sounds come from the harp and antique cymbals. Debussy's emphasis on solo instruments develops a sense of intimacy. Pay particular attention to the floating sonorities and how one moves to the next. Building delicate textures and sonorities took precedence over structuring a compelling, functional chord progression.

muted
darkening or softening the tone of instruments by using mutes. Brass instruments place mutes in the bell while strings use wooden clamps on the bridge.

0:00   The first section (A) opens with a solo flute that will dominate the various instrumental colors of this section. Harp arpeggios and other solo winds build a delicate texture.

1:37   A brief orchestral tutti swells the texture, only to be followed again by solo instruments, especially flute and clarinet. The harp returns with arpeggios.

2:00   Flute returns with harp and strings.

2:41   The theme returns again in the flute part.

3:23   The clarinet enters with a contrasting idea with more rhythmic motion; muted brass.

3:56   The middle section (B) begins with the oboe. The harmonies seem more defined. The alternation between soloists and string section continues.

4:48   Peaceful moment contrasts the more developmental passages that started (B).

5:39   Sudden melodic change (strings) with slow harp arpeggios.

6:21   Solo French horn, solo violin, and solo clarinet. Oboe enters; harp arpeggios accompany the original theme (flute).

7:05   Oboe statement begins a brief moment of energy.

7:35   Developmental section continues with full orchestra intertwined with solo winds.

7:59   Last section (A'), original theme (flute), solo violin, with lush string accompaniment. Small cymbal rings.

8:42   Flute continues; slow harp arpeggios, solo violin.

9:12   The oboe continues the dialogue.

9:32	Cadence, feeling of stability.
9:56	Solo flute, light cymbal rings, soft strings bring the work to an end.
10:18	End.

At the same time impressionism was developing in Europe other styles were also emerging with similar goals: to forge a new tonal language in rebellion to the overblown characteristics of romanticism. In the music of Igor Stravinsky we see a continuation of nationalism followed by primitivism, neoclassicism, and finally serialism. Stravinsky grew up in Russia, then became a citizen of France and finally of the United States. His writing made a dramatic impact on the direction of music.

 ## *Nationalism Continues*

Nationalism played an important role in the first period of Stravinsky's life. His Russian heritage provided a wealth of Eastern melodic structures that invaded his writing for the Russian Ballet. His ballet *Petrushka* captures the spirit and culture of Russian life by using folk songs and dances in a surprising story of puppets brought to life by a magician. Due to its sheer orchestral beauty and power the music has become a concert work. After Mussorgsky, Stravinsky became the most famous nationalistic composer from Russia.

 ## *Primitivism*

primitivism
in music, a twentieth-century style inspired by primitive works of art where music is combined with rhythmic and melodic angularity.

During his nationalistic period, Stravinsky wrote his most famous ballet, *The Rite of Spring*. This work is an example of **primitivism** because of its score and staging. The original choreography was angular and almost grotesque, the costumes were made of brown burlap, and the music sounded primitive with its pounding, irregular rhythms, sharp dissonances, and unique orchestral colors. The desire to rebel against the strictures of modern culture and once again enjoy the unstructured life of primitive cultures was made startlingly clear by this work. This style was an aggressive break from romanticism. This music was so startling that at the première of *The Rite of Spring* the audience reacted so strongly that fighting erupted.

A scene from Stravinsky's ballet *The Rite of Spring*

Listening Notes

Igor Stravinsky, *Le Sacre du printemps* (The Rite of Spring) (1913).

This ballet is unique both to dance repertoire and to Stravinsky's other works. The story tells of primitive Russian peasants celebrating the coming of spring through the sacrifice of a virgin who dances herself to death as the elders watch. The tribal setting depicts the cruelty and brutality associated with such a primitive culture.

The music begins with a solo bassoon playing in its extreme high register. Solo French horn and solo clarinets create an innocent and transparent texture, beckoning the beginning of spring. As they weave around each other the soloistic sounds of woodwinds and brass provide sparkling orchestral colors.

The element that shocked and offended first-time listeners was the violent use of accents. These accents appear in irregular patterns, often over percussive repetitions of chords. As the dissonant chords repeat, the accents move on and off the beat, providing angular rhythms for the twisted motions of the dancers.

Stravinsky's block approach to structure is typified in this work. He built blocks of sound by using strings of repeated chords, superimposed with accents, to form long ostinatos, repeated rhythmic ideas. These ostinatos create the image of primitive drumming from some forgotten rite.

This ballet is structured into two large parts, each of which is made up of several scenes. Part I is entitled *The Adoration of the Earth* and Part II is *The Sacrifice.* Listen to the colorful "Introduction" and the first section titled "Dance of the Adolescents." In this excerpt are moments of irregular metric patterns, ostinatos, repetitive chords, and sharp dissonances. Notice the aggressive, percussive orchestral writing; it is a sharp contrast to the impressionistic orchestrations of Debussy. The orchestra is enormous, with expanded woodwind, brass, and percussion sections.

0:00	Bassoon plays in its highest register, a gentle call, the beginning of spring. The other woodwinds enter slowly.
0:35	Bassoon plays another phrase that is completed by the English horn.
1:15	Strings enter with pizzicato accents; the woodwinds become very polyphonic.
1:54	Another thick woodwind passage is started by the flute. No brass or percussion.
2:35	More aggressive lines; the trumpet joins the texture.
2:55	Return to the high bassoon. Woodwind trills and pizzicato strings.
3:30	Heavy string ostinato. "Auguries of Spring: Dances of the Young Girls." Solo woodwinds and brass (muted) dance above the repeated rhythm.
4:10	Repeated chords with angular accents. Solo statements from the bassoon and trombone break up the repetitions.
4:48	Loud articulation followed by falling lines in the woodwinds and brass. "The Ritual of Abduction."
5:10	Ostinato in the strings (pizzicato) continues; French horn starts a series of solo statements from woodwinds and brass.
5:47	Texture thickens with brass, bells, and drums.
6:10	The texture becomes more frantic.
6:55	Very fast trumpet calls followed by trombone and horn calls. Drums make powerful accents.

7:36	The texture begins to unify and gives way to a single flute trill.
8:15	"Roundelays of Spring." A restful melody (clarinets) opens this next section.
8:43	New low string repetition (slow).
9:35	Solo passages float above the low string ostinato.
10:15	The gong begins a sudden increase in tension, the ostinato continues, dissonant chords and screaming brass lead to a cadence of very dissonant chords.
11:03	The music picks up energy and momentum.
11:19	All stop except a flute trill and a peaceful melody in the high clarinet.
11:50	Low brass introduce another intense texture. Different sections set up a continuing dialogue.
12:48	New ostinato drives the music.
13:21	Strings begin a new rhythmically complex texture.
13:57	Climactic polyrhythm.
14:16	Sudden release of tension.
14:40	Huge crescendo, brass punches, gong.
15:07	Fast rhythmic activities from all the sections, crescendo.
15:47	End.

Igor Stravinsky
(1882–1971)

DATELINE	BIOGRAPHY
1882	Igor Stravinsky was born near St. Petersburg, the son of a Russian opera singer who encouraged him in music, provided him with piano lessons, and exposed him to many ballet and opera performances.
1903	While studying law at St. Petersburg University, Stravinsky met Nicholai Rimsky-Korsakov and had the opportunity to study musical technique and composition with him for several years. These studies laid the foundation for all Stravinsky's later compositions.
1906	He married his cousin Catherine Gabrielle.

1910   Stravinsky met Sergei Diaghilev, the director of the Russian Ballet, in Paris in 1909 and subsequently composed three ballets specifically for the Russian dance company. In 1910 the successful performance of *The Fire Bird* established Stravinsky as a major composer. The ballet *Petrushka,* based on Russian folklore, was performed in 1911, also in Paris.

1913   The première of the ballet *Rite of Spring* caused the audience to riot in response to the unconventional methods of orchestration, the dissonance, and the primitivism expressed in the rhythms and costumes. Despite this reaction the ballet remained successful, and Stravinsky's reputation as a master of composition grew to worldwide recognition.

1914   Stravinsky fled to Switzerland at the beginning of World War I. To support himself under war conditions he began composing for smaller ensembles, as evidenced in the theater work *L'histoire du soldat.*

1920   After moving to Paris at the end of the war he wrote the ballet *Pulcinella,* based on sonatas written by Pergolesi, and using more traditional compositional techniques. He became a French citizen in 1934.

1940s   After the outbreak of World War II Stravinsky moved permanently to the United States, settled in California, and became a U.S. citizen in 1945. He continued writing, performing, and conducting, including some work for the film industry.

1950s   Stravinsky surprised the musical world by using a modified version of the twelve-tone technique of Schoenberg in his compositions.

1962   Stravinsky visited Russia after having been away for almost fifty years.

1971   The last decades of his life were spent touring the world as a renowned pianist and conductor. He died in New York at the age of eighty-eight.

 Neoclassicism

neoclassicism
music of the early twentieth century inspired by the restraint and control exhibited in the eighteenth century. This style was partially a response to the overly emotional music of the late twentieth century.

absolute music
instrumental music not associated with a poem, story, or title.

Characteristics of **neoclassicism** are based equally on philosophy and technique. Composers desired to return to the structures and order typical of eighteenth-century composition. The music still contained the dissonance of modern composition; however, composers left the world of emotionalism and romanticism and returned to the restraint and control exhibited by **absolute music** of the eighteenth century. Writing concertos and fugues, composers adopted older forms and styles. For example, harpsichord pieces by François Couperin were used to build a suite in Baroque style set brilliantly for orchestra by Richard Strauss. Another excellent example is Stravinsky's ballet *Pulcinella* written after *The Rite of Spring*; the work was based on music by an early composer

Béla Bartók
(1881–1945)

DATELINE	BIOGRAPHY

1881   Béla Bartók was born in a small town in Hungary. At the age of five, his mother began giving him piano lessons.

1891   His father died and Bartók's mother got a job as a schoolteacher in Bratislava, where he began seriously studying piano and composition.

1899   Bartók entered the Royal Academy of Music in Budapest, where he soon got caught up in the nationalist movement prevalent in politics, music, art, and literature during the early 1900s.

1903   Bartók's first major composition was *Kossuth*, an orchestral tone poem written to honor the Hungarian nationalist leader of the 1848 revolution.

1905   Bartók met and became good friends with Zoltán Kodály, with whom he shared a deep interest in the collection, study, and analysis of Hungarian folk songs.

1902–7   Bartók toured Europe as a concert pianist and did research in Hungary, Rumania, and other Slavic countries for his folk-song collection.

1907   He was employed as a piano teacher at the Budapest Academy, a position he held for twenty-seven years.

1909   Bartók married Márta Ziegler, one of his piano students; they were divorced in 1923. He subsequently married another piano student, Ditta Pásztory, with whom he later performed and toured.

1926–37   Bartók composed a series of 153 piano pieces called *Mikrokosmos*, a six-volume work including pieces ranging from beginner level to extremely advanced piano technique.

1940   After Nazi Germany annexed Austria, Bartók, fearful that the same fate would befall Hungary, fled to the United States. Although in poor health he researched folk music at Columbia University and continued to compose.

1945   Bartók died of leukemia in New York.

Giovanni Pergolesi. Although the music borrowed structures and melodies from the eighteenth century it continued to grow in levels of dissonance with increasing rhythmic angularity.

Neoclassicism splintered into many directions. At one extreme are the highly theoretical and tonal writings of Paul Hindemith; his tonality is filled with biting dissonances. At the other end is the Russian composer Sergei Prokofiev, who wrote in a more classical sense. His famous *Peter and the Wolf*, written for children, shows a tendency toward a tuneful, romantic style. His Symphony no. 1 (*Classical*) is yet another contrasting example of Neoclassical composition.

A renewed interest in studying the stylistic development of music, **musicology,** emerged with the proliferation of styles in the twentieth century. It was not only of interest to plot the growth of the new styles, but also to research the development from older styles. The study of music specific to different cultures is called **ethnomusicology.** Béla Bartók was both a brilliant composer and ethnomusicologist. His studies permeated his compositions, producing a refreshing new blend of sounds from folk music of Eastern European countries and modern composition. He rarely quoted folk material exactly but borrowed its structure and essence freely.

Because of his ability to write at the breaking edge of tonality, Bartók as a composer holds a unique place in history. The dissonance is often severe and to the beginner's ear sounds atonal; however, threads of tonality existed in his writing. He was reluctant to give up traditionally proven formal structures. Although his melodies and rhythms were inspired by his nationalism and the simplicity of folk music, his accompaniments were very sophisticated, using highly developed chords and rhythms.

musicology
the study of musical styles, both historically and theoretically.

ethnomusicology
the study of music history in light of ethnic group and cultural identities.

Listening Notes

Béla Bartók, *Concerto for Orchestra* (1943).
First Movement: Introduction—*andante non troppo; allegro vivace*

This selection is typical of the extended writing techniques of Bartók. The movement begins with a solemn idea in the low strings. The slow introduction is a steady crescendo of activity and range. Notice how the different melodic ideas move from the low strings into the soft upper flute range. Finally, out of a stronger statement in the strings, the *allegro vivace* section begins. This fast section's form is quasi sonata-allegro.

Typical of the period, the themes are fragmented and presented in an ever-changing meter. It is common for Bartók to change the meter signature as often as every other measure. Notice how difficult it is to establish a steady beat as you listen; as the music shifts meter the pulse is destroyed. The second theme is less active and shows folk influences. Its simplicity of melody (centered around two notes) and the repetitive accompaniment are characteristic of folk music. From the development section to the end the music begins to soar. The texture becomes polyphonic and the theme is passed around the large brass section. The two themes return, out of order, and the movement ends with a solid brass statement.

0:00 Slow introduction, low strings. Violins shimmer softly and the phrase ends with soft woodwinds.

0:35 Next phrase, similar to the first.

1:07 Unison string line, again with the same ending texture.

1:53 Trumpets enter over a soft but active string texture.

2:33 Strong string melody in counterpoint with the lower strings.

3:07 Acceleration in tempo up to the first theme.

3:23 First theme. Notice the irregular rhythm groupings.

3:50 Softer statement; strings are still the most predominant.

4:09 A wind texture develops with solo parts, beginning with the trombone.

4:24 Second theme, built primarily on two notes. A softer, more soloistic texture.

5:15 The second theme begins to break up, lower strings.

5:47 Sudden *forte* begins a highly developmental texture. Polyphony intensifies.

6:20 Contrasting clarinet solo texture. Other woodwind solo passages follow.

7:04 The polyphonic texture returns in the brass section.

7:40 Crescendo builds to a climax.

7:53 Recapitulation. Texture suddenly thins with clarinet statements based on the second theme.

8:16 The oboe and flute take over the melody.

8:50 The texture becomes more erratic, building in volume and activity.

9:18 First theme.

9:32 Final brass statement derived from the first theme.

9:36 End.

Expressionism and Serialism

Expressionism is a German school of thought in which artists attempt to expose their innermost thoughts and experiences. This movement was more an extension of, rather than a reaction to, romanticism. The expressions were often distorted and explosive. Feelings of frustration, guilt, and terror became topics for artists. In music, atonality became the chief characteristic of expressionism.

Music and tonality were severed completely by a compositional system developed by Arnold Schoenberg. He first touched on a new system of atonality when he wrote his prophetic *Pierrot lunaire* (Moonstruck Pierrot). Not until nearly ten years later did he crystallize a system where independent pitches could be liberated from a tonal center. Three names all describe the same system: **serialism, twelve-tone technique,** and **dodecaphony.**

The equality of each note is the basis for this system. See the discussion of tonality and atonality in Chapter 3. Using all twelve notes available in the octave equally is the critical element. Basically the rules of serial composition are the following:

1. First, a **series** or **tone row** using *all* twelve notes in the octave must be composed.
2. The order of the notes in the row determines the order they appear in the composition.
3. Chords are built by combining adjacent notes from the row. For example, a three-note chord might be the notes 5, 6, and 7 of the row.
4. The row can be written
   a. backwards (**retrograde**),
   b. upside down (**inversion**),
   c. upside down and backwards (**retrograde-inversion**), or
   d. starting on a different pitch (**transposition**).

This system allows no single pitch to sound more stable than another. Because no one pitch is emphasized over another, the possibility of a tonal center is eliminated. Schoenberg also developed a new technique for vocalists called ***Sprechstimme*** (speech voice). A vocalist presents the text in a half-spoken, half-sung voice.

Two American composers, Charles Ives and Henry Cowell, although quite different in style, used new, more experimental techniques at about the same time. The use of **tone clusters,** several notes separated by the interval of a second and played simultaneously, appeared in the compositions of both, but for different reasons. In Cowell's *The Tides of Mananaun* the palm of the hand or arm plays these clusters to portray

serialism
a modern classical system for writing music. Devised by Schoenberg, it arranges the twelve tones of the octave into a tone row or series. Because all twelve notes of the octave are used, tonality is destroyed. Atonal composition is also called twelve-tone technique and dodecaphony.

series
notes, rhythms, and dynamics can be used to build a serial composition and can provide an order for melodic and rhythmic activities. The series can be played forward, backwards (retrograde), upside down (inversion), and upside down and backwards (retrograde-inversion) or can start on a different pitch (transposition).

tone row
an ordering of the twelve notes in an octave. The row will be the basis of a serial composition.

Sprechstimme
a singing technique used in the twentieth century. The voice half-sang and half-spoke the melody. The result is similar to very animated speech.

tone cluster
several notes, separated only by major or minor second intervals, are played simultaneously to form dissonant clusters of sound, a twentieth-century technique.

Arnold Schoenberg
(1874–1951)

DATELINE	BIOGRAPHY
1874	Arnold Schoenberg was born in Vienna to a Jewish family. He began playing violin at the age of eight.
1898– 1900	He wrote several songs, including the string sextet *Verklärte Nacht*, the first real piece of program music written for a chamber group.
1901	He married the daughter of his counterpoint teacher and moved to Berlin to become conductor of the Buntes Theater.
1903	He returned to Vienna and continued teaching and writing songs, ballads, and string quartets. Alban Berg and Anton Webern were among his first pupils.
1908	Schoenberg attracted worldwide attention by composing atonal works.
1912	He wrote *Pierrot lunaire*, a highly expressionistic song cycle using twenty-one German poems and introducing the technique of *Sprechstimme*.
1923	He formulated the twelve-tone method of composition.
1933	After losing his post as professor at the Prussian Academy of Fine Arts in Berlin due to the German occupation, Schoenberg moved to Paris, then to the United States where he made his American conducting debut with the Boston Symphony Orchestra.
1934	He moved to Los Angeles and became a professor at the University of Southern California, composing choral and orchestral works as well as piano and string concertos.
1951	Schoenberg died in July, ironically on Friday the thirteenth, a day he superstitiously dreaded.

the sounds of the roaring ocean. Ives, in his Piano Sonata no. 2 (*Concord*), uses a short board to create clusters that sound like the upper harmonics of some very low note. The techniques of the two are similar, but the effects are quite different. Both of these early twentieth-century composers expressed the experimental mood developing in America.

Also at the beginning of the century another American style was developing that would eventually lead to an entirely new stylistic stream.

Listening Notes

Arnold Schoenberg, *Pierrot lunaire* (Moonstruck Pierrot) (1912).

The instrumentation in this piece is typical of chamber music; however, the interplay seems far more independent. The work is scored for piano, flute (or piccolo), clarinet (or bass clarinet), violin (or viola), cello, and voice. Notice how the very high notes of the piano, flute, and clarinet blend with the pizzicato of the violin into a delicate, spatial sprinkling of notes. Tuneful or soaring melody is lost.

This cycle of songs encompasses the fascination with the moon and its literary association to lunacy. The song "Mondestrunken," the first of twenty-one songs, presents a very thin, soloistic texture, and the use of *Sprechstimme* and atonality enhance the mysterious image of the moon. This surprising vocal technique takes on the qualities of an exaggerated recitation of a story or poem. The relationship of the instruments to the voice might appear distant, to say the least; the texture, however, is extremely well balanced. Notice how the texture of the music parallels the dreamlike nature of the text. It tells of how the moon pours wine on the waves of the sea, the very wine we drink with our eyes.

0:00 Ostinato pattern, light and delicate, piano and pizzicato violin.

0:03 Voice enters with *Sprechstimme*. Notice the lack of sustained pitch. The flute is the only melodic part.

0:12 The texture becomes very animated, starting with the piano and voice. The vocal range rises and falls in a glissando to two very low final notes.

0:25 Instrumental interlude. Short melodic statement from the flute, followed by the cello.

0:43 Second verse. Very independent melodic lines accompany.

0:57 Short breaks in the texture.

1:02 Descending lines, cadence (pizzicato returns).

1:10 Third verse begins with a sudden loud chord in the piano.

1:25 The texture relaxes.

1:30 A high note in the violin falls in a glissando.

1:39 After a short return to the ostinato from the opening measures is the final cadence.

Jazz, rock 'n' roll, rhythm and blues, and country and western would emerge from the unique sounds of the early blues.

Blues and Jazz (1900–50)

The beginning of jazz cannot be easily placed in time. Jazz, like all art forms before it, materialized without focus or definition. Music and culture from many countries pollinated the music America received from Europe. The early slave trade brought individuals from Africa and the Indies to North America in 1619. Members of each African tribe brought a separate cultural identity, including memories of their own customs, religion, and music. This blend of cultural and artistic images provided the seeds necessary for a new American art form.

Two elements brought from West Africa helped spark the development of jazz. The first is an emphasis on complex rhythms and combinations of rhythms, called **polyrhythms.** Second is greater participation in the musical experience by those from African cultures. Listeners never hesitated to join the flow of music with singing, hand

polyrhythm
the simultaneous use of two or more contrasting rhythms. Such rhythms often conflict with and blur the beat.

A unique musical style was born in America with the advent of the blues. Rhythm and blues, jazz, and rock all blossomed from this personal solo style of singing. The styles that developed out of the poor underclass in America gave expression to diverse and unique cultural attributes in the United States.

clapping, and dancing. Their music continued in work, worship, and play. When these influences met the musical structures from Europe a sophisticated give-and-take relationship between the lead singer and those who responded developed. Jazz musicians have applied the term ***call-response*** to this shared experience.

call-response
a musical dialogue between two musical statements; one musician states a phrase and the other fills in the gaps between the phrases. In early American religious traditions it was called "lining out": A leader would sing a line of text and the congregation would respond with the same line.

blues, country and city
a vocal style that uses blue notes and inflections. Country blues is a free and less disciplined style of blues. City blues is more structured and involves several musicians playing accompaniment.

Plantation owners controlled the amount and nature of the music the slaves could use. Some slaves were forbidden to perform their own music; others were allowed to use their instruments but not their own melodies and rhythms. European melodies and rhythms were foreign to most slaves and the harmonies seemed complex and confusing. The simplification of African rhythms and melodies along with the simplification of European harmonies led to a unique repertoire of folk music. This developing style, the **blues,** combined the rhythmic freedom of call-response with the structured world of chord progressions.

Blue notes get their name from the melodic quality of a note that is lowered in pitch for expressive reasons. The most common notes of the major scale to be "blued" are the third and seventh. To sing in a blues style requires blue notes and other expressive vocal ornaments and affectations.

Blues Scale:

In all cultures singing songs and playing instruments have always been wonderful outlets for expression. The instruments of early blues, around 1910, were not sophisticated; spoons, washboards, harmonicas, and guitars were more available than the European instruments found in more affluent settings. Blues singers used what they found or what was available. Instrumentation helped categorize the style of blues being performed.

There are two categories of blues: country and city. **Country blues** has a very sparse accompaniment, usually only a guitar. Rhythmically and metrically it can be very free. The singing style is equally free and dealt with the hardships of the downtrodden. A dramatic example of this earthy style is Robert Johnson's historic performance of "Hellhound on My Trail."

City blues is more controlled than country blues. The meter is strict and the singing style is more refined. Rather than just a guitar, three or four musicians accompany the singer. Vaudeville shows traveling around the country produced some of the most notable singers of the day. Bessie Smith, an excellent example of city blues, had a powerful voice with the musicality to communicate personally to large audiences. "St. Louis Blues" with Bessie Smith and Louis Armstrong (*Smithsonian Collection of Classic Jazz*) is a brilliant display of call-response and a city blues performance.

The blues still has a profound influence on today's music. Singers such as Ray Charles, B. B. King, and Eric Clapton have established definitive personal styles based on a foundation in the blues. Blues inflections are present in all styles of commercial and folk music. Throughout the history of jazz and commercial music the blues has taken on new shapes and sounds; however, the basic structure with its simple chord flow has remained.

Art Tatum
(1910–56)

DATELINE	BIOGRAPHY
1910	Art Tatum was born in Toledo, Ohio. Afflicted at birth by cataracts, he lost the sight in his left eye and had only slight vision in the right.
1923	After an unsuccessful attempt to learn violin, he switched to piano and by his early teens was playing at local parties.
1927	Tatum was hired as a staff pianist at radio station WSPD in Toledo and was given a fifteen-minute show that was broadcast nationwide. He began playing in local nightclubs for extra money.
1932	After arriving in New York as accompanist for singer Adelaide Hall, Tatum began playing in the small nightclubs along Manhattan's West 52nd Street. He was already gaining a reputation for being a phenomenally talented jazz improviser, amazing his audiences with his lightning speed technique.
1933	Tatum recorded the first of many solo piano recordings.
1938	He performed successfully in London, having gained an international reputation as a solo jazz pianist.
1943	Tatum formed a trio with Slam Stewart on bass and Tiny Grimes on guitar; he rarely performed as a soloist after this year.
1956	Tatum died of uremia in Los Angeles.

Blues and Jazz Piano Styles

boogie-woogie

a blues piano style where the left hand repeats a rhythmic melodic pattern (ostinato) that supplies the harmony. The right hand improvises above.

ostinato

a repeated, usually short, rhythmic musical figure. In boogie-woogie it is an eight-note pattern.

riff

a melodic motive used in jazz to build larger melodic structures.

ragtime

a compositional form based on European dance forms. It later became a style used for improvisation on the piano.

stride piano

a highly improvisatory, technically developed form of ragtime piano.

The piano was equally influential in developing jazz styles. Blues was played on the piano as early as 1900 and became popular in the 1930s in the form of **boogie-woogie.** The twelve-measure format of the blues spawned melodic repetition and rhythmic interplay. Boogie-woogie is built on an **ostinato** in the left hand (usually an eight-note pattern) with syncopated rhythms and **riffs** or motives in the right hand. In the hands of an accomplished player such as Meade "Lux" Lewis, the rhythmic tension between the two hands is extraordinary. Listen to his "Honky Tonk Train."

A piano style that developed from European dance forms was **ragtime.** This music is not improvised; it has a strict form of AA BB CC DD. The characteristic left-hand pattern of a low note followed by a chord identifies this relaxed but highly syncopated style. Scott Joplin, the most famous of all ragtime composers, even wrote an opera in this style. He hoped this style would eventually become America's new music. It was not long before the music was no longer played as written but improvised like other piano styles. The rigid form of ragtime became freer and more soloistic. Ragtime style sounds like ragtime; however, it is improvised rather than performed as written. Compare the recording of "Maple Leaf Rag" as written by Joplin to the improvisation of the same tune by Jelly Roll Morton.

When more advanced piano technique appeared in jazz (1930s), the style became known as **stride piano.** It used many of the techniques specific to the piano. Perhaps the most gifted performer of this style was Art Tatum. His technique and musical imagination were second to none. Listen to "Willow Weep for Me" for an example of his ability to reshape a simple song into a sophisticated arrangement. (The above selections can be found on the *Smithsonian Collection of Classic Jazz.*)

Dixieland

Dixieland

the term musicians gave to New Orleans jazz after it had been brought north to Chicago and other cities.

collective improvisation

the process where several musicians improvise a melodic or rhythmic part that combines to form a unified, polyphonic texture; for example, Dixieland.

By the 1920s an instrumental style had developed that remains popular today. **Dixieland** is a combination of instruments sharing musical space, each in its own range. All instruments improvise melodies and rhythms, creating a balanced musical texture. This activity is called **collective improvisation.** The most common instrumentation has only six players.

1. The trumpet is the most dominant instrument and plays the main melody.
2. The clarinet plays above the trumpet, improvising a melody to complement the trumpet.

3. The trombone plays a slower melody below the trumpet and helps define the harmonies by supplying important notes of the chords.

4. The drums provide rhythm and accent. They become more aggressive as the style develops.

5. The piano, which replaced the banjo, provides both rhythm and chords to accompany the three melodies from the winds.

6. The tuba and later the string bass supply the fundamental of the chord and short, simple melodic ideas between chords.

Listening Notes

Louis Armstrong and his Hot Five, ''West End Blues'' (1928).

Notice how this style of Dixieland provides a well-balanced texture in which all the horns are heard clearly. The piano (Earl Hines) is only heard during its solo. The drumming is very sparse compared to more contemporary styles. This recording represents Dixieland at a moment when the music was maturing from an earlier New Orleans style to the more contemporary Chicago style. The musicians all needed improvisational skills to perform this music. The texture is a product of collective improvisation.

0:00 Double-time (twice as fast as the normal beat) introduction by trumpet (solo improvisation).

0:14 Flat-four rhythm section (even accents on each beat); trumpet leads the texture, clarinet and trombone play slower melodies in accompaniment.

0:49 Trombone solo. Drummer uses wood blocks, banjo continues 4/4 beat, right hand trills in piano accompaniment.

1:22 Call-response between clarinet and voice. Voice improvises double-time melodies like those in the introduction; banjo strums a flat-four beat.

1:55 Piano solo, melodic right hand (double time).

2:07 Octaves in right hand make melody more forceful.

2:28 All horns play long notes, banjo and piano play a flat-four beat.

2:40 Trumpet solo with double-time melodies over long notes by clarinet and trombone.

2:52 Piano interlude.

3:00 Ending.

Swing

The late 1920s held experiments in instrumentation by arrangers such as Fletcher Henderson, who was instrumental in establishing more control by the composer/arranger, not the performer, over the music. This led to a change in the ensemble. The biggest change was in the size of the ensemble. The big bands of the swing era grew to fifteen or more members, now with sections of instruments like those in an orchestra. For this reason many of the original bands were called dance orchestras. Each section replaced one of the winds found in the Dixieland bands.

Benny Goodman
(1909–86)

DATELINE	BIOGRAPHY
1909	Benny Goodman was born into a poor Jewish family in the Chicago ghetto; he was the eighth of eleven children. He and two brothers studied music at the Hull House, a social services institution. He took up classical clarinet and studied for two years with Franz Schoeppe, clarinetist with the Chicago Symphony.
1921	At the age of twelve he appeared on stage in Chicago with Benny Maroffin.
1925–28	Goodman toured with Ben Pollack's band.
1929	He made his first solo recording, "He's the Last Word," in 1929. Goodman left Pollack's band and went to New York, where he began working as a studio-recording and pit-band musician.
1934	Goodman organized his first big swing band, which performed on "Let's Dance," a national NBC radio show. The band toured across the country and ended up in Los Angeles in the spring of 1935. Their performance at the Palomar Ballroom was a huge success.
1936–44	Goodman's band became the most popular swing dance band in America; in 1938 they were the first swing band to perform in Carnegie Hall.
1936	Racial taboos were broken when Goodman introduced African Americans Teddy Wilson (piano) and Lionel Hampton (vibes and drums) into his group.

1939   Goodman was the first jazz musician to solo with symphony orchestras. He commissioned several classical composers, including Béla Bartók, Aaron Copland, and Paul Hindemith, to write pieces for him.

1941   Goodman married Alice Duckworth, sister of John Hammond, a wealthy promoter of many jazz musicians and a personal friend and patron of Goodman's.

1950   The Benny Goodman Sextet toured Europe; throughout the years, Goodman's small groups ranged from trios to septets.

1956   Goodman became the first jazz soloist to be the subject of a full-length motion picture, *The Benny Goodman Story*, starring Steve Allen.

1956–62   The Goodman band toured all over the world on behalf of the U.S. State Department, including trips to the Far East, Europe, Central America, South America, and Russia. His success was international.

1958–59   Goodman hosted his own television show, "Swing into Spring."

1960–85   He continued to perform at concerts and jazz festivals; he toured extensively with his band and sextet.

1986   The King of Swing died after enjoying a lifetime of international celebrity.

There was a saxophone section with players who could also play clarinet, a trumpet section, a trombone section, and a rhythm section made up of piano, bass, and drums. Collective improvisation was impossible with so many players, so written-out arrangements and compositions were needed to organize the ensemble. Even small groups of three, four, or five musicians arranged their music to take on a more contemporary sound, moving away from the spontaneity of collective improvisation.

The Rhythm Section

By the time swing became the dominant style in jazz, the rhythm section had also been more clearly defined. The swinging feeling associated with jazz in the 1920s was created by playing two equal valued notes (in this case, eighth notes) as long-short instead of as equal divisions of the beat. Melodic lines **swing** with this long-short rhythm and become even more personalized by a technique called **layback.** A soloist would play or sing slightly behind the beat, allowing the rhythm section to push ahead. Singers such as Billie Holiday were characterized by this layback style. Her sound was very personal and intimate. The layback technique developed from the blues style singers and remains an important part of most jazz, rock, and commercial styles.

swing
a style of playing two notes of equal value within a beat. A classical musician interprets the duration of each note as equal; a jazz musician makes the first note last longer than the second. The result is a swinging, dancelike feeling of long-short, long-short.

layback
melodies played slightly behind the beat; the effect imparts a feeling of improvisation to a solo.

The instruments in the rhythm section became standardized by the swing era, each with its own role. The drummer maintains a constant pulse and adds color through the use of cymbals, tom-toms, and bells. The bass player helps generate the metric pulse while furnishing the fundamental harmonic progression. The piano or guitar supplies chords freely in a rhythmic fashion called **comping.**

Rhythm sections work together to create various styles such as swing, rock, and Latin. They improvise these textures, knowing when to make the eighth notes swing or when to make them equal. Rock and Latin jazz styles require even eighth notes while swing requires the long-short interpretation. The energy of a solo or ensemble relies on the activity level provided by the rhythm section.

The swing period produced many great bands and individual soloists. A great jazz performer had to be an expert improviser. Band leaders required soloists in their bands to add personality; the Benny Goodman, Duke Ellington, and Count Basie big bands enjoyed great soloists such as Lester Young, Cootie Williams, and Johnny Hodges.

comping, comps
a rhythmic activity supplied by the chording instruments and the drummer to help fill in the texture. The left hand of the pianist supplies chords that complement the melodic activity. A guitarist comps with chords sounding much like the pianist's left hand. The drummer uses the snare drum, playing rhythms similar to those used by the pianist and the guitarist.

Listening Notes

Duke Ellington, ''In a Mellotone'' (1940).

Notice the organization of the musical material and how collective improvisation has been replaced by a predetermined interplay between sections. The two soloists, Cootie Williams on trumpet and Johnny Hodges on alto sax, improvise around the arranged parts of the other players. Pay particular attention to the use of inflections and mutes to personalize the music. These elements were often freely added by the performers and not notated by the arranger.

0:00 Piano introduction, bass fills.

0:12 Saxes play melody in unison, fills by trombones in solos, rhythm section activity is bass and brushes on the snare drum.

0:41 Second chorus. Same scoring.

1:08 Piano interlude.

1:10 Cootie Williams (trumpet solo) uses the straight mute and the plunger, saxes fill in solos; a balanced dialogue is established.

1:43 Growl in solo.

1:54 More growls in solo, saxes are more active.

Music Around the World

A Kenyan harpist
(M & E Bernheim/Woodfin Camp & Associates)

A punk rocker, Harajuku Park, Tokyo
(Catherine Karnow/Woodfin Camp & Associates)

An Aborigine playing a didgeridoo
(Penny Tweedie/Woodfin Camp & Associates)

The late Dizzy Gillespie
(Craig Lovell/Viesti Associates)

Bruce Springsteen
(Michael S. Yamashita/Woodfin Camp & Associates)

A Turkish lute player in Istanbul
(R & S Michaud/Woodfin Camp & Associates)

Swiss Alphorns
(Paolo Koch/Photo Researchers, Inc.)

Musicians in Ladakh, Tibet
(Craig Lovell/Viesti Associates)

A Spanish guitarist in Seville
(Kim Newton/Woodfin Camp & Associates)

Traditional musicians in Jaisalmer, Rajasthan, India
(Robert Frerck/Woodfin Camp & Associates)

Kenyan Wa-kamba dancers
(Mario Fantin/Photo Researchers, Inc.)

Musicians playing at a festival in Marrakech, Morocco
(Dick Rowan/Photo Researchers, Inc.)

A festival in Bali
(Lindsay Hebberb/Woodfin Camp & Associates)

An orchestra on market day in Pisac, Peru
(Peter Buckley/Photo Researchers, Inc.)

Music jamboree, Smithville Tennessee
(Karen Kasmauski/Woodfin Camp & Associates)

Classical opera at Chengchow, Honan Province, China
(George Holton/Photo Researchers, Inc.)

2:10	Tutti (same rhythm, different notes).
2:17	Johnny Hodges (alto sax solo) uses double-time phrasing; the piano plays accompaniment for the first time.
2:32	Brass section plays long notes in accompaniment.
2:36	Solo break in double time.
2:45	Solo remains in double time.
2:54	Tutti band plays the melody, solo fills by the alto sax.
3:09	End.

Bebop

Jazz took a sudden turn in direction as musicians revolted against the confinement of swing music, especially that of big bands. The new style, called **bebop,** was also a revolt against the popularity of musicians who the new beboppers thought were musically weak. All in all, the new style demanded virtuoso techniques in combination with a well-developed background in music theory. The playing style was based on songs from the swing era, usually with new melodies. Original compositions from this period were usually in an A A B A form. The emphasis was on powerful and often very fast improvisation. The B section of bebop compositions usually had no written melody; it was replaced by an improvised solo. Two soloists towered above the others from this period: Charlie Parker on alto sax and Dizzy Gillespie on trumpet.

bebop
jazz style from the middle and late 1940s. The music is characterized by its technical virtuosity and angular compositions.

Charlie Parker
(1920–55)

DATELINE	BIOGRAPHY
1920	Charlie Parker was born in Kansas City; his mother supported him by working at night, which left young Parker unsupervised. As a young teenager he was already caught up in the world of jazz nightclubs, including the drug scene.
1931	Parker's mother scraped together $45 to buy him an ancient, beat-up alto saxophone. He began teaching himself how to play.

1935	He gave up school and married Rebecca Ruffing, nineteen years old; she was the first of his four mates. In 1936 his son Leon was born.
1937	He got a job playing in a band at a resort in the Ozarks. He spent the summer listening to Lester Young records and memorizing the solos.
1939	Parker left for New York City and found a job as a dishwasher at Jimmy's Chicken Shack in Harlem where Art Tatum was playing.
1940–43	Parker played and toured with several bands, including Jay McShann's and Earl Hines's, where he met Dizzy Gillespie. He and Dizzy spent many off-hours together playing brass and woodwind instructional studies as unison lines at lightning speed.
1945–46	These years were spent playing in small groups with Dizzy and other bebop players. Their sextet was coolly received in Hollywood and the group, sans Parker, returned to New York. He had turned in his return ticket for drug money. An addiction that had started at age fifteen was taking control of his life.
1946–47	After a complete physical and emotional breakdown at a recording session, he was admitted to Camarillo State Hospital for the mentally disordered.
1947–50	Although his health was declining, marked with bouts of ulcers and cirrhosis of the liver, these years were very productive musically. Parker wrote, performed, and recorded continuously.
1954	After a concert at Birdland, a jazz club named after Parker, he went home and attempted suicide. He was revived at Bellevue Hospital, after which he committed himself to the Psychiatric Pavilion.
1955	After a heart seizure, Charlie "Bird" Parker died in New York at the home of a friend. Although he was not yet thirty-five, the coroner estimated his age at the time of death as fifty-five.

Listening Notes

Charlie Parker, "KoKo" (1945).

This selection is not entirely a new piece as Parker composed a new melody to the popular standard "Cherokee." The melody requires great technical skill and acts as a springboard to fast, fluid solos. Parker and Gillespie play the melody in flawless unison. The drummer, Max Roach, creates a steady roar with his stick work. He delivers a complex polyrhythmic texture typical of bebop drumming. The form of the written melody is A A B A with the B section being improvised. Solos make up the bulk of the performance. Notice the activity of the rhythm section. The bass player **walks,** one note per beat chosen from scale and chord patterns. The drummer is very aggressive and plays **bombs,** loud accents that help build excitement. The piano player **comps** chords.

0:00	Introduction begins with a double-time unison melody by the alto sax and the muted trumpet (Dizzy Gillespie).
0:05	Trumpet solo with drum accompaniment (brushes); notice the bombs.
0:12	Sax solo with drums.
0:18	Duet (harmonized melody), drums continue; notice the uniformity of inflections as both play the last double-time phrase.
0:22	First chorus (A A): Alto sax solo, bass walks, drums play ride pattern, piano comps.
0:50	Bridge (B): Notice the last notes of each phrase (melodic extensions).
1:03	Last (A) of the first chorus.
1:14	Second solo chorus (A A).
1:40	Bridge (B): A very complicated melodic pattern.
1:52	Last (A) of second chorus.
2:05	Drum solo (Max Roach): Bass drum and snare drum, accents on the snare drum; the beat becomes increasingly difficult to find.
2:27	Unison melody line returns.
2:34	Muted trumpet solo with drum (cymbals) accompaniment.
2:39	Sax solo with drums.
2:45	Duet ending.
2:48	End.

walks, walking
a rhythmic-melodic activity employed by a swing-style bass player. When a note is played on every beat of the measure and notes move in a scale pattern, the impression is one of "walking" up and down the scale. A walking bass provides harmonic support for the rest of the ensemble.

bombs, dropping bombs
a bebop drumming technique. Bombs are accented notes that do not correspond with other rhythmic ideas in the ensemble. They supply energy and excitement in the texture.

Chapter 11

NEW MUSIC:
1960 to the Present

Music Outline of the Late Twentieth Century

1. The driving force behind many changes in composition was based on philosophies about the meaning of music and its role in society.

2. **Total serialism** applied the techniques of Schoenberg to every controllable element of composition.

3. **Indeterminate music** combined random elements with elements controlled by the composer.

4. **Electronic music** developed with computers and sophisticated recording equipment and techniques.

5. **Experimental/theoretical music** focused on a changing relationship between the composing experience and the product. The act of composing became the single most important element in music.

6. **Minimalism** was a move toward simplicity in composition and performance.

7. New notational systems developed to interpret the new procedures of performance.

8. **Neoromanticism** arose as an answer to the problem of less and less communication between composer and listener. Music refocused on the listener.

9. Jazz sought a new direction, a **third stream,** by combining elements of jazz and classical.

10. Elements of rock and commercial music combined with jazz in a very popular style first called **fusion,** then **crossover.**

 ## *A Questioning Time*

Now more than ever the academic community examines the learning process and how it impacts the arts. Not only is the sound of a composition important to twentieth-century composers, but the manner in which it was conceived has become equally important. All these developing systems of composition share a common expression: a response to the composers' need to place music in a new perspective. Previously, composing had become increasingly academic and intellectual. Following are brief discussions of some of the various schools of thought concerning composition and how specific composers viewed their art.

 ## *Total Serialism*

total serialism
an extended use of serialism. In addition to using pitches in a series, dynamics and rhythms are also serialized.

The organizational ideas offered by the serialism of Schoenberg continued to expand, especially with the increased control offered the composer through the technological advances in the 1950s. The short works of Schoenberg and his students Berg and Webern were primarily structured around the serialism of pitches. The technique can be applied to other musical elements as well; that is, a work can also use a predetermined series of rhythms or dynamics, giving further control to the composer. The goal is to coordinate the various series through a comprehensive plan, very often mathematical.

The first to expand the concept of serialism and successfully systematize rhythm, articulations, timbre, dynamics, and pitch was Milton Babbitt. In 1949 his *Composition for Twelve Instruments* typified an objective approach to composition of total serialism. Eventually he took total control over composition and performance in his writings for the computer. The computer requires the composer to control all variances, whether gradual or expansive. With the computer, series of dynamics, rhythms, and pitches can be ordered in an infinite number of ways.

Karlheinz Stockhausen was interested in the development of serialism and its application to other elements of music. Rather than using themes to unify his works, he created large works unified by series of pitches, rhythms, and even dynamics. At times his works involved a large number of musicians; in *Gruppen* (1955–57) he used three orchestras.

 Indeterminacy

indeterminate music
partially composed music. The performer is required to make decisions while playing. The level of decision-making varies considerably, from choosing what note to play to deciding what the overall structure will be.
aleatory, chance music
other terms for indeterminate music.

The control offered through total serialism stands in sharp contrast to a style where chance, based on random factors, is woven into the performance. This style has several names: **indeterminate music, aleatory,** or **chance music.** In these performances the musician is required to make decisions during the performance in sections where the composer purposely gives little or no notation; the performer is obligated to complete the compositional ideas. The unpredictable elements of this music ensure variety in each performance. At times control is even removed from the performers and random musical events are left to chance. For example, a note played on an instrument may be used to trigger a computer that would in turn randomly select another note.

Like serialism, indeterminacy can play an important role in computer composition. Indeterminate compositional concepts led composers to write computer programs where the composer may choose to give up control; the computer then finishes the idea by pulling data randomly from a bank of possibilities. Computer composition allows composers to control the outcome or to give up control at nearly every level. The term for programming control away from the composer and into the computer is **artificial intelligence.** There are serious efforts today to develop a compositional environment where artificial intelligence could realize in specific detail the larger ideas of the composer, but such an activity requires extensive knowledge of computer programming by the composer. These composers look at the computer as another instrument in their immediate world of music.

artificial intelligence
a computer environment where decisions in creation and direction are determined by software. These systems develop and expand simple ideas into complex structures.

John Cage was a leader in indeterminate music. He developed a modified piano where small objects are placed in between the strings; when notes are played, percussive sounds add to the texture of the music

John Cage
(1912–92)

DATELINE	BIOGRAPHY
1912	John Cage was born in Los Angeles. He was educated at Pomona College and studied piano with Fannie Charles Dillon in Los Angeles and Lazare-Levy in Paris.
1930s	After studying with Charles Ives and Henry Cowell, Cage became interested in experimental music. His love of percussion led him to organize and perform concerts with percussion orchestras.
1940s	By attaching foreign objects to the piano strings to change the pitch and timbre Cage invented the "prepared piano." His *Sonatas and Interludes* for prepared piano was performed at Carnegie Hall in 1949.
1949	Cage was awarded the Guggenheim Fellowship and the Award of the Society of Arts and Letters.
1951	After studying the philosophy of Zen Buddhism, Cage began to write compositions based on chance. He used charts from the ancient Chinese book *I Ching*, along with the tossing of dice, to select the random choices involved in the compositions. His *Imaginary Landscape No. 4* involved the random playing of twelve radios with different wavelengths, volumes, and durations.
1952	His silent composition *4' 33"* called for the performer to do absolutely nothing for four minutes and thirty-three seconds, thereby allowing the composition to be determined solely by environmental sounds.
1950s	Cage began composing in the recording studio, using magnetic tape to produce the sounds he desired. His *William Mix* (1952) is a mixture of sounds taken from everyday life and assembled on tape.
1970s	He continued to produce works determined by chance and/or choices by the performers themselves as to duration, rhythms, and instruments used. In almost all pieces the visual experience is as important or more important than the actual sounds produced. The piece *Etudes astrales* (1974–75) is based on cosmic star studies.
1980s	Cage, the master of nonthematic experimental music, turned to computers to provide random options and new computer-generated sounds.
1992	Cage died in New York City.

Listening Notes

John Cage, *Solo for Sliding Trombone,* from Piano Concert (1957–58), combined with *Fontana Mix* (1958).

This work has many variables. The trombone solo has great liberties in setting structure and determining texture. The sounds used by the trombonist encompass dramatic extremes. The soloist here is James Fulkerson. He never plays a melodic line; he spends most of his time playing single notes which are sustained and manipulated by mutes for tone and the slide for pitch change. The primary focus is placed on the quality of single notes in different ranges.

Different trombonists, with different determinations, can change the outcome considerably; however, the overall structure would still be recognizable. The score of the *Fontana Mix* consists of transparent sheets, some with dots and others with curved lines. When placed on top of each other, the curves and points yield images used to create "tape music," vocal music, and theatrical events. This score resulted in the tape used here as an accompaniment to the Trombone.

0:00 Water sounds with a high buzz begins the performance.

0:08 Long notes, first in the low range then higher; low rumbling background sounds.

0:23 Electronic sounds in the background.

0:38 Low notes on the trombone, called pedal tones.

0:43 Voices talking (high long note).

0:54 Trombone plays a middle range note.

0:59 Trombone varies the pitch on a note.

1:02 Dogs barking.

1:16 Very high pitch (white noise in the background).

1:25 Backwards sounds, trombone plays a middle range note.

1:40 Low guttural sounds from the trombone.

1:46 Hiss predominates the texture.

1:53 Another long note.

2:00 Rattle and buzzes, trombone plays another long note; more backwards sounds in the background.

2:20 Number of notes played by the trombone increases.

2:50	Squeaks predominate.
3:04	Low then middle range notes.
3:30	Silence.
3:34	Single note with amplitude changes (vibrato-like).
3:50	Very high note.
3:59	Trombone makes sliding sounds and mutes the sound.
4:19	More sliding sounds.
4:28	Dogs barking.
4:30	Fade out.

(for example, *Sonatas and Interludes*). The "prepared piano" introduced new and unpredictable sounds. Cage's interest in Zen Buddhism led him to detach his writing from the traditional concept of music composition and to introduce Oriental sounds, especially percussion.

His music is structured around programmed activities that are organized under a single directive. A prime example of Cage's interest in elements out of his or anyone's control is his unique work called *4′ 33″*. A pianist sits in silence at an open piano for four minutes and thirty-three seconds. The sounds in the room and the audience itself become the musical experience. The pianist leaves the stage without having played at all.

Indeterminacy has worked well in combination with the other budding compositional schools of the late twentieth century. Serial composers such as Boulez and Stockhausen have found indeterminate aspects valuable to their music. The impact of Cage's music has proven as powerful as any from this period. His influence continues to excite young experimental musicians.

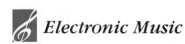 *Electronic Music*

By the 1960s composers became more aware of the possibilities of electronics and music. At first their image of it was more like science fiction than reality. Music and electronics merged slowly. Instead of creating electronically generated sounds, composers first recorded sounds from nature on tape and through the process of **tape manipulation** created musical compositions. Tapes can be spliced and reordered, slowed down, sped up, run backwards, distorted, filtered, and rerecorded. This technique is called ***musique concrète.***

tape manipulation
used to affect recorded sounds. Tapes can be slowed down, sped up, run backwards, or cut and reassembled in a different order.

musique concrète
music composed from recorded and electronically affected acoustic sounds and tape manipulation.

The technique is expanded to include sound generators in a work by Edgard Varèse entitled *Poème électronique* (Electronic Poem) written in 1958. This piece is less than ten minutes long and has recorded sounds drawn from animals, humans, and nature. Written for a performance at the World's Fair in Brussels, it was accompanied by photographs projected on the walls of a large pavilion. There were 425 speakers placed around the room, and the sounds were manipulated so that their original sources were unrecognizable. Varése composed music using and varying sound sources, a compositional concept known as "liberation of sound."

Once sound synthesis came of age, composers such as Milton Babbitt used electronically generated sounds in combination with live performance. His *Philomel* presents a single singer in a performance with recorded synthetic sounds composed in a strict serial style. The early computer-driven compositions could only be produced in expensive facilities such as the Columbia-Princeton Electronic Music Center. Today even more complex computers and sound generators are accessible to professional and amateur musicians alike at a fraction of the cost. Sound tracks to movies, music videos, and live performances are now organized, processed, and stored digitally. Synthesizers are then

Milton Babbitt at the RCA Synthesizer

used to repeat the music at will. Synthesizers have become required tools for composers of all styles of music, and the commercial and educational music worlds have adopted their usage extensively since the mid-1980s.

Listening Notes

Milton Babbitt, *Composition for Synthesizer* (1960–61).

This work is a serial composition based on a twelve-tone row and a series of rhythms. The sounds and textures here were very new to music. The crispness and speed of some of the figures are only capable with synthesizer performance. This work was written and performed on the RCA synthesizer. The computer was enormous for its day and thrilled Babbitt because of the control offered the composer. Babbitt believed that the control of the primary musical elements was as important as the resulting sound.

What sounds like noise is really pitches and combinations of pitches that phase and conflict, leaving sweeping, noiselike sounds. The elements of music discussed in Part I (''Physics of Sound'') are especially important here. The composer is concerned with rhythm, melody, chords or clusters, dynamics, and structure.

0:00	Chimelike sounds begin the composition. Repeated metal-sounding accents are bridged by statements of the row.
0:52	Shimmer sounds surrounded by bell sounds.
1:07	A mixture of electronic sounds and shimmers along with a sound much like a bassoon.
1:45	Combination of very high and low pitches.
2:10	Bassoon sound surrounded by pitches with interesting attacks and decays.
2:35	Shimmer sounds increase.
2:46	Very low pitches enter the texture.
3:25	Bassoon sound returns with shimmers.
4:18	High-register melodic activity predominates briefly.
4:57	New sounds.

5:28	Change in texture, trills; move to the treble range.
5:48	Notice the stereo image. Sounds dance from side to side.
6:05	New sounds, sustained pitches.
7:06	New sounds, this time percussive in nature; white noise.
7:23	Sounds with clear pitches enter and fade out.
8:00	Interesting stereo image.
8:10	Pitched notes return briefly.
8:35	Return to texture built on sounds with pitch.
9:25	Periodic ringing metal sounds return.
10:06	New sounds, the texture begins to change rapidly, movement increases.
10:30	End.

 ## *Experimental/Theoretical Music*

Research remains an unquestionably important part of the academic world. Universities are homes for research, and each discipline is pushed and probed for meaning, historical significance, and future possibilities. Music has not escaped such investigation. In fact, some of the most problematic encounters in the arts have come with experimental music. Questions not previously asked have taken front stage, further stimulating the musical arts. For instance, is it necessary for music to have sound as part of its definition? Is sound merely the byproduct of the creative act? Is composition more important than performance? Is structure necessary? Is there room for chance and improvisation? Is the notational system adequate? The questions go on and on.

The most common product of experimentation is failure. Only a few experiments provide the desired result. However, one learns from the results of all experiments. Theory produces ideas on which performance is based. There is even the element of risk in using traditional notation. Will and should the performer accurately interpret the composer's intent? Why? Experimental music has produced compositions such as *General Speech* by Robert Erickson in which a trombonist is asked to recite a speech, dressed in uniform and playing the trombone. There is always the thrill that something wonderful will happen, something beyond the expected and still within the realm of musicality.

Stuart Dempster performing Robert Erickson's *General Speech*.
Commissioned by Stuart Dempster, this performance requires the trombonist to integrate music, speech, and theater. The performer must coordinate difficult melodic passages with verbal articulations that are spoken through the trombone while playing. The verbal quotes come from General Douglas MacArthur's retirement speech at West Point. The use of costume, speech, and musical notation creates an arena similar to musical theater. To eliminate any of these elements would reduce the effect of the performance. The standard dress code of a symphony orchestra is quiet black gowns and suits to focus attention on the music and not the performers. This work purposely negates this tradition.

Along with compositional experimentation came extended performing techniques. Instrumentalists are now asked to sing one part while playing another. This technique can be extended even further; for example, for flutists who can sing one part, whistle another, and play a third. There are even compositions that are physically impossible to perform; it is the object of the musician to play as much as possible. Some works are written for a player piano because no single person can play the complex rhythms and meters. The concept of virtuosity has been extended to near superhuman levels. Clarinetists can control two or three notes at once on an instrument previously thought able to produce only one note at a time.

This activity is true to the definition of research. Composers and performers have always looked for new ways to liberate sound from traditional concepts. Louis Armstrong extended the range of the trumpet; Edgard Varèse liberated sound by using a siren in classical composition. Henry Cowell and Krzysztof Penderecki used several notes only half-steps apart in clusters, creating blocks of sound instead of chords. All these sounds are born of the same spirit of experimentation.

 Minimalism

With the pendulum swinging toward an ever-increasing world of technology and complexity, a reaction arose. Exaggerated styles such as romanticism and serialism have bred equally strong reactions. Minimalism is an extreme in itself. Karlheinz Stockhausen composed *Stimmung* in 1968, a work that is representative of the goals of minimalism. In this work, six vocalists sing one chord for nearly sixty minutes; the purpose is to have a single event last for large periods of time. The chord in this example changes only as it goes in and out of tune. This movement was partly reflective of a new interest in Eastern ideals and religion, as seen recently in the music of Steve Reich and Philip Glass.

Listening Notes

Steve Reich, *Music for Mallet Instruments, Voices and Organ* (1973).

This excerpt is from a work approximately sixteen minutes long and scored for a colorful combination of instruments. One level of "activity" comes from the continuous patterns from the mallet instruments. The other level is very slow by comparison. The tonal center is established by the slow movement between two notes in the organ. When the voices enter, they blend into the texture with activity similar to the mallet instruments. The almost hypnotic music has no sudden changes in dynamics or texture. Reich's study of African drumming influenced his repetitive writing style. The sustained notes give his music a weak sense of tonality; however, it is difficult to perceive the chords as a traditional harmonic progression. Tonal stability is established by repetition.

0:00	Selection begins with melodic/rhythmic patterns played out of phase by the marimbas; the organ moves between two notes (a minor third). The lowest note establishes a tonal center. There is a high note each time the organ begins its low two-note pattern.
1:16	Slight rhythmic variations in the mallet instruments; the length of notes in the organ become very long (augmentation).
1:30	Soft voice part in the middle of the mallet texture.
2:57	The voice sings in unison with the marimba.
3:20	High sustained note returns as the organ bass notes speed up.
3:43	The organ notes quicken. Two high notes change with the organ notes.
4:03	Sudden tonal shift upward. Bass notes speed up again. More sustained notes in the treble range using a two note pattern.
4:20	Return to original texture. Organ will vary the length of the two notes.
5:19	Low notes in the organ slow dramatically; voices enter with melodic patterns similar to the mallet instruments.
6:00	Fade.

Neoromanticism

The research and experimentation in music led to a detachment from audiences that are more interested in traditional musical styles. Audiences seldom hear that the music is a product of logic and concept. The need for composers to communicate to listeners has become an increasing concern. Music based on intellectual theory and experimental performance techniques is rarely understood by the average concertgoer. The music is stimulating and rewarding when put into perspective, and the intellectualism in which it is conceived is extraordinary. However, music for the very few is lonely, to say the least. The resurgence of commercial music and the unbelievable response to music produced outside the educational environment has nudged composers to reevaluate the impact of their music on their audiences. They have had to reevaluate their audiences and find an avenue to their listening needs. Ellen Zwilich in 1983 (see Topic 5) and Roger Reynolds in 1989, both winners of the Pulitzer Prize, have shown this redirection. The music has incorporated a sense of emotionalism reminiscent of the Romantic period and a move to tonality.

🎼 *Jazz: 1950 to the Present*

Third Stream and Free

cool jazz
a post-bebop style that
softened some of the
aggressive elements of bebop.
The melody was played in a
more comfortable range, the
rhythm section used fewer
explosive sounds, and the
tempos were more relaxed
than in bebop. Also called
West Coast jazz.

hard bop
a bebop style with elements of
blues along with a less angular
sense of melody. Also called
straight-ahead jazz.

third stream
jazz that incorporates elements
of classical music such as
modern sounds, orchestral
instruments, and composing
techniques.

The 1950s produced a wealth of different styles in jazz. **Cool jazz** developed on the West Coast in an effort to calm down the hard driving bebop style of Charlie Parker and Dizzy Gillespie. Melodic lines were less explosive and range was limited, giving the music a less aggressive sound than bebop. Meanwhile, **hard bop** reintroduced elements of blues inflections into the soloing. The virtuosity of jazz attracted many classically trained musicians who brought additional skills and knowledge to the field, further impacting the development of jazz. A **third stream** of music blossomed briefly, a wedding of jazz and classical. There are four elements of this elusive style:

1. Jazz used instruments associated with classical music, for example, French horn, violin, cello, or flute.
2. Compositional techniques associated with classical music such as serialism were adopted.
3. Classical forms such as concerto or sonata-allegro form might be used.
4. Jazz compositions might sound like classical music, using ensembles similar to symphony orchestras.

Miles Davis recorded cool and third stream works in the fifties and sixties. Gil Evans pitted the solo sound of Davis against orchestral ensembles using strings and woodwinds not commonly associated with jazz. The *Porgy and Bess* album is a wonderful combination of the compositional skills of Gershwin, the arranging skills of Evans, and the improvisational skills of Davis. The range of possible techniques in third stream is expansive. For example, jazz composers such as George Russell and Thelonius Monk used tone clusters like Cowell and dissonances associated with serial composition.

Much like the activities in twentieth-century classical composition, third stream was and continues to be experimental. New combinations of instruments played newly designed melodies supported by less-patterned rhythm sections. Third stream became associated with the avant-garde and was soon identified with another growing style, **free jazz.**

free jazz
a modern jazz style that
questions traditional melodic
and harmonic rules.
Performers are free to play
anything at anytime they feel is
musical.

In the 1960s a movement toward free jazz was based on questioning all traditional jazz styles. This movement incorporated a high level of atonality and abandoned the structures of patterned rhythm and meter.

Like classical music at this time, instrumental techniques were pushed to an experimental level, manipulating tone color and performance techniques. A work by Chick Corea called "The Law of Falling and Catching Up" is performed inside a piano but not using the keys; strings are plucked and strummed and hit with hands and mallets.

Avant-garde classical and free jazz come very close to being the same. The sounds and activities of each are very similar. The only difference is that one group is composed of jazz musicians while the other is comprised of classical musicians. Another element that parallels classical music is the move to collective improvisation. For jazz it is a return; for classical it is new. The composer has very little control over these performances, and the performers are free to add or subtract ideas at will in response to the other musicians.

Ornette Coleman
(1930–   )

DATELINE	BIOGRAPHY
1930	Ornette Coleman was born into a poor family in Ft. Worth, Texas. His mother was a seamstress and his father died when he was seven. Coleman took odd jobs after school to help the family.
1944	His mother bought him an alto saxophone. He basically taught himself how to play with the help of a cousin and the high school band program.
1946	At the age of sixteen, Coleman began playing in the R & B nightclubs around Fort Worth; he listened to and copied the bebop style of Charlie Parker.
1949	Coleman toured with a traveling minstrel show called "Silas Green from New Orleans," the Clarence Samuels's Traveling Rhythm and Blues Band, and Pee Wee Crayton's band, which took him to Los Angeles. His credibility as a jazz musician already was being questioned as Ornette began to develop his own atonal style.
1952–59	Unable to support himself as a musician, Coleman worked as a porter, an elevator operator, and a stock clerk. He married Jayne Cortez and had a son, Ornette Denardo. He studied harmony and theory but preferred free jazz over the conventional methods of improvisation based on chord patterns.

1959   Having relocated in New York, Coleman formed a quartet with trumpet player Don Cherry and bassist Charlie Haden; they recorded for Atlantic Records. Supported and encouraged by Percy Heath of the Modern Jazz Quartet, Coleman and Haden attended the Lenox School of Jazz in the summer of 1959.

1960s   Coleman performed in nightclubs in New York playing a white plastic sax; he also took up the trumpet and the violin, providing him with the opportunity to produce new, distinctive sounds. His music was either applauded with enthusiasm or totally rejected.

1965   He took his quartet on a European tour. In 1967 and 1974 he received Guggenheim fellowships for his compositions.

1972   Coleman's quartet performed his piece *Skies of America* with a symphonic orchestra at a New York jazz festival.

1986   Coleman collaborated with Pat Metheny on the album *Song X* and worked regularly with his electric ensemble, Prime Time, which includes his son Denardo on drums.

1987   Coleman reassembled his original quartet with Don Cherry, Charlie Haden, and Billy Higgins and recorded the album *In All Languages;* they went on the road.

1990s   Coleman continues to perform at concerts and jazz festivals; his style of free jazz has come to be taken seriously in the music world.

Listening Notes

Ornette Coleman, excerpt from "Free Jazz" (1960).

This excerpt is an extended solo by Coleman on alto sax with accompaniment ideas supplied by the other players. Notice the freedom of the other musicians to comment freely as the music progresses. The accompaniment figures fade in and out of the very loose texture. The group is a double quartet, sax and bass clarinet, two trumpets, two drummers, and two bass players. The texture is independent and at times very thick. Notice the swinging nature of Coleman's solo; the long-short flow of eighth notes is a direct heritage from his rhythm and blues background.

0:00   Introduction: Everyone plays slowly; long notes.

0:11   Organized section: Bebop melody provides ideas for the following long improvisation.

0:22	Alto sax solo: Bass walks, drummers play patterns that produce a strong feeling of swing.
1:10	Horns enter with accompaniment ideas (backup figures).
1:20	One bass player plays high, fast scales, while the other plays a more traditional bass line.
1:28	First climactic point: Backup figures are free improvisations.
1:40	New backup ideas: Bass clarinet plays long notes.
2:45	New backup ideas: Coleman continues the hard, rhythmic swing feeling.
3:00	Notice the bass.
3:22	Bebop pattern.
3:35	Horns enter again with related but independent ideas.
3:43	New backup ideas.
4:10	Fast solo work by Coleman, new climax.
4:20	The bowed string bass plays a separate idea.
4:40	All the horns play, increasing the density and energy.
5:00	Climax.
5:10	"Jingle Bells" quote, perhaps by accident.
5:38	Sharing of melodic ideas started by Coleman.
6:43	Very free section in which all the horns become near-equal soloists, each playing an independent idea.
7:15	Coleman takes solo role again.
7:43	All play fast notes, increasing energy.
8:45	Horns pass around motive from the first part of this section.
9:15	Building to another climax.
9:40	Return to the bebop melody first heard at the beginning of this excerpt; horns play in unison.
9:51	Fade out.

Fusion and Crossover

Swing was the most popular period in jazz history. It had a well-defined rhythm section supporting easily comprehensible melodies. The reaction to bebop, third stream, and free jazz was decisive and powerful. Jazz gained new popularity with yet another wedding, this time to rock. Rock contributed the long-missed regularity of a predictable rhythm section upon which melody reigned supreme. **Fusion** was the combination of jazz structures, improvisation, and theory with the rigidity and drive of rock patterns. Electronics, especially developing keyboards, intrigued the creative imaginations of performers such as Herbie Hancock, Chick Corea, and Joe Zawinul.

Groups such as Weather Report and Return to Forever set the pace by which jazz players would enter this new style. Musicians now had to deal with the problems of electronic instruments, massive volume levels, and a new balance between the soloists and the rhythm section. As the

Michael Brecker
(1949–)

DATELINE	BIOGRAPHY
1949	Michael Brecker was born in Philadelphia, into a musical family. His father and sister are both pianists, and his brother, Randy, is a well-known trumpeter.
1965–69	Brecker studied saxophone with Vince Trombetta, a sax player on the Mike Douglas Show for sixteen years; he also took up flute, soprano sax, drums, and piano, although tenor sax was to be his primary instrument.
1969	Brecker moved to New York City to establish himself in the jazz scene. Influenced by John Coltrane, he spent hours jamming with sax players such as Dave Liebman and Steve Grossman.
1970–73	He formed a fusion group Dreams with his brother Randy on trumpet.
1975–80	The Brecker Brothers recorded six albums on the Arista label.
1981	Brecker recorded ''Cityscape,'' an orchestra project written and arranged for him by Claus Ogerman.
1983–84	He played in the house band for ''Saturday Night Live'' while continuing to record almost 400 albums for such names as James Taylor, John Lennon, Billy Joel, Spiro Gyra, David Sanborn, Frank Sinatra, and Billy Cobham.
1989	Brecker's first solo jazz album, *Michael Brecker,* was recorded with Charlie Haden and Pat Metheny. He continues to perform and record with his group Steps Ahead.

Listening Notes

Michael Brecker and Don Grolnick, "Itsbynne Reel" from *Don't Try This at Home* MCAD-42229 (1989).

This selection displays the use of a wind controller (Akai EWI) capable of playing any of the settings available to keyboard synthesizers. It is played like a saxophone and is capable of breath accents and articulations. The opening duet that sounds like bluegrass features Brecker on EWI and Mark O'Connor on violin. Mike Stern on guitar represents the influence of rock soloing styles. All the musicians have virtuoso technique and perform together in an improvisational texture. Their communication is extraordinary and very responsive to the soloist, and their ability to improvise large architectural solos is remarkable. The rhythmic patterns supporting the texture are a hybrid of rock and jazz, and the fusion of the two styles is complete.

0:00   Introduction, solo melody (EWI), hoedown style melody.

0:08   Violin joins the EWI.

0:16   Piano pattern is added.

0:54   The violin and the EWI become independent; they dialogue back and forth.

2:12   Full rhythm section, drums, bass, and keyboards, extended rock rhythmic patterns. Brecker now plays tenor sax.

2:40   Chordal sounds from the sax and synthesizers.

3:17   Notice the acoustic piano sounds.

3:40   Complex ensemble patterns, drummer accents all ensemble patterns.

4:18   Tenor sax solo (improvised).

4:47   Tenor sax plays rhythms with the ensemble background momentarily.

5:25   Rhythm section maintains a static harmonic texture with varying accents. Brecker builds the melodic line to a climax.

6:11   Climax of solo.

6:20   Return to hoedown theme, violin joins the melody.

6:56   Repeat of theme with slight variations.

7:01   Violin and sax become very soloistic and independent.

7:40   End.

style matured the role of the soloist changed. In the more jazz-oriented groups, the rhythm section continued to improvise around the soloist and often took turns soloing. In the more commercial groups like David Sanborn, the rhythm section might be "programmed" ahead of the performance while the soloist assumes the entire role of improvisation.

Performers like Michael Brecker have extended technique beyond fast bebop or fusion. His use of a wind controller to drive synthesizers has given a new dimension to electronic soloing for winds. He also records with a wide cross section of musicians such as Mike Stern, who has brought a highly developed rock guitar style to jazz. Until recently the strongest soloists were generally trained in jazz; however, the number of young rock players entering the jazz/rock world has opened up the definition of **crossover.** This style is a hybrid of jazz, rock, and commercial techniques, bringing the best players of each style into an arena of mutual communication.

crossover
a jazz style where jazz and rock combine with the newest of commercial instruments and recording techniques.

Chapter 12

ROCK:
1950 to the Present

Music Outline of Rock

1. Rock 'n' roll shared the same heritage as jazz. The three basic styles that spawned rock are country and western, popular, and rhythm and blues.

2. Rhythm section concepts borrowed from rhythm and blues along with the emotionalism of black gospel music produced a new sound. The amplified sound of the rhythm section is an identifying factor of rock.

3. Rock emerged as a new style in the 1950s and diversified politically, culturally, and musically in the 1960s.

4. Rock musicians were leaders in dealing with amplified sound and electronic effects.

5. Rock shares an identity with commercial and pop music.

6. Sophisticated recording techniques developed in the 1960s and expanded in the 1990s with digital sound and music videos.

7. Rock 'n' roll, folk rock, and soft rock developed into progressive styles such as art rock, progressive rock, and fusion.

In the early 1950s a musical style evolved that shared many of the same roots as jazz. Although it has been suggested that rock 'n' roll is a descendant of jazz, it actually developed independently, but along similar paths. In recent years the two styles have converged and, in places, merged.

Jazz and rock share a heritage of country blues, rhythm and blues, work songs, rags, gospel, and even country and western. As both styles matured, they grew apart stylistically; not until the 1970s did they combine. These two styles mingle today in the recording studio where electronic effects have become essential. In this atmosphere, the wedding of jazz and rock into a popular musical fusion was natural. The terms *commercial, jazz/rock, rock/jazz,* or *contemporary fusion* are negative terms to some traditionalists, but they still accurately describe rock's place in society today. Elements of rock can be found in most aspects of commercial writing such as film scores, commercials, radio jingles, albums, and videos. Although it has infiltrated much of the music in our society, it has maintained a singular stream of development.

> **Commercial Music**
> Several terms used today describe different parts of the popular music industry and are often used interchangeably. Commercial music usually refers to movie soundtracks and jingles; however, it has grown to include activities in the music industry such as playing in studios for soundtracks and popular songs. The term is used when the music business is a primary concern. Popular music is an even bigger term encompassing packaged music that enjoys a large listening audience. Many musical styles make up the larger category of pop music. One could even say the waltzes of Strauss fell into a definition of popular music. Although rock is a large part of the popular and commercial music world it must share that position with country and western, jazz (especially swing), folk, and even contemporary gospel.

 The Fifties

Pop music (1920s) from Tin Pan Alley, an area of music publishing in New York City, provided a basis for lyric development in the popular songs of the day. In the popular ballads of the 1940s lyrics of songs reigned supreme. Again in the 1950s lyrics were essential to the shaping of rock's musical style. The lyrics were not provocative and usually centered on romance and falling in love.

Bill Haley and the Comets used a combination of rhythm and blues and country to forge the beginning of a new vocal sound. Elvis Presley further intensified and personalized it with inflections from the black tradition borrowed from the blues. The techniques used by these performers contributed to the library of inflections that identify rock performers today. **Rhythm and blues** singers such as Chuck Berry and Bo Diddley gave further definition to the 1950s sound of rock 'n' roll. By adding amplified sound, early rock became aggressive and vibrant.

rhythm and blues
a rhythmic dance form of the blues. It led to the development of rock 'n roll.

Like jazz, rock adopted the tenor sax as the major melodic instrument. Unlike jazz, brass instruments were seldom heard. The tenor saxophone still plays a primary role in both styles. The rhythm section mirrored the structure of rhythm and blues bands. The following table compares a typical 1950s small jazz group to a rock 'n' roll band of the time.

Table of Rhythm Sections Comparison

TRADITIONAL JAZZ INSTRUMENTATION	ROCK INSTRUMENTATION AND FUNCTION
Piano	Rhythm guitar (comps by playing simple strummed patterns)
String bass	Electric bass (less active melodically, usually 4/4 patterns built around the chord)
Drums	Drums, expanded sets (rigid patterns with simple but forceful fills)
Solo horns (trumpet and sax)	Lead guitar, saxophone (cell-response to the vocal part, relatively short solos, repeated riffs as accompaniment to voice)

The importance of the twelve-bar blues and the style of rhythm and blues cannot be underestimated. These two structures provided an environment for new vocal sounds, new lyrics, and new recording techniques. The twelve-bar blues structure is basic. Rock, using such a simple structure, could easily be passed from individual to individual by imitating records. Everything was imitated, the music, vocal inflections, guitar styles, even accompaniment figures. There was little need for notated music.

Teenage audiences of the 1950s did not discriminate between the rock offerings of Buddy Holly and Little Richard and the more conservative popular music produced by singers like Pat Boone and Paul Anka. Then, as now, the line between soft-rock and rock music is always difficult to draw. The lines between jazz and rock, or rhythm and blues

Elvis Presley
(1935–77)

DATELINE	BIOGRAPHY
1935	Elvis Presley was born in Tupelo, Mississippi. His early musical education consisted of exposure to church music, gospel concerts, and country music.
1945	He first appeared in public at a State Fair talent contest.
1950s	Presley formed a band through connections at Sun Studios in Memphis; they toured the South and became locally popular.
1954	Colonel Tom Parker became Presley's manager and began to build a solid career for him based on personal appearances, recordings, and films. RCA-Victor purchased Presley's contract from Sun Studios.
1956	The recording "Heartbreak Hotel" catapulted him into stardom; he made his first of thirty-three motion pictures this year, *Love Me Tender.*
1956–61	Nearly all his recordings during these years made the top ten in the United States, including such hits as "All Shook Up," "Don't Be Cruel," "Hound Dog," "Jailhouse Rock," and "Love Me Tender"; he successfully combined elements of country and western with rhythm and blues and was a tremendous influence on rock performers in the United States and England.
1958–60	Presley was drafted into the U.S. Army and served two years in Germany.
1967	He married Priscilla Beaulieu, daughter of an Army officer; they had a daughter, Lisa Marie.
1970s	His popularity declined, although he still had a large following of faithful fans who packed his Las Vegas stage shows and bought his recordings.
1977	Presley died in Memphis, Tennessee; although his death was officially declared a result of natural causes, his long dependency on drugs undoubtedly led to his early death at the age of forty-two.

for that matter, have been equally indistinct. For instance, historians justifiably consider Ray Charles and Muddy Waters vital contributors to both rock and jazz.

The Sixties

The 1960s brought a new generation of listeners and several different cultural identities which would impact the direction of rock. The Beatles probably exemplified this era most prominently. Their worldwide, lasting impact was unprecedented, and rereleases of their albums on compact disc twenty years later sparked unbelievable sales.

The Beatles took rock 'n' roll into uncharted territory. They explored the use of classical concepts (rock's third stream), new recording techniques, jazz ideas, and experimental sounds. As John Lennon, Paul McCartney, George Harrison, and Ringo Starr matured musically, their importance became more and more far-reaching. Their musical styles fall into three periods, the first involving simple lyrics and musical arrangements, the second dealing with lyrical symbols and growing electronic experimentation, and the third with well-rehearsed and studio-perfect performances that dealt with mystical and abstract ideas.

The sixties rock group Jefferson Airplane

Paul McCartney
(1942–)

DATELINE	BIOGRAPHY
1942	Paul McCartney was born in Liverpool, England. Influenced as a teenager by Elvis Presley, he traded in the trumpet his father gave him for a bass guitar.
1957	He joined his friend John Lennon in the group the Quarrymen; they began writing music together and played locally in pubs.
1961	Lennon picked the name "Beatles" after Buddy Holly of the Crickets died in a plane crash; this same year the group was discovered by Brian Epstein, who became their manager and promoter.
1963	Capitol Records released "I Want to Hold Your Hand"; already popular in the British Isles and Europe, the group gained American recognition.
1964	The Beatles' debut in the United States brought them instant fame; between 1962 and 1970 they recorded several hit albums, including, *A Hard Day's Night, Rubber Soul, Revolver, Sgt. Pepper's Lonely Hearts Club Band,* and *Abbey Road.*
1970	McCartney took the other Beatles to court to have their partnership legally dissolved; he released his first solo album, *McCartney.*
1971	McCartney formed the group Wings, with his wife Linda on keyboards and vocals. Their most successful album was *Band on the Run.*
1980	He was arrested on drug charges at the beginning of a Japanese tour.
1982	He recorded a hit duet, "The Girl Is Mine," with Michael Jackson.
1985	His movie production *Give My Regards to Broad Street* was a commercial failure.
1991	With the associate conductor of the London Philharmonic, McCartney composed the *Liverpool Oratorio.* The work was commissioned and premièred by the Royal Liverpool Philharmonic. The West Coast première was in 1992.
1992	A multimillionaire, McCartney continues to write music and perform. He runs his own company out of an office in London.

By 1965 the success of The Beatles allowed them to take their audience with them as they experimented with new instrumental combinations and song structures. Such activities normally blurred a group's identity, spelling failure in the marketplace. The pinnacle album of The Beatles and of all rock at that time was *Sgt. Pepper's Lonely Hearts Club Band,* a concept album based on scenes from a concert with heavy psychedelic overtones. The album has sitars (a stringed instrument from India), strings, brass, crowd noises, and sound effects and also showed new recording techniques that would stimulate the recording industry for years.

Rock 'n' roll, like jazz, has had many tangent styles that have met with varying degrees of acceptance. Sudden improvements in recording techniques encouraged variations of singing and playing that were not possible before; sound effects like echo and distortion were the first to appear. Groups also began to reflect geographical locations and cultural backgrounds. For example, surfing music became associated with good times and security whereas acid rock spoke of rebellion and a demand for change. The untroubled and dissident worlds, respectively, of the Beach Boys and Jefferson Airplane seem even farther apart now than when they were both active on the West Coast. West Coast or cool jazz was centered in Los Angeles at the same time and place as surfing music, while in San Francisco, acid or psychedelic rock flourished. The sixties was indeed a time for rock styles to splinter from the earlier twelve-bar rhythm and blues structures.

Cultural diversity was expressed in another segment of sixties rock, **soul.** Soul was a mixture of the emotions of gospel, rhythm and blues, and the urban black community. The music was produced largely in Detroit by the record company Motown. The name of the company became a stylistic term. **Motown** stars such as Stevie Wonder, Diana Ross, Smokey Robinson, and eventually Michael Jackson carry a strong lineage of the emotion-packed style of soul.

The guitar has remained the most important instrument in rock and was given new definition by Jimi Hendrix in the late 1960s. His ability to coordinate the new electronic effects such as the **wah-wah pedal,** the toggle switch, and the tremolo bar set standards for guitarists today. His use of feedback as a musical sound shocked some and excited others. He delivered an historic performance of the "The Star-Spangled Banner" at Woodstock using feedback almost exclusively.

The Vietnam War greatly affected the youth of the sixties and was reflected in the music. Individuals in each era adopt avenues of escape and encounter through their music. It is no coincidence that music from the times when the United States was at war has always inspired nostalgia

soul
a blues style defined by the black musical tradition of slow rock (1970s) that emanated from Detroit (Motown).

Motown
a name for the musical style that emanated from Detroit. It is a black rock style with a strong emphasis on rock rhythms.

wah-wah pedal
the pedal used by guitarists to vary the level of distortion and volume from their guitar amplifier. It can sound like vocal inflections.

A scene from the sixties rock-opera *Hair*

for those who lived through the turmoil and insecurity. Many folk rock singers of the sixties and seventies sang of individual freedom and respect and decried governmental structures that denied them a sense of identity.

 The Seventies

The 1970s produced technological advances in music with better recording techniques and more realistic products. The goal to imitate "live" music was no longer the single purpose of the studio. The music business became a leader in experimenting with the storage, synthesis, and processing of sound. The art of studio recording had matured far beyond the revolutionary recordings of The Beatles. The jazz and classical communities were initially uncomfortable with electric applications for their instruments. Amplification's association to rock 'n' roll was considered demeaning. Today, however, jazz and classical artists do not hesitate to acquire sound systems and sound engineers to help enhance otherwise totally acoustic performances.

American and English musicians and their promoters controlled rock 'n' roll's direction. English groups and artists like the Rolling Stones, Elton John, and The Who became models for young players in America to emulate. Meanwhile in America, musicians like Peter, Paul and Mary, Joni Mitchell, and Bob Dylan pursued a more folk-oriented rock style. Jazz, having had a strong hold in Europe and Scandinavia since the 1920s, continued to exert an ever-increasing influence on modern rock. Instrumental soloists, especially on sax, were increasingly showing backgrounds in jazz.

Progressive rock in the late seventies expanded musical structures and developed more complicated musical textures. This was the beginning of rock's journey toward fusion. Groups started to use brass instruments. Blood, Sweat and Tears and Chicago are prime examples of the move to using several horn players. Blues and jazz ideas began to appear within the standard rock 'n' roll structures. Then to further modify the style, Santana, among others, introduced Latin rhythms into rock. The elements of jazz-rock were at hand.

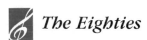 ## The Eighties

Rock styles of the 1980s returned to a danceable format. Like jazz, rock's most popular styles were those associated with dance rhythms. **Disco,** perhaps the most obvious dance rhythm, was the popular music industry's answer to progressive rock. New Wave groups like the Stray Cats brought back the simplicity of Elvis Presley. Punk, an aggressive and extremely loud style of basic rock, and several parallel styles in England carried on the rock tradition of cultural separation from the perceived establishment.

But most important, musicians with true virtuoso abilities, such as John McLaughlin, emerged from rock and were capable of bridging the gap to jazz convincingly. The floodgates then seemed to open, and musicians such as keyboardist Herbie Hancock and violinist Jean-Luc Ponty were able to generate great musical excitement in both worlds of rock and jazz. In the later part of the 1980s musicians were passing from rock to jazz as freely as from jazz to rock. Such previous jazz hard-liners as Miles Davis and Chick Corea blended musicians of both worlds into groups that became headline attractions.

disco
a dance style typified by a heavy bass drum on each beat of the measure. A contemporary style of the late 1970s.

Elton John
(1947–   )

DATELINE	BIOGRAPHY
1947	Elton John was born Reginald Kenneth Dwight in Middlesex, England. He began studying the piano at an early age.
1964	After graduating from high school, John worked as a messenger for a music publisher and played piano at night in the local pubs.
1965	He joined the band Bluesology, which provided backup for American soul stars touring England.
1967	John began collaborating with lyricist Bernie Taupin. After working for several other groups, they began writing for John's voice, and in 1969 his first song, "Lady Samantha," was released; this led to his first album, *Empty Sky*.
1970	The album *Elton John* became a hit in England and the United States; the Elton John Band was a huge success at the Troubadour Club in Los Angeles.
1971	The album *Madman Across the Water* made the top ten in the United States and Europe.
1971–76	During these years, John became one of the world's most famous and highest paid solo rock performers; he performed to packed audiences who were drawn by the elaborate stage sets and costumes as well as the music.
1973	John established his own record company, Rocket Records.
1974	He performed on stage in New York with John Lennon singing "Lucy in the Sky with Diamonds"; it was Lennon's last public performance.
1975	John performed in the film musical *Tommy* as the Pinball Wizard.
1976–80s	He continued to tour and perform throughout the United States and Europe; his visit to Russia inspired the 1985 hit "Nikita."
1987	Throat surgery performed in Australia was successful, and Elton John continues to thrill audiences and fans all over the world.

Record production and **multitrack** recording possibilities have restructured the definition of bands. It is common for one individual to perform more than one musical part and store it on tape to be **mixed** together later. As a result, many recordings have only two or three musicians who sound like five or six. The job of producing albums is critically important and is often done by someone not in the band. The producers' objectivity and knowledge of the industry and the market make them critical to the success of a project. Producers such as George Martin for The Beatles, Berry Gordy for Motown, and Quincy Jones for Michael Jackson are prime examples of the importance of producers in the recording industry.

 ## Heavy Metal and Rap

Rock, like any musical style, has branched into separate entities that contrast with each other and parts of its heritage. Heavy metal has come into focus in the last few years. Acid rock, an extremely loud and basic style in the 1960s, led to the metal styles. Metal uses high volume levels and projects a very thick texture of electronic power. The vocals are mixed into the texture without the upfront placement of more commercial rock. The topics of the songs further separate metal from mainstream rock, discussing more rebellious topics associated with street culture. Until recently, the music had been simple and direct; however, with groups like Queensrÿche the style has developed musically and technically with larger, more sophisticated forms. Queensrÿche's album *Operation: mindcrime* is an excellent example of a concept album where the composers and musicians alike display mature musical and studio techniques. As has happened with other groups from this genre, the songs, volume, topics, and performances have been dismissed as outside of sophisticated musical taste; however, heavy metal has found quite a large audience.

Alongside these metal groups is an international music underground of highly experimental rock, punk, and metal. The recordings are home-grown and sold mostly in a tape format. The east and west coasts of America and London are the primary areas of activity. The music is caustic and angry, pulling away from mainstream cultural identity. The subject matter is threatening and can be interpreted as revolutionary. This musical style is very possibly the most removed stream of musical development from academic environments. In fact, the academic world is often not even aware of its existence.

multitrack (recording)
the process of recording individual parts separately and mixing them together at a later time. Modern studios have as many as sixty-four tracks available to record and mix later.

mix (mixed)
the process of blending instruments together into a musical whole. In the modern studio the mixing is performed electronically by engineers. In orchestras and ensembles the mixing is performed by the instrumentalists.

Michael Jackson
(1958–   )

DATELINE	BIOGRAPHY
1958	Michael Jackson was born in Gary, Indiana, into a large family of performers. Still a young child, he stepped in as the youngest brother of the original Jackson Five singing group. His sisters, LaToya and Janet, later became solo stars in their own right.
1971	At the age of thirteen, Jackson had his first solo hit, "Got to Be There."
1971–76	During these years he recorded six best-selling albums with the Motown label.
1976	He starred with Diana Ross in the movie *The Wiz*, from which came the hit duet "Ease on Down the Road."
1979	Jackson teamed up with producer Quincy Jones for his solo album *Off the Wall*; this was the beginning of a long-standing personal friendship and professional relationship.
1982	Jackson recorded the hit duet "The Girl Is Mine" with Paul McCartney.
1982	Quincy Jones produced Jackson's hit album *Thriller*, which sold over thirty million copies and produced several hit singles as well; the video "Thriller," directed by John Landis, showcased Jackson's unique dancing style.
1987	The album *Bad*, also produced by Jones, rivaled *Thriller* in sales and popularity.
1988	Jackson's popularity was at an all-time high when he went on world tour.
1989–92	Although Jackson was reputed to be somewhat of a recluse during these years, his music continued to thrill fans all over the world.
1993	Jackson "resurfaced" to perform in three major televised events in early 1993: the inaugural concert for President Bill Clinton, the half-time extravaganza at the Super Bowl, and an unprecedented 90-minute live interview with talk show host Oprah Winfrey. His sister, Janet, presented him with the Grammy Legend Award at this year's Grammy ceremonies in Los Angeles.

Rap is at the other end of the acceptance spectrum from metal. It enjoys great popularity, especially as an expression of black identity. Rap first appeared in the 1940s and was associated with the beginning of bebop. It may be easier to describe rap performances as a rhythmic literary form rather than a developed musical structure. Rap minimizes harmonic motion and intensifies rhythmic and metric patterns. Speech patterns with minimal melodic shape ride above the rhythm with soloistic freedom. Like metal, rap is strongly associated with cultural pockets in America, often quasi-revolutionary and angry. To a lesser degree, the style has recently invaded more mainstream commercial rock, with artists such as Vanilla Ice.

 ## Music Video

The most dramatic addition to rock in the 1980s was the development of **music videos.** This format is indeed a theatrical musical entity. At first, videos merely showed performances. Later they became elaborate interpretive extensions of the song. Some are entertaining, provocative, or bizarre. The video alone can change a listener's impression about a

music video
a video production that accompanies or interprets a song.

The recording of "We Are the World" was an enormous hit and its video that followed soon after was equally successful. It showed a unity of performers from several different styles within the popular music world. The topic, world hunger, was emotionally ever-present. This video brought good feelings and security to its viewers/listeners with a melody that was singable by everyone. Popular culture found itself singing together for the first time in years.

song or about the group that wrote and performed it. Videos are a vital part of some performers' outputs. Many groups do not perform live; they just produce recordings and videos. The music industry has changed dramatically from the days of the early rock 'n' roll bands of the fifties. Music is now presented visually, adding new and extended interpretation. As in the study of opera and tone poems the debate once again surfaces: Should music be able to stand alone without other elements such as staging, text, or video?

Today many commercial styles of rock are associated with a vast number of cultural developments. Many styles, such as reggae, Latin, rhythm and blues, gospel, and even experimental, show elements of folk music. Rock is immediately responsive to trends in society and culture. Both rock and jazz have spawned many tangential styles that became popular and were then absorbed into the more global commercial music industry. These trends give music historians and critics much food for thought, argument, and occasionally despair, but they are healthy indications of the viability of the art. New styles and new names will continue to reflect societal changes, cultural shifts, and world conditions.

Part III

TOPICS

Musical Ideas and Developments

Composers are often humorously pictured as individuals who possess an unexplained motivation, are moved by extraordinary emotion, and, with head back, play or write music under the guidance of some external creative force. This stereotype is obviously a fantasy; however, it does contain an element of truth. Composers are driven by an inner creative urge. The absent-minded composer who seems out of touch with reality is often the very person who controls a world of specifics beyond the concept of many listeners, specifics that can make all the difference in how the music is perceived.

As portrayed in the cluttered scene from the house of the professor in the movie *Back to the Future*, creative people often surround themselves with half-completed ideas, projects yet to be started, even remnants of failed projects. Out of this looseness many new ideas arise. A new idea or problem, once exposed, becomes the object of intense activity. At this point the composer turns to shaping and polishing until the product takes on character and uniqueness. Such processes of creativity produce spectacular works of art.

Part III introduces several composers along with their unique approaches to musical problem solving. It will also explain how composers from different periods deal with similar compositional ideas or problems. Musical concerns that thread through several historical periods are the basis of the topics presented here. The nature of the compositions gives us insight to the composers' motivation, energy, and expression. Although composers found inspiration in traditional forms they were not slaves to them. Many liberties were taken as their works took shape.

The following ten topics for discussion will introduce compositional limitations and inspirations experienced by some of the most well-known composers from all parts of history. You will want to refer to the survey of historical periods presented in Part II as you study these composers and concepts. Refer to the listening notes and compare these works with the standardized forms discussed in Part I.

Rather than the study of history itself, it is the examination of style development and the works from different historical periods and countries that thrills musicologists. Bridging time, you can see a common purpose that seems to drive all active musicians. As you survey the concepts of composition discussed in these topics your perception of contemporary music will be enriched. The musical world unifies when parallels are drawn across the boundaries of time and style. Part III is the window for such discoveries.

This part follows no chronological order. Some topics of musical interest develop through two or more historical periods; others, because the music of the twentieth century is so diverse and encompasses so many different stylistic trends, deal with comparisons within a relatively short time frame. Feel free to study all or part of them in any order as time permits.

■ 205

Topic 1

IMPROVISATION AND COMPOSITION FROM THE KEYBOARD

 Scarlatti, Liszt, and Evans

Throughout the last several hundred years of music history there has been a dominant instrument at which composers prefer to work. At first it was the harpsichord and organ, then the pianoforte, and now electronic keyboards. In all cases, these instruments have provided the means to hear more than one part at a time. The advantages for composers using a keyboard over instruments such as the clarinet or oboe are obvious. In many cases composers were not exceptional keyboard players; however, they did have enough skill to develop ideas using the keyboard whether they were writing for piano, chamber ensembles, or full orchestras.

If a composer is writing for orchestra, ideas must be written down away from the very group that will perform them; at a later time, they must be tried by the group to assure that the intended sounds were **scored** accurately. Skilled composers are sure of the sounds without having to hear the orchestra perform them. The orchestra is their instrument. This approach to composition is extremely common. In fact,

scored
the process of placing each instrument into the musical texture.

Jackson Pollock (1950).
This photograph shows a painter working on a project that is not at all representative of nature. Pollock's intent is to express the moment of creation. He is actively creating. His technique mirrors the improvisational techniques inherent in all art forms. His activity and involvement preclude the building concern for premeditated intellectual planning.

many ideas are discovered by composers through their own performance. A performer's hands are capable of building new ideas using familiar patterns learned through years of practice. Melodies and themes are discovered and developed before a pen is put to paper. Composition is both an intellectual and tactile experience.

Many composers have been excellent performers with the ability to improvise new material without rehearsal. **Improvisation** is the instantaneous creation of melody, rhythm, and harmony. Improvisations are usually very expressive and have unique stylistic elements because they contain ideas specific to the performer's technique. The nature of this uniqueness comes partly from melodic **ornaments** that personalize each performance. Ornaments, as the name implies, are simply decorations. They enhance and enrich melodic ideas. In the Baroque period, ornamentation became a means of displaying virtuoso technique. In da capo arias, for instance, the singer would heavily ornament the return of the last A section. The display of virtuosity quickly moved the performance to a realm of improvisation that excited listeners.

From these ornaments, composers discovered new, and unintended, ideas. These accidental ideas are more common than you might first think. Many simple and complex motives and even entire melodies are discovered while improvising. There is a wealth of vocabulary in the hands of a trained musician. Improvisation is a means of unleashing potential ideas.

improvisation
the instantaneous creation of music. Players improvise melodies, harmonies, bass lines, and rhythms. Texture is improvised by all the musicians working together.

ornament
a melodic device that accentuates a melodic idea. Found in every style of music, ornaments are either rehearsed or added freely by the performer, depending upon the style.

Improvisations can be based on a variety of musical ideas, and the thrill of improvisation has been a constant source of excitement throughout music history. For instance, it was traditional for pianists such as Mozart or Chopin to build improvisations on short melodic ideas given to them by a member of their audience, often royalty. The melody was presented to them at the time of the concert, removing any chance of advance preparation. The resulting performance was a display of compositional and technical skill.

The type of improvisation just described became increasingly scarce in the late nineteenth and early twentieth centuries for a number of reasons. Composers were often not performing their own works but were writing for other virtuoso performers. Even with increased virtuosity, soloists felt that it was too difficult to improvise a **cadenza** in a concerto at a level equal to what had been written by the composer. The soloists who performed the works were often not composers themselves. Finally, there has developed a fear by contemporary performers that they may not be worthy of making improvisational comments in a work by such great composers as Beethoven or Schumann. Moments in concertos that had previously been improvised are now commonly rehearsed. The spark, the gamble, the excitement of improvisation slowly disappeared. During the Baroque, Classical, and Romantic periods, improvisation was the high point of a performance by such great composer/performers as Scarlatti, Mozart, Beethoven, Chopin, and Liszt. It is now very difficult to find a highly skilled classical pianist who is willing to improvise on stage.

Improvisation has, however, remained very active with classical organists. Today, in some of the churches where most large pipe organs exist, organists still thrill listeners with improvisations during parts of worship services. The most common place for improvisation is between verses of a hymn. The more creative improvisers develop material presented in the hymn much like a composer would develop themes in a sonata-allegro form. One must remember that J. S. Bach was known during his lifetime as a brilliant improviser on organ. One can speculate that many of the wonderful ideas he wrote were discovered during improvisations.

Likewise Scarlatti was known for his powers of improvisation and near acrobatic abilities at the harpsichord. His compositions exhibit this flamboyant keyboard style and carry a spirit of improvisation even when performed by harpsichordists and pianists today.

cadenza
an unaccompanied solo that is rhythmically very free in both pulse and meter. Cadenzas are most commonly associated with the concerto form.

Listening Notes

Domenico Scarlatti, Sonata in C-Sharp minor K. 247.

This single-movement sonata is an example of what Scarlatti called his *Essercizi* (Exercises). It surpasses the scope of a mere technique builder, however. The music here has fluctuations in tempo and mood more commonly associated with piano works from the 19th century. The dramatic swings of mood are more representative of improvisation than a precisely structured work from the Baroque period.

This sonata uses a three note motive in the treble which is answered by a two note motive in the tenor or bass range. The five note idea is developed throughout. There are four larger sections; each begins with an expressive melody, varies the five note motive, and ends with fast scales in the right hand. The overall impression is one of variation and development.

0:00	Melody begins with large skips.
0:13	2nd phrase uses the five note idea.
0:35	3rd idea, built on the original idea.
0:44	Melody now based on an inversion of the previously falling melodic idea.
0:52	Fast melodic lines end the first section.
0:58	More expressive melodic lines begin the second section.
1:37	Return to the fundamental melodic motive.
1:49	Fast scale ends the second section.
1:56	New section.
2:26	New melodic variations based on the original melodic motive.
2:46	Developmental section using the primary motive.
2:54	Scale runs end the third section.
3:00	Strong cadence.
3:33	Expressive moment where the performer uses rubato.
3:51	Return to the motive and cadence.
4:11	End.

Giuseppe Domenico Scarlatti
(1685–1757)

DATELINE	BIOGRAPHY
1685	Giuseppe Domenico Scarlatti was born in Naples into a large Italian musical family, one of nine children born to composer Allesandro Scarlatti. J. S. Bach and Handel were also born this year.
1700(?)	Scarlatti became organist at the royal chapel where his father was maestro di cappella.
1708	He met Handel in Venice and the two became good friends, often challenging each other to keyboard competitions, both having acquired phenomenal improvisational skills on the harpsichord.
1709–14	He composed several operas for Maria Casimira, queen of Poland, during her stay in Rome.
1717	Domenico gained full legal independence from his father.
1720(21?)	He was appointed maestro of the royal chapel at Lisbon, returning to Rome and Naples on several occasions, once in 1728 to marry Maria Caterina Gentile.
1729	Scarlatti was brought to the Spanish court at Madrid by Maria Barbara, the Infanta of Portugal, to teach and compose.
1738	He published a collection of approximately 550 harpsichord sonatas, which established him as a virtuoso of the new keyboard execution and effects.
1757	Addicted to gambling, Scarlatti died in Madrid, leaving his second wife and children with no money or means of support other than a pension given to them by the queen of Spain.

 ## From Improvisation to Notation

The spirit of improvising on the piano is easily translated to other instruments and ensembles. Franz Liszt, known as one of the most powerful pianists and improvisers of the late nineteenth century, was equally known for his orchestral writings. His innovative orchestral writing can be heard in his tone poem *Les Préludes*. This is an emotionally charged work filled with harmonic moments which are both interesting and puzzling. Some of the ideas were very possibly born of his technique at the piano and honed by his intellect. A melody or harmony becomes fluid when thrown into an improvisational environ-

Franz Liszt
(1811–86)

DATELINE	BIOGRAPHY
1811	Franz Liszt was born in Raiding, Hungary. His father, a steward for the Esterhazy family, began teaching him piano at the age of six.
1821	The family moved to Vienna, where Liszt studied with Carl Czerny; he also had the opportunity to meet Beethoven and Schubert.
1822	By the age of eleven Liszt was performing all over Europe as a child prodigy.
1830	While in Paris Liszt heard a Paganini violin recital and decided that he would become a virtuoso of the piano, just as Paganini had mastered the violin.
1830s	Liszt, handsome, long-haired, and hopelessly attractive to women, carried on several affairs during his lifetime; he became romantically involved with the writer George Sand and had a ten-year relationship with Countess d'Agoult. One of their daughters, Cosima, later married Wagner.
1839–47	During these years Liszt toured Europe nonstop, conducting operas and concerts and dazzling audiences with his keyboard showmanship. He composed volumes of piano pieces, including *Hungarian Rhapsodies* and *Les Préludes*.
1848	Liszt retired to the Duchy of Weimar where he became the court music conductor; Weimar became the musical center of Europe under his direction. He sponsored Wagner's theater productions and produced several operas, including *Benvenuto Cellini* by Berlioz.
1865	Liszt traveled to Rome and joined the Franciscan priests; in 1866 Pope Pius IX gave him the title of Abbe.
1886	During his last concert tour of Europe Liszt played for Queen Victoria in London; he died the same year while in Bayreuth attending a Wagner festival.

ment. The player is able to work out the possibilities before committing them to notation. Thematic variation is a normal improvisational process; in composition, themes are varied using a technique called **thematic transformation.** The transformations found in this work are reminiscent of the kind of thematic development in a long improvisation. This compositional technique was not new with Liszt. Schumann and even Berlioz, a non-pianist, used this technique very effectively (See chapter 9).

thematic transformation
changing a theme to take on a different character or personality each time it returns in the movement or work.

Listening Notes

Franz Liszt, *Les Préludes* (1854).

This famous tone poem is based on a poem by Alphonse de Lamartine, a French romantic poet. The program pulled from Lamartine's work is full of dramatic and contrasting moods. Following is an excerpt from the program.

> What else is life but a series of preludes to that unknown song whose first solemn note is intoned by death. Love is the enchanted dawn of all existence; but what destiny is there whose first delights of love are not interrupted by some storm? . . . after such a storm, does not try to soothe its memories in the gentle calm of country life? . . . to find in combat the full awareness of himself and the complete possession of his powers.

This single-movement work was written during a period when Liszt was not concertizing. The structure is made up of four large sections preceded by a slow introduction. A simple three-note motive (long-short-long) is the basis for thematic transformation. It first appears in the strings and moves to the brass. From there it is transformed into two different love themes. The storm follows the love themes with militarylike transformations of both love themes.

The use of thematic transformation is not only a means to consciously unify long works, it is a natural developmental process in improvisation. Liszt's command of this technique as a composer and performer proposed exciting new horizons for dramatic orchestral writing. Wagner was among the benefactors of the expanding harmonic and melodic style heralded in this work.

0:00	Two pizzicato notes. Theme starts with the three-note motive in the strings.
0:44	Repeat of pizzicato notes and theme. Strings and woodwinds echo each other.
1:35	Theme is repeated several times, up one step each time, crescendo.
2:25	The texture builds to a majestic theme (Love/Death), lower brass, strings play arpeggios.
3:18	First love theme, strings. Basses respond. Horn takes over the melody.
4:42	Second love theme, French horns. The harp and violas play a warm accompaniment figure.
5:22	Woodwinds play second theme with responses by the violins.
5:50	Crescendo. Suddenly the woodwinds play softly but are interrupted by aggressive statements from the strings.
6:33	Second theme in the violins and horns.
6:49	Soft woodwinds, harp. Transformation of the majestic theme.
7:08	Storm sequence begins with the cellos section. Strings move up in range and volume.
7:45	Full orchestra. The thematic material is highly developed.
8:34	The fanfare brass herald the climax of the storm. The orchestra slows and softens.
9:12	Oboe brings back the first love theme accompanied by the woodwinds and harp.
10:24	Pastoral section features the horn, harp, and woodwinds.
11:06	Themes are broken into little parts.
11:57	Second love theme, duet. The theme builds until the entire orchestra is playing.
13:57	Trumpet fanfare, call to battle. Strings soar through scale passages.
14:27	March to battle, percussion and brass take the lead.
15:55	A long-term crescendo begins to build.
15:26	Self-Realization. The combination of themes in a very full orchestral setting leads to the final chords.
16:37	End.

This photograph shows Liszt performing in a chamber setting. He is playing a Bösendorfer, one of the most famous pianos of his day. This piano was one of the first high-tension instruments that was capable of a large range of dynamics. The new piano helped build the image of Liszt as a powerful and dynamic pianist. The audience is large and pictured sitting in unrealistic proximity to one another.

The degree of influence leveraged on improvising composers by their technique will never be known. However, these composers must have found insight and inspiration from ideas that appeared in their playing. To be sure, the musical ear of an improviser in combination with musical training in the techniques of composition have produced some of history's most exciting music.

Improvisation Continues

Improvisation did not vanish when it became less active in traditional concert music. It is a natural development by anyone who sings or plays music. When a song is well known and sung over and over, it is eventually changed, often without knowing. These variations are essentially improvisations. The most active musical styles for improvisation today are jazz and experimental classical. Indeterminate music discussed earlier requires a great deal of improvisation on the part of the performers. Those aspects of the music not specifically notated must be improvised.

In jazz there are many **standards,** or favorite songs, that continue to be the basis for improvisation. The original melody is quickly abandoned for new, improvised melodies. There have been many great pianists in jazz, each with a personalized style based on ornaments, inflections, and use of music theory.

Bill Evans was very influential in setting a new improvising style for pianists starting in the 1950s. His new harmonic ideas and sense of melodic line have made him a model for jazz improvisation on piano. His compositions were not notated traditionally but in a more commercial shorthand, and his written melodies would be accompanied by chord symbols with **harmonic extensions.** His compositional activities were centered around his improvisations, many of which have been preserved on recordings. As a result it is very difficult, if not impossible, to reproduce his compositions without imitating the performances themselves.

standards
songs from musicals, jazz, or commercial music that are used as a basis for jazz improvisations. They are standards because most jazz players know them and they are standard to the literature.

harmonic extensions
notes that are dissonant to a chord's fundamental three notes but are still theoretically related to the chord.

Listening Notes

"Pavane," based on a theme by Gabriel Fauré, arranged by Claus Ogerman, with improvisations by Bill Evans (1965).

This unique setting of a jazz trio as part of a symphonic structure was a very successful experiment. The themes used at this recording session were taken from composers crossing four centuries: Bach, Chopin, Scriabin, Granados, and Fauré. The themes presented by these great composers were freely arranged by Claus Ogerman. He understood the conditions necessary to stimulate an improvising pianist of Evans's caliber. The intent of these arrangements was to provide a musical environment for improvisation, not to reproduce the original piano works.

The jazz trio and the orchestra often work in dialogue. The piece begins with a statement from the drums and is followed immediately by a statement from the piano that is answered by lush chords in the strings. The piano remains rhythmically free to swing the theme. The strings are rhythmically strict. They stop while the trio improvises jazz variations on the thematic material but return, playing long flowing lines, while the trio replaces the swinging rhythms with Latin rhythms.

This music has both structure and freedom. The process is very similar to improvising freely on a standard.

0:00   Introduction begins with brushes on drums, the piano and bass enter. The trio is using Latin rhythm patterns.

0:18	First statement of the theme. The rhythm turns to swing patterns.
0:31	Strings play the theme, the bass and drums continue.
0:45	Piano takes over.
0:59	The dialogue continues again with the strings creating a polyphonic texture.
1:13	Strings stop and the trio continues.
1:28	Chord melody (a chord is played beneath each note of the melody), drums more active.
1:40	Woodwinds enter with the theme.
1:55	High strings play melody, woodwinds support with lush chords.
2:11	Tempo slows to a cadence.
2:14	Piano improvises a jazz solo; no orchestration, just trio.
2:49	Double-time melody (right hand).
3:10	Trio moves to Latin rhythm patterns.
3:19	Strings enter with the melody, the trio maintains the Latin patterns.
3:36	Final cadence. The piano plays an ascending arpeggio over the last chord.
3:51	End.

Central to all levels of improvisation is some form of unity. The structure of the improvisation may be determined by the chords of a song, a specific length of time, or even a simple rhythm. The freedom inherent in improvisation varies considerably. Ornamentation of a written melody is a limited form of improvisation. Playing anything desired for one minute and four seconds is very free by comparison. Interpretation is yet another level of improvisation when it is applied freely and spontaneously to a performance. Although music is often fully notated as in the example of Liszt, liberties exist in the areas of tempo and dynamics for the performer. Freedom in interpretation communicates a performance more powerfully to a listener. As listeners, we are very receptive to music that sounds spontaneous and freely expressive.

Bill Evans
(1929–1980)

DATELINE	BIOGRAPHY
1929	Born in Plainfield, New Jersey, Bill Evans studied flute, violin, and piano as a boy. He graduated from Southeast Louisiana College and spent four years in the Army.
1954	When he was discharged in 1954, he went to New York and began his professional career with George Russell, a well-known jazz (third stream) composer and pianist.
1958	Evans burst into prominence when he teamed with Miles Davis in the sextet that recorded the landmark album *Kind of Blue*.
1959–61	He formed a trio with Scott La Faro on bass and Paul Motian on drums, producing some of his most reflective and impressionistic recordings. After La Faro was killed in a car accident in 1961, Evans went into seclusion for almost a year. When he emerged he formed a new trio with Eddie Gomez (bass) and Marty Morell (drums). They worked together for nine years.
1963–71	During this period he won five Grammys as Best Soloist and Best Jazz Performance by a Group. He published three books of original compositions and transcriptions of solos.
1975	After defeating a twenty-year drug habit, he remarried and his music became less introspective and melancholy. His career and music became more enthusiastic and positive.
1980	His health began to deteriorate badly in the late 1970s, and in September of 1980 he died of a massive bleeding ulcer while in New York.

Topic 2

COMPOSING FOR THE LARGE ORCHESTRA

 Beethoven and Mahler

The modern orchestra has many colors, with sounds ranging from solo instruments to subtle instrumental combinations. The large orchestra is equally capable of large, loud sounds and small, delicate sounds. Over the years, with the introduction of each newly accepted instrument, the sound of the orchestra has changed. The most recent instrument to find acceptance in the modern orchestra is the saxophone, which appeared in 1936.

Much earlier Beethoven introduced the trombone, the piccolo, and the contrabassoon to the orchestra. Although compositions for choir and orchestra were common, he combined them in his Ninth Symphony to the surprise of everyone. There was no precedent in symphonic writing for combining vocal and instrumental forces. Mahler not only added choruses in his symphonies but also introduced clever instrumental combinations and expanded the percussion section. He took the orchestra of Beethoven and introduced interesting instruments such as the mandolin, the guitar, the celesta, and even the cowbell. These composers, and others such as Berlioz in the nineteenth century, exhibited the compositional belief that there are always new sounds to be found.

Both Beethoven and Mahler were not content to work with the orchestral format inherited from their predecessors. They were busy searching for new timbres from new instruments and new combinations of traditional instruments. By the time Mahler was writing in the early twentieth century, many of the traditional orchestral instruments had been improved. The string family had a more projecting tone and the introduction of valves on brass instruments allowed far more flexibility than Beethoven ever experienced. Naturally, composers took full advantage of all these new possibilities.

These two composers wrote and conducted music nearly 100 years apart, and their music, although associated with different musical periods, is similar in structure and medium. Although they composed many varied forms, they are known today as composers of the greatest magnitude, especially in the development of the symphony.

The Developmental Process

The symphonies of Beethoven and Mahler are exciting examples of how composers can expand the basic structure of the symphony without weakening it. The traditional structure of four movements in a symphony became the first target for change. Next, the relationship of the movements to the whole were further developed by both composers. The use of development was not limited to motives or themes. Structural development within single movements and as a total of all the movements was a major concern of both these musicians.

First, we will look at Beethoven's Fifth Symphony, a work that reduces like a fraction to one single element. The common denominator is the four-note **motive** Beethoven called "fate knocking at the door." He was not the first to use development of the same motive in more than one movement, but he was unequaled in weaving a single idea into the fabric of an entire large work. His symphonic writing style exemplifies organic composition. As you listen to this work, keep in mind that the rhythm of the opening four notes reappears in all four movements. The progression of the entire work is so integrated that to leave out one movement or not finish the entire symphony weakens the drama inherent in the work.

motive
a small musical unit made up of a short identifiable rhythm encompassing a few pitches. The most famous motive is the opening of Beethoven's Fifth Symphony.

Beethoven made many changes that must have appeared dramatic in their day. For instance, he changed the third movement from a minuet to a scherzo, adding drive and tension that find resolution only in the last movement. To accomplish this Beethoven removed the traditional break between the last two movements, accelerating the scherzo into the fanfarelike beginning of the last movement. To further unify the structure he carried the motive throughout the four movements and recalled themes from the third movement in the last movement.

To say that the large structure of this work is typical of the period is misleading. Beethoven's greatest ideas were more global than motives or themes. As in many of his works, the Fifth Symphony defines its own structure. It is possible to find an altered **sonata-allegro form** in the first movement, a theme and variations in the second, and a minuet form in the third movement; however, some deviation from standard form is a significant characteristic of Beethoven.

sonata-allegro form the primary large structure used for the first movement of a symphony. Themes are exposed, developed, and recapitulated. See Part II.

Listening Notes

Ludwig van Beethoven, Symphony No. 5 in C minor, op. 67 (1808).

 I. Allegro con brio,
 II. Andante con moto,
III. Allegro (scherzo),
IV. Allegro.

Beethoven used dramatic changes in dynamics to give his symphonic writing a unique flavor. No composer before had such orchestration skills. He fashioned aggressive orchestral tuttis, injecting a percussive quality greater than either Haydn's or Mozart's works. The four-note motive, which has been described as "fate knocking at the door," opens the symphony as a unison statement. The ensuing first thematic area is a pyramid of the motive. The first movement is in a sonata-allegro form with an enlarged development section. The basic motive proves so organic that even the coda of the work acts as another development section.

Another unique feature is the short oboe solo that acts as a cadenza, not at all a common occurrence in a symphony. The *forte* entrance by the French horn that announces the upcoming recapitulation is likewise an innovation, so much so that it was once thought of as an error in the score. The development section is brilliant in that the motive is not only a building block, it is itself broken down to a two-note idea. This movement expanded previous notions of motivic development and symphonic form.

0:00 Opening statements (two) of the four-note motive. An overlapping of the motive builds until the last note is held, ending the phrase.

0:18 Second phrase, similar structure.

0:43 French horn (motive plus three more notes that will be developed later).

0:47 Second theme, contrasting long melodic lines.

1:05 Transition theme to end the exposition.

1:25 Exposition repeats completely (both theme groups).

2:12 Second theme (repeat).

2:31 Transition theme, this time leading into the development.

2:51 Development begins with the motive (French horns) and continues, developing the motive with melodic fragments (strings) from the more flowing second theme.

3:15 Echoes between the woodwinds and strings (four-note rhythm).

3:20 Tutti rhythm, full orchestra.

3:30 Fugal texture.

3:40 Two-note echoes.

3:49 One-note echoes, softening.

4:01 Suddenly loud for a brief moment then back to one-note echoes.

4:10 Loud tutti orchestra, four-note motive, ending the development section.

4:15 Recapitulation.

4:32 Oboe cadenza (brief).

4:45 Texture builds using the motive.

5:07 Second theme.

5:33 Move from minor to major.

5:51 Coda becomes a transition theme and false ending.

6:02 Extension, developmental texture.

6:05 Low strings start the motive, the orchestra joins into a tutti descending melodic line.

6:32 New thematic material is echoed through the orchestra.

6:56 Final coda. Sounds like another recapitulation but spins out and quickly loses momentum.

7:09 Final cadence.

7:15 End.

The second movement is in 3/8 and is a **theme and variations** (see Chapter 4 for a diagram). In this movement the rhythmic four-note motive supplies the accompaniment in slow repetitive statements. As in the third movement, which is also three beats to the measure, the motive takes all three beats of one measure and ends over the bar line with the emphasis on the down beat, the fourth note. If you count as the orchestra plays, you will feel the motive and hear it appear everywhere.

The third movement is a **scherzo,** which means "joke." The minuet form is traditionally the third movement of a symphony. The only difference here is that the word "minuet" in the form is replaced by the word "scherzo" (see Chapter 4 for a diagram). The minuet that gave birth to the scherzo was a dance with a lilting 3/4 meter. The scherzo is no longer dancelike; perhaps this is the joke. It moves with aggression and builds powerfully and connects to the last movement without stopping. The transition to the last movement is one of the most dramatic moments in the work. The last two movements blend into a soaring and heroic finale. The movement from the key of C minor to C major underscores the victory.

theme and variation
a formal structure of a single work or movement of a larger work. Once a theme is stated, it is varied to the point of obscurity and is usually restated at the end of the selection.

scherzo and trio
a musical form designed after the minuet form. Scherzos are usually followed by a trio which returns to the scherzo themes. See Part II.

In addition to his famous symphonies, Mahler wrote many large works. He completed three operas and many songs using either piano or orchestral accompaniments. His greatest fame during his lifetime came from his conducting of large operatic works in Austria and Germany. Praise for his conducting came from other composers of his time, including Brahms. The bulk of his conducting was of works by other composers; he was especially known for his control of detail and interpretation of the operas of Mozart and Wagner. His success as a conductor brought him to America as director of the New York Philharmonic Society in 1908. His opera direction continued at the Metropolitan Opera House in New York.

Such extravagant conducting success speaks to Mahler's extraordinary ability to understand and interpret historical and contemporary works. This knowledge gave him the background to manipulate instrumentation and structure in his own compositions. Unfortunately, his own compositions never had much of an impact on the musical

The Musical Ear

Realizing that Beethoven was nearly or totally deaf when he wrote some of his most famous works makes us question the nature of the musical ear. A composer must hear inside his or her head what the product of the writing might be. The better the composer, the more accurate the inner ear is in comparison to the actual performance. For instance, when a melody is written, it can sound dramatically different if performed on different instruments; that is, if the melody *Mary Had a Little Lamb* were first played on the piano, how would it sound played on a tuba? An oboe? A violin? Composers must go another step farther. How would it sound if it were played by a tuba and a violin together? Orchestral composers must be familiar with combined sounds and be able to project the sound of newly discovered combinations.

Beethoven's progressive deafness forced him to stop playing and eventually to stop conducting. However, it did not stop his composing. His depression from the loneliness of deafness was overcome by his art. He admitted that his music was made more difficult by his deafness, but not impossible. His ''inner ear'' was so highly developed before deafness overtook him that he could continue to perceive and feel what he was composing.

So great was his musical ear that in a world of silence he continued to produce great works. His last string quartets are masterful works of construction and thematic development. His last symphonies are performed by modern orchestras with a brilliance more typical of today than during his lifetime. Did Beethoven hear an orchestra of the future? Did he forget the limitations of his present-day orchestra? His confidence was such that he added chorus and four vocal soloists to his last symphony, creating brilliant new effects which inspired future composers, including Mahler.

The sound in the inner ear is not real sound, but it has a relationship to real performance in a unique way. The musical ear is the rhythmic interplay of notes and melodies, harmonies and meter, tension and release. An active musical ear sings and dances in a world of consonance and dissonance. It is not sound; it is the activity of creative imagination.

society while he was alive. Now, however, they are considered brilliant examples of orchestral writing.

Mahler's Sixth Symphony extended the innovations of Beethoven, again using organically fertile motives and themes, nearly 100 years later. Like Beethoven's Fifth, the last movement becomes the culmination of the three preceding movements. Contrapuntal writing, especially in the last movement, is a dominant element in this symphony and gives the thematic material new personality. The thematic development, however, differs considerably from Beethoven's Fifth. Instead of a motive permeating the entire work, Mahler exposes grand themes that soar in the first and last movements and are contrasted by small ensemble sounds more commonly associated with **chamber music.**

chamber music
another term for ensemble music. It is designed to be played in smaller rooms where large choirs and orchestras would not be suitable. Chamber music usually has only one individual on each part.

Michelangelo, *The Crossed-Legged Captive* (c1530–34). Marble. 7' 6½".
This unfinished sculpture shows an interesting aspect of creativity in motion. Notice that parts of the body are not only recognizable but finished and polished. The artist had a specific image in mind and did not hesitate toward the goal. Michelangelo believed he was liberating the figure, not chipping down to it. The image remains a captive in the stone. Similarly, composers have ideas that demand liberation and development; they work toward that end until each idea stands with unique identity. (Academy, Florence)

Although Mahler's Sixth Symphony is nearly ninety minutes long, it is not his longest. His Eighth Symphony lasts one and one-half hours and requires eight vocal soloists, two choruses, a boys choir, and an enormous orchestra. The most dramatic quality of Mahler's music arises from his ability to control a vast orchestra, utilizing all its many colors. The large orchestra of Mahler performed equally large musical forms. As Beethoven expanded the length and scope of the symphony in his day, Mahler expanded it again in his.

Gustav Mahler
(1860–1911)

DATELINE	BIOGRAPHY
1860	Gustav Mahler was born July 7 in Kalist, Austria.
1875	He began study at the Conservatory in Vienna.
1877	He studied history, philosophy, and the history of music at the University of Vienna.
1880	He became *Kapellmeister* in the summer at Hall, Austria, and finished his first major composition, ''Das klagende Lied.''
1880–90	He moved from post to post as conductor and *Kapellmeister* throughout Austria and Germany.
1891–97	As *Kapellmeister* in the theater at Hamburg, Mahler found time to compose and work with opera productions.
1897	Through a recommendation from Brahms, Mahler was appointed *Kapellmeister* at the Court Opera in Vienna.
1908	He moved to America and worked as conductor of the New York Philharmonic Society.
1911	Mahler returned to Austria, where he died.

Listening Notes

Gustav Mahler, Symphony No. 6 (1904).

 I. Allegro energico, ma non troppo,
 II. Scherzo: Wuchtig,
 III. Andante,
 IV. Finale: Allegro moderato.

To understand the significance of Mahler's writing we must witness his ability to develop musical material in large works. The enlarged orchestra offered new textures and colors. This work expands the wind sections with four oboes, piccolo clarinet, E♭ and B♭ clarinets, four bassoons, bass trombone, bass tuba, and an enlarged percussion section including cowbells, deep bells, gong, birch rod, hammer, xylophone, two harps, and a celesta. The cowbells are used in each movement except the scherzo as an offstage sound leading into more delicate themes, a unique sound in symphonic literature. The militarylike themes in the first and last movements and the use of colorful low brass and percussion are typical of Mahler's writing. They add drama and contrast to the often subtle and intimate sound of the woodwinds and strings.

Although this work has no formal program or storyline, traditional interpretations are placed on three of the movements. The first movement was an attempt to express his wife, Alma, in a theme. The theme ends the first movement and contrasts with the opening military march theme. The second movement is a scherzo, moved from its traditional position as the third movement. This movement depicts two children, his own, playing arhythmic games running and laughing in the sand. The movement turns increasingly more tragic and ends in a whimper. The last movement is perhaps the most powerful and intensely scored of them all. In this movement Mahler depicts the "three great blows of fate." The tragedy in his life undoubtedly had an impact on this work. What the three blows of fate represent is arguable; however, there is little argument as to their relationship to the loss of a five-year-old daughter and Mahler's own deteriorating health. For these reasons and more, the symphony has unofficially taken on the name Tragic. There is no better way to defend this title than by the ending of the fourth movement in its extraordinary intensity.

0:00	Cadence after a large climax (approximately seventeen minutes into the movement). Horns play fate motive against a descending bass line; woodwinds play short arpeggios.
0:55	Chimes and trombone begin a short section of solo instruments. The tempo slowly increases.
1:50	The rhythm settles with an oboe solo that is soon taken over by a violin.
2:15	String section plays the theme.
2:35	Crescendo.
2:44	Full orchestra with horn lead.
2:55	Brass section begins a long crescendo.
3:35	The motive is continually transformed.

3:51	Ripping horns play motive, the other brass instruments enter.
4:08	Bells and woodwinds.
4:18	Marchlike treatment of the theme.
4:51	Climax of tragic theme; development continues.
5:34	More horn rips followed by a very high range melodic line.
5:50	Crescendo in activity.
6:15	Horns play a more stable theme that is passed around the orchestra.
6:35	The theme is passed around the sections again.
7:16	Momentary restful chord and texture but builds immediately.
7:33	Loud blow of fate followed by a string line; momentum seems to stop.
8:10	Strong cadence. Beginning of coda, tragic minor theme. Trombones and tuba play a short, dissonant fugato.
8:55	The theme is slowly passed around as the orchestra fades.
9:20	Final slow statement in the low instruments.
10:08	Last transformed statement of the theme is a fortissimo chord.
10:21	End.

Topic 3

WORDS AND MUSIC

Should music be subservient to the words of a piece? Should it play only a role of accompaniment? Or should words and music establish an equal partnership? Such questions have dominated the minds of musicians and poets alike for hundreds of years. With every significant musical change in style the issue has resurfaced. Many elements complicate the issue. For example, could the successful balance between the Italian language and eighteenth-century operatic melodies be repeated using French or German? The arguments were not just between the poets and the musicians; listeners, conductors, and performers could not agree.

In early chant, **monophony,** where texts were first set clearly in a one note, one syllable declamatory style the text was not impeded by musical activities. Several notes per syllable, **melismas,** grew in importance and extended the musical time spent on each syllable. Several notes per syllable emphasized and ornamented special words and ideas. Soon the relationship between music and words met a greater test. In early polyphony, a ***cantus firmus*** was borrowed from a sacred text, usually a chant, and served as the unifying element of the composition. It was slowed almost to a drone and the text remained in Latin. The words were mostly unintelligible because the syllables were so spread out that the entire text could not always be sung. Above this slow Latin text were faster more easily understood texts. The thick settings

monophony
a single melody with no other musical accompaniment; for example, a Gregorian chant.

melisma
singing several notes per syllable. Some melismas are very long with many notes sung using one syllable of text.

cantus firmus
a melody, most often a Gregorian chant, used as the lowest part, the **tenor.** Other parts were written above, creating a form of polyphonic music.

typical of these motets represent a move toward focusing on the music over the meaning of each word.

During the Renaissance, as secular madrigals became more popular, the *cantus firmus* technique changed again. Although the text of the *cantus firmus* remained in Latin, the parts above were usually in the vernacular. This meant that French, Italian, or German was combined with Latin. There are even examples of three languages being sung at the same time.

Clement Jannequin and Word Painting

Every composer had to make decisions about words and their relationship to the music. From the earliest music to the present the decision has not been an easy one. The composer's interest in describing words through musical sounds is especially evident in Renaissance **madrigals** with **word painting.** Jannequin's chansons are clear examples of a composer's attempt to imitate the meaning of words accurately. In this example sounds of birds are literally imitated by the vocal text. The sounds are entertaining although rather excessive and obvious to our modern ear.

Listening Notes

Clement Jannequin, "Song of the Birds" *(Chant des oiseaux)* (1529).

Word painting was the interpretation of specific words by the music. Literal interpretation of words can be found in this chanson. Bird sounds are imitated vocally with trills and two-note motives, and polyphonic textures are contrasted with homophonic sections, typical of chansons and madrigals. The **points of imitation** and **cadences** are easily identified. The imitation is simpler than would be found in contemporary **motets.** The vocal sound effects and short rhythmic motives **(madrigalisms)**, compared with the large motets, give this music an immediate secular identity.

0:00   The madrigal begins with a point of imitation. Notice how the entrances are spaced irregularly.

0:24   Another point of imitation. Voices enter in another order.

madrigal
a secular poem about love popular in the Renaissance set in a polyphonic texture with contrasting homophonic sections. Word painting was prevalent.

word painting
a word stressed musically to make it stand out from the other words before and after it. The emphasis is made to interpret the special meaning of the word.

point of imitation
the moment a new phrase begins where each part enters using the same melodic idea. The entrances are staggered, creating a thick polyphonic style.

cadence
the end of a musical idea both large and small. It can be the end of a phrase, theme group, or movement.

motet
polyphonic settings of a Latin text. An essential part of Renaissance music, they are sacred choral works but are not part of the Mass.

madrigalisms
specific words or feelings are emphasized musically. Associated with word painting.

0:44	New texture, more vocal accents, text moves faster.
0:59	Point of imitation.
1:22	Cadence, all parts sing unison.
1:24	Smoother melodic lines but soon become more agitated.
1:43	First bird imitations, short repetitive ideas.
1:56	Texture increases with fast delivery of text and fast points of imitation.
2:34	Cadence followed by a new point of imitation. Notice the trilled notes.
2:57	More bird imitations.
3:10	More trills with quick overlap of repeated text.
3:37	Trills intensify.
3:47	Return to polyphonic lines without sound effects.
4:07	Cadence, point of imitation.
4:29	Imitation of the cuckoo.
4:54	Point of imitation.
5:00	Last polyphonic section. The imitative texture remains full.
5:33	End.

Only a few years later the sacred music of Palestrina responded to the determinations of the Council of Trent, where music was intentionally being redirected toward a more conservative texture without the theatrical effects of the madrigals and motets.

Again, in the Baroque era, focus on a single line melody established a new balance between music and words called **monody.** The vocal line is accompanied by chords creating a homophonic texture. The **Camerata** strove to establish a new musical style that would free the words from a thick polyphonic texture. Words were important to the literary society and poets were an important part of the Camerata. No other time in history was music so successfully steered into a new direction by an intellectual concern. This movement did not eliminate polyphony. Composers such as Bach and Handel continued to compose using monody and polyphony. Their often dense, powerful choral style and the newly developed monody appeared side by side in religious works such as cantatas, masses, and passions.

monody, monodic style
a new vocal technique of solo voice and basso continuo developed by the Camerata.

Camerata (Florentine)
a group of composers and poets who gathered in 1575 to develop a new dramatic relationship between music and text.

Songs of the Romantic period exhibit some of the clearest examples of aligning musical composition and poetry (the spinning wheel in *Gretchen am Spinnrade* or the galloping horse in *Erlkönig;* see Chapter 9). Interpretation of the words in general and the painting of specific words was a foremost concern of composers such as Schumann and Schubert. In the twentieth century the word-music concern was again addressed through the use of *Sprechstimme* as seen in *Pierrot Lunaire* by Schoenberg. The animated half spoken, half sung vocalizations compromise true pitch yielding a very expressive performance (See chapter 10).

Popular music styles today still deal with the issue of words and music. Different contemporary styles have different needs. For example, country and western music has always placed great importance on hearing the words above the instruments; on the other hand, heavy metal rock places the voice in a thick, loud texture where it is more difficult to understand the words without reading them. Rap is totally word-oriented. Romantic ballads are based on the meaning of the words. Dance music in commercial pop takes a music first, words second attitude. Listeners automatically focus on words above everything else. When the words are masked or buried in the music, the number of people who choose to listen diminishes. Throughout music history purely instrumental music has only been a fraction of the music demanded by the public.

 ## *The Composer and the Libretto*

A composer must consider a variety of elements in choosing a text for a song, musical, or opera. Naturally the subject matter is of ultimate concern; however, the text must have musical potential as well. A librettist is required to transform text into patterns of words that offer rhythms and sounds to stimulate the composer. The actual sound of a word affects the tone and texture of a composition. Some words sound soft, such as "free" or "man"; others are percussive and rhythmic, such as "startle" and "people." To replace the words with synonyms could severely change the sound of the music. Thus many argue that translating any music from its original language destroys the artistic portrayal of the original composition.

Another consideration is repetition of text. The "Hallelujah Chorus" from Handel's *Messiah* is essentially built on a single word and a few phrases of text. The "Amen Chorus," which concludes the same work, uses the repetition of the single word *amen*. When text repetition is made possible by the libretto, the music takes precedent over the text. The "Amen Chorus" mentioned above is a well-crafted fugue; because there is only one word, there is no need for concern that the thick fugal texture will cover the words. Repetition allows for a higher degree of rhythmic activity than is normal in speech. It also expands the melodic line beyond the scope of the poetic phrase.

When text is needed to tell a story or clearly describe dialogue, the opposite is true. In the recitative settings of Baroque and Classical opera, the text dictates the rhythm and there is very little repetition of text. The aria, on the other hand, is generally more expressive and the words are expanded with melismas and soaring melodies. The level of repetition increases as well.

Musically thick textures, such as in the choruses of Baroque cantatas, present another consideration for composers. Because the texts were drawn from the Bible or from hymns, listeners were usually familiar with the text and the music could dominate the text without argument. Today fewer people are familiar with these words, making them more difficult to understand. In fact, singing styles themselves can make understanding one's own language difficult. The debate still exists as to singing music in its original language or translating to the vernacular. However, singing an opera in English does little for following the story line. To project one's voice over a large orchestra without injuring the voice, singers must pronounce the vowels more like European languages. As a result the pronunciation is just different enough to make it difficult to understand.

Unlike smaller vocal forms, opera deals with many different elements. Music and words work together for explaining actions, describing events, establishing dialogue, and expressing a variety of emotions. Review the listening examples for Verdi and Wagner in Chapter 9 and notice how the composers dealt with setting words in their respective language. The differences in their concept of writing melody to express the words made these two composers very different. Wagner wrote his own libretto, not trusting anyone else to understand his needs. Verdi, on the other hand, worked with a very fine librettist, Arrigo Boïto, who was a composer himself and was very sympathetic to the problems of setting text. Verdi felt strongly about the need to support and interpret the words without dominating them. His orchestrations maintained a sense of clarity and brilliance for this very purpose. Wagner relied heavily on the emotional power of his orchestra and would escape into instrumental sections expounding on emotions drawn from the text.

Giacomo Puccini and Alban Berg

Giacomo Puccini and Alban Berg, although nearly contemporaries, offer very contrasting operatic styles for two reasons. First is a striking difference in compositional techniques. Puccini wrote tonal music in the tradition of Mozart and Verdi using opera's favorite language, Italian. Berg, on the other hand, used atonal techniques from the school of expressionism using German. Second, the subjects of the operas are extremely different. Puccini sets a simple love story where reality is blurred by romance. Berg takes a depressing subject of frustrated love and life and gives it a remarkable expressionistic setting. Both, however, proved very effective in composing dramatic works where a marriage between words and music reigned supreme.

A scene from Puccini's opera *La Boheme*

Giacomo Puccini
(1858–1924)

DATELINE	BIOGRAPHY
1858	Giacomo Puccini was born in Lucca, Italy, into a family of professional musicians that spanned four generations. Although he showed no early interest in music, his family insisted on formal musical training.
1872	At the age of fourteen he became organist at the San Martino Church in Lucca.
1880–83	Puccini studied at the Milan Conservatory on a scholarship granted to him by the queen of Italy.
1883	He wrote his first opera, *Le villi,* and entered it in a competition; it received little notice but was performed in Milan in 1884 and at La Scala in 1885. Its success led to commissions for further works.
1893	The opera *Manon Lescaut* was Puccini's first major triumph.
1896	The opera *La Bohème,* the simple love story about Bohemian life in Paris, established him as a great composer as well as making him wealthy and world famous.
1900	Puccini focused on realism **(verismo)** in his works; he portrayed ordinary people in real situations, unlike earlier operas that dealt with mythological themes or heroic figures. His opera *Tosca* is especially representative of the verismo movement.
1904	The debut of *Madame Butterfly,* the story of an American serviceman and a Japanese geisha, was rejected by the Italian audience; however, the work became popular outside of Italy.
1918	Puccini wrote *Il Trittico,* a collection of three one-act operas first performed at the Metropolitan Opera in New York.
1924	Puccini died in Brussels after suffering a heart attack; he had gone there to have surgery for throat cancer and was still working on his last opera, *Turandot.* The work was finished by a friend, Franco Alfano, and was first performed in 1926.

verismo
a movement centered around realism in the late nineteenth century. Operas (such as Puccini's) depicted realistic situations incorporating a wide range of emotions.

Listening Notes

Giacomo Puccini, End of Act I from *La Bohème* (1896).

This scene is perhaps Puccini's most famous. The music supports the hesitation and excitement of Rodolfo and Mimi as they fall in love. While searching in the dark for a lost key, Rodolfo slowly reaches out to touch Mimi's hand and their love innocently begins to soar. Mimi tries to pretend that nothing is happening, but as the scene progresses their love is undeniable; the scene ends with them hopelessly in love. The dialogue leading up to Rodolfo's aria is effectively speechlike but still melodic. This selection begins with Rudolfo's aria on page 236. The ending of Rodolfo's aria is followed by Mimi's aria. He sings of hopes and dreams and she sings of her humble life and her anticipation of spring. The final duet is emotional and overwhelming.

     The plot of the opera is based on a Bohemian romance; its emotional settings and dramatic developments give Puccini a vehicle for beautifully crafted melodies. The power of this duet is carried to the end of the opera as Mimi dies from consumption in the arms of Rodolfo. Puccini's ability to develop characters is extraordinary and has made this work one of the most successful romances in Italian opera.

Chi é lá? —Scusi. Una donna! (Who's there? — Excuse me. . . . A woman!)

0:00   This short section is an animated accompanied recitative. Notice how the orchestra builds from the first to the harp glissando. The momentum is supplied by the orchestra.

0:49   Oboe solo followed by a very thin texture as Rodolfo sings; the text speeds up.

1:33   The vocal parts become more melodic. Rodolfo and Mimi are polite to one another but are aware of their attraction for each other.

2:03   End of recitative section. (Immediate segue.)

Oh! sventata! (Oh! foolish me!)

0:00   This part is immediately more melodic with full orchestral support.

0:18   Mimi's candle goes out. She asks for help to find the key she has lost.

0:34   She teasingly calls Rodolfo a bothersome neighbor because both their candles have gone out and they cannot find the key.

1:01   Rodolfo finds the key but puts it in his pocket. He acts as if he did not find it.

1:09 While searching in the dark their hands touch. The orchestra swells dynamically.

1:34 The orchestra ends the section.

Che gelida manina. (What a little cold hand.)

0:00 **Rodolfo's aria begins with a single note.**

0:30 Harp and soft strings provide the only accompaniment.

1:09 Melodic climax supported by full orchestra. He tells her that he is a poet and that he lives in his happy poverty.

1:33 Texture thins.

1:57 Text becomes more declamatory.

2:15 Orchestra and voice build into the love theme.

2:28 The most passionate melodic line of the aria swells with full string accompaniment including harp.

3:26 The strings play the love theme while Rodolfo sings above.

4:15 Final cadence.

Mi chiamano Mimí. (They call me Mimi.)

0:00 Mimi begins her aria. The beginning is like an accompanied recitative.

0:52 "I love all things, That have a gentle *magic*" (word painting with the harp).

1:11 A very high note sung with restraint.

1:47 Mimi asks if he understands her. He responds affirmatively.

2:06 A sudden tempo increase followed by an unaccompanied moment. (This repeats.)

2:40 A new slow melodic line that builds with the strings and French horns; Mimi sings of the beauty of spring.

2:58 "The first kiss, Of April is mine!"

3:50 "Petal to petal. So lovely" (a melodic climax).

4:20 The aria cadences with a final recitativelike statement. A short recitative dialogue (thirty-eight seconds) between Rodolfo and his friends (outside) connects Mimi's aria with the final love duet.

O soave fanciulla, o dolce viso. (Oh! lovely girl, oh! sweet face.)

0:00 The love duet begins with Rodolfo, begins with the harp.

0:41	He is soon joined by Mimi in the most climatic phrase of the duet. ("Already I taste in spirit, The Heights of tenderness! Love trembles in our kiss!")
1:37	The texture thins as the two melodies fall into a dialogue.
1:52	Sustained strings and harp arpeggios.
2:36	Music from Rodolfo's aria.
3:08	Harp and light strings support the ending where they profess love for each other.
3:54	End.

A powerful melody or theme, when repeated, is immediately nostalgic and continues to be a source for character identity and development. Themes return and are modified to reflect changes in the plot. The singable melodies written by Puccini in *La Bohème* help listeners identify with the couple, their love, and their tragedy. Music from the love duet between Rodolfo and Mimi builds and transforms throughout the opera, although they never sing it again themselves. The importance of the music set to the words of love in Act I remains alive and viable to the very end of the opera. Only when music works with words can the effect of those words last so long.

The opera *Wozzeck* is easily the most significant expressionistic opera written. It is organized according to traditional forms. There is a large superstructure of three acts described by Berg as Exposition, Development, and Catastrophe. Each act in turn is made up of scenes that are structured like a single movement of an instrumental work. For example, the long second act has five scenes, each of which is structured like a movement from a symphony:

1. sonata-allegro
2. fantasia and fugue
3. largo
4. scherzo
5. rondo

The third act is also made up of five scenes, but in this case they are a series of variations. In order, the scenes are

1. variations on a theme,
2. variations on a single tone,
3. variations on a rhythmic pattern,
4. variations on a chord, and
5. variations on continuous running notes.

Alban Berg
(1885–1935)

DATELINE	BIOGRAPHY
1885	Alban Berg was born in Vienna, Austria. His family provided a musical atmosphere that led him to consider composition at an early age.
1900	By the age of fifteen Berg had already composed over seventy songs.
1904–11	Berg studied with Arnold Schoenberg, who was to become not only his teacher and mentor, but a good friend. Berg later adopted the twelve-tone method of composition.
1911	He married Helene Nahowski, who supported his work throughout their marriage.
1915–17	Berg served in the Austrian army during World War I.
1918–21	He became codirector (with Schoenberg) of the Society for Private Music Performance in Vienna.
1923	He wrote "Kammerkonzert," a chamber music piece that he dedicated to Schoenberg.
1925	The première of the opera *Wozzeck* at the Berlin State Opera House brought Berg instant acclaim.
1929	He began work on the opera *Lulu,* which was never completed; he had the opportunity to hear several parts of it performed just a few days before his death.
1935	Berg died on Christmas Eve in Vienna; he had been chronically ill for years.

This sense of structure and organization is part of the expressionistic thinking adopted by serialistic composers. Such organizational care was also an effort to restore a sense of order and organization lost when tonality was abandoned.

Although based on a play written by Georg Büchner in the early 1830s, the plot is very contemporary. The libretto is a brilliant piecemeal product of Berg. It is as different literally from Puccini as the opera is musically. It offers tremendous latitude for setting dialogue and orchestral development.

A scene from the first performance of Berg's opera *Wozzeck*

Listening Notes

Alban Berg, *Wozzeck,* Act III (1917–1921).

Scene 4: Wozzeck, in anguish, returns to the dark forest where he had stabbed his mistress. As he washes his hands he drowns while the captain and the doctor who tormented him so seem unmoved. The orchestra sounds fateful throughout this scene and continues with a powerful interlude before the next scene, which paints a picture of the tragedy of Wozzeck's life and death.

Scene 5: Wozzeck's son goes to see the body of his mother with the other children. The music sounds like twisted nursery rhymes. The inevitability of the situation gives rise to hopelessness and depression. The end of the scene and the opera is subtle and without fanfare. It ends as if it were just another day in the life of the troubled.

As you listen, notice the characteristics that are typical of modern melody and harmony. Although this opera is primarily atonal, it is more romantic than the works of other serial composers. This work is not a twelve-tone composition. For contrast and emotional impact, Berg takes excursions into tonal areas, both major and minor. The interlude before Scene 5 is one of these moments where the music sounds more like late Romantic opera than atonality. Another trait of this period is the various singing styles used by Berg, such as *Sprechstimme,* speaking, and emotional shrieking. The melodies themselves are angular with large leaps and awkward twists. Dynamics are extreme, from ***pppp*** to ***ffff.*** The large orchestra moves from soloistic melodies to explosive tutti ensembles. The orchestra with its expanded pitch range is used by Berg to create unusual sonorities and sound effects, increasing the impact of the libretto.

0:00 Scene 4 begins with a single chord. Wozzeck enters and searches for the knife.

0:11 Spoken dialogue, but still animated, very thin orchestration.

0:38 The orchestra builds as Wozzeck shouts ''Murder.''

0:47 He discovers the body of Marie; strings accompany.

1:14 ''Murder! Murder!'' is shouted within a *Sprechstimme* setting.

1:23 He finds the knife and throws it in the water; the orchestra plays a falling harmonic passage.

1:49 The moon rises and is dark red. Wozzeck sees blood everywhere.

2:23 He wades into the pond to hide the knife and wash off the blood. He believes he is washing in blood. He drowns. The orchestra rises in pitch, slows and softens.

2:50 The doctor and captain enter.

3:35 They discover the drowning but do nothing; descending melodic line played by the celesta.

4:05 The orchestra stops completely.

4:24 Orchestral interlude starts with the low strings and low woodwinds. Polyphonic texture builds gradually.

5:13 Building intensity.

5:20 Horn melody followed by the harp and dissonant chords.

6:15 Sudden increase in activity and volume; texture becomes more dissonant.

6:54 Percussion instruments feed the building texture.

7:22 Full orchestra leading to a climax and slow decrescendo.

7:50 Restful final cadence.

8:01	Scene 5 begins with children's voices playing.
8:27	Marie's child, riding a hobbyhorse, is told that her mother is dead.
8:53	The children run to see; Marie's child stays on the horse.
9:08	The music winds down and stops. The child runs off after the other children.

The music and words balance beautifully, yielding a tragic and cynical work. The plot is simple but powerful. Wozzeck is a victim of others and himself. As a soldier he was subjected to a cruel captain, experimented on by an eccentric doctor, and betrayed by his mistress. The range of emotion in this work is phenomenal. The emotions of despair, frustration, uselessness, and lack of worth add to the more traditional emotions of love, yearning, anger, and hate. Wozzeck eventually stabs and kills his mistress and drowns himself trying to wash the blood from his hands. The dialogue and the settings are realistic, the music is dissonant and contorted, and the orchestra is huge. With this opera language and music found a new balance in the twentieth century.

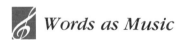

Words as Music

In the twentieth century words and their sounds have been further explored by both poets and composers. The unique work *FA:M' ANIESGEWOW* (1959) by Hans Helms uses sounds common to both Russian and English. He manipulates the text so that, while reciting a Russian text, meaningful words of another language can be heard, a technique known as synthetic polyglot and verbal polyphony. Another excellent example is *Sonate* by Kurt Schwitters in which the sound of the words and syllables create the music, a technique called **sound poetry.** Pitch and rhythm are a product of the recitation. The text is written below and can be performed in a variety of rhythms and tempos. Notice that there is repetition and contrast similar to the use of themes in the binary and ternary structures studied earlier. The realm of poetry and music are combined so completely here that it is arguable whether this is a musical work or a literary work. Its beauty is due partly to this blur of art forms. Music and words will forever be intertwined. The perception of the artist and performer will remain as a guide to the resolution of tensions between the two.

sound poetry
a literary style of writing words and/or syllables for their sound alone. The meaning of the text may be irrelevant to the performance of the recitation.

Kurt Schwitters, *Sonate* (1919)

Grim	glim	gnim	bimbim
grim	glim	gnim	bimbim
grim	glim	gnim	bimbim
grim	glim	gnim	bimbim
grim	glim	gnim	bimbim
grim	glim	gnim	bimbim
grim	glim	gnim	bimbim
grim	glim	gnim	bimbim
bum	bimbim	bam	bimbim
bum	bimbim	bam	bimbim
bum	bimbim	bam	bimbim
bum	bimbim	bam	bimbim
grim	glim	gnim	bimbim
grim	glim	gnim	bimbim
grim	glim	gnim	bimbim
grim	glim	gnim	bimbim
bum	bimbim	bam	bimbim
bum	bimbim	bam	bimbim
bum	bimbim	bam	bimbim
bum	bimbim	bam	bimbim
Tila	lola	lula	lola
tila	lula	lola	lola
tila	lola	lula	lola
tila	lula	lola	lola
Grim	glim	gnim	bimbim
grim	glim	gnim	bimbim
grim	glim	gnim	bimbim
grim	glim	gnim	bimbim
bem		bem	
bem		bem	
bem		bem	
bem		bem	

Tata	tata	tui	E	tui	E		
tata	tata	tui	E	tui	E		
tata	tata	tui	E	tui	E		
tata	tata	tui	E	tui	E		
Tillalala	tillalala						
tillalala		tillalala					
tata	tata	tui	E	tui	E		
tata	tata	tui	E	tui	E		
Tillalala	tillalala						
Tillalala	tillalala						
Tui	tui	tui	tui	tui	tui	tui	tui
te	te	te	te	te	te	te	te
tui	tui	tui	tui	tui	tui	tui	tui
te	te	te	te	te	te	te	te
Tata	tata	tui	E	tui	E		
tata	tata	tui	E	tui	E		
Tillalala	Tilla	lala					
tillalala		tilla	lala				
Tui	tui	tui	tui	tui	tui	tui	tui
te	te	te	te	te	te	te	te
tui	tui	tui	tui	tui	tui	tui	tui
te	te	te	te	te	te	te	te
O be	o be	o be	o be				
o be	o be	o be	o be				

Topic 4

THE CONDUCTOR AND COMPOSITION

Conductors are commonly considered to be an important part of any performance involving a large musical group; however, conductors were not required in early periods of music history. The need for a conductor emerged over time. Originally composers wrote music that required little variance in tempo and few, if any, dynamic changes. One of the most obvious examples is **terraced dynamics** from the Baroque era. Changes in dynamic levels were sharp and sudden. When loud sounds were needed the composer wrote for more musicians to play; soft sounds were made by using a small number of musicians. Composers did not consider the possibility of gradually changing the dynamic levels from one extreme to another, **crescendo** and **decrescendo.** It is difficult to say whether conductors led to new musical styles or whether new musical styles required direction and therefore conductors. It is safe to say, however, that as music styles developed so did conducting styles and techniques.

terraced dynamics
a technique used in the Baroque era to change dynamics. More players or more stops on the organ were added, resulting in sudden rather than gradually dynamic changes.

crescendo
a gradual increase in dynamic level from soft to loud.

decrescendo
a gradual decrease in dynamic level from loud to soft.

The Development of Conducting Techniques

The need for organization became increasingly important as the size of choirs and orchestras grew. The first recorded method of conducting can be traced back to the fifteenth century where the chief singer in the

Tact, taktus
the up-and-down motion made by early conductors intended to guide the musicians rhythmically.

Sistine Chapel choir used a roll of paper called a sol-fa to beat time for the musicians to stay together. The motion was called a **"Tact"** and the beat was called **"taktus."** The simple beating of time was assuredly used most often when the performers had a difficult time staying together. Because the number of musicians used in church music in the early periods was not yet very large the art of conducting was not at all established. The roll of paper soon turned to the bow of a violin or other "stick" that moved up and down to parallel the motion of the music so that all could see.

The Cane Incident

Some technique of direction and time keeping undoubtedly existed in every historical period. In the Baroque period, for example, Jean-Baptiste Lully would beat time on the floor using a cane or stick. With more than 150 musicians participating in a celebration concert for the recovery of King Louis XIV, Lully hit one of his toes with the cane. The injury resulted in gangrene and led to his death the same year, 1687.

By the eighteenth century the stick had disappeared and the leadership role had moved to the harpsichordist. The harpsichordist was often the composer who used the keyboard to steer the ensemble. The music of Mozart and Haydn was usually performed under the direction of the harpsichordist. As the harpsichord was dropped from the orchestra and string ensembles grew in size, the leadership moved once again to the **concert master,** who was traditionally the best violinist. The concert master would not beat time all the time. When the ensemble needed direction, he or she would stand and move the bow up and down with the beat to bring the players together. When all was going well, the concert master would play.

concert master
the assistant to the conductor of an orchestra. Traditionally, the first chair violinist is automatically the concert master.

The first chair violinist is still the one musician who enters the stage last and proceeds to organize the tuning procedures before the concert begins. The concert master is also the single orchestra member with whom the conductor shakes hands after the concert is over. He or she receives a separate bow for overseeing the orchestra.

One of the most dramatic changes in conducting came with Mendelssohn, who helped to define the conductor as an interpreter of music at the Gewandhaus concerts between 1835 and 1843. The "Mendelssohn tradition" of conducting placed the conductor at a music stand in front of the orchestra, once again with a stick or baton. The conductor's control over the ensemble had grown to the point that tempo changes and dynamic levels were now clearly seen by performers and audience alike.

Levels of volume in the orchestra are determined by the conductor's personal interpretation of what is most musically correct. If the melody appears in the violins, everyone else is directed to play softer. The number of decisions made by the conductor grew over the years.

Wagner has been considered the first modern conductor because of his insistence on controlling all aspects of a performance, from rehearsal to concert. Because he was interpreting his own compositions his control exceeded even most conductors today. He worked carefully to rehearse the musicians so that, in his words, the melody was never lost and the tempo was always correct. By this time in the late nineteenth century the role of the conductor had been determined.

 ## *Style of Conducting*

Review the conducting patterns in Chapter 4. These patterns are used to indicate the location of each beat in the measure. However, when musicians are well trained and do not get lost easily, then the strict beating of a pattern by the conductor is not always necessary. In that case conductors leave the standard patterns and move to body motions that elicit higher levels of expression. In fact, some conductors from Hungary and London have given up all time-beating patterns; they merely push the air in slow motions, outlining the overall development of phrases and dynamics. They seem disassociated from the momentary rhythmic activities; they are concerned with larger musical elements. These conductors require their musicians to be excellent performers who can play their part in total response to the conductor's indications. All conductors occasionally give up beating time to indicate overall expressive goals. Remember that small chamber groups such as a string quartet still do not need a director. They respond to each other in light of the decisions made during rehearsals. While performing, they use small body motions to unify the ensemble rhythmically and stylistically.

 ## *Responsibilities of the Conductor*

Originally the role of conductor as interpreter was not universally accepted. New questions arose, such as: Should the goal of the conductor be to accurately represent the intent of the composer? How much of a

Arturo Toscanini
(1867–1957)

DATELINE	BIOGRAPHY
1867	Arturo Toscanini was born in Parma, Italy. As a youth he studied cello and piano at the music conservatories in Parma and Milan.
1886	At the age of nineteen Toscanini was playing cello with an opera company in Rio de Janiero, Brazil, when he had the opportunity to replace the conductor for a performance of Verdi's *Aida*. He conducted brilliantly from memory; thus began his career as possibly the greatest conductor of all time.
1896	After conducting orchestras throughout Italy he became the artistic director of the La Scala opera house in Milan.
1908–15	Toscanini came to the United States to become conductor of the Metropolitan Opera.
1922–29	He returned to La Scala but left Italy in 1929 after refusing to conduct the fascist song ''Giovinezza''; his hatred of the fascist governmental policies led him to return to the United States.
1929–36	Toscanini was principal conductor of the New York Philharmonic Orchestra; his philosophy that the performers were mere servants of the composer was the foundation for his brilliant interpretations of the composers' intentions. His reputation for conducting Beethoven, Brahms, Debussy, Verdi, Wagner, and early Stravinsky was unrivaled.
1930–31	He was the first non-German conductor to be invited to Bayreuth to conduct Wagner's operas *Tristan, Die Meistersinger von Nürnberg,* and *Parsifal.*
1937	His humble disposition led him to refuse a doctorate of music degree offered to him by Oxford University.
1937–54	Toscanini directed the NBC Symphony Orchestra, with which he toured and performed extensively until his retirement at the age of eighty-seven.
1957	Toscanini, the most influential symphony orchestra and opera conductor of his time, died after spending seventy years as musical interpreter of the great composers.

performance should be a product of the personal interpretation of the conductor? If the conductor does not agree with the composer's intent, which is more important: the composer's original ideas or the contemporary interpretation of the conductor? These questions present difficult performance decisions. Critics, composers, performers, and conductors do not always agree. Various solutions to these questions have given remarkably different performances of the same works over the last two hundred years.

The preparation for conducting today is very extensive. Conductors must analyze an extraordinary amount of music and study rehearsal techniques so that they can communicate effectively with the players and use valuable rehearsal time effectively. Some conductors do their best work in rehearsals. At the concert the orchestra knows in advance what it must do. Other conductors are excellent at making last-minute decisions during a performance to make the music responsive to the moment. Styles of conducting are very personal.

Because of the vast number of works available to study and perform, some conductors have specialized in the works of specific composers; they develop an innate understanding of, and a love for, these compositions. Although most conductors are capable of conducting

Simon Rattle conducting the Birmingham Symphony Orchestra

much of the standard literature, they tend to show greater intensity when conducting works to which they are personally committed. As a result many listeners not only have favorite works but favorite conductors for those works.

The job of a conductor has grown in importance far beyond the normal requirements of rehearsal and performance. As orchestras perform, the conductor is a visual representation of what is happening and what will be the next important musical element. With eager anticipation we are shown to whom a **cue** is given and await the result. Great conductors are tour guides for the audience. The communication of musical ideas has become a three-way experience: conductor, performers, and audience. The conductor reaffirms wishes to the orchestra while showing to the onlookers what to expect. The popularity of many successful conductors hinges on their ability to excite the audience as well as the orchestra.

cue
a visual motion given by the conductor to instruct a performer of an entrance or needed musical effect.

Of course, the personality of a conductor also helps to build symphony organizations, drawing potential listeners and musicians. There are many fundraising projects that are a necessary part of each symphony orchestra foundation; concerts and recordings alone will not support all the musicians and facilities. Luncheons, auxiliaries, auctions, and banquets help subsidize the ongoing musical seasons. The conductor is not required to organize all these activities but must be agreeable and attend. The conductor's primary concern is still to program interesting music so that people will renew their subscriptions. Some of the most successful conductors have learned to manipulate the musical arena and support functions as well. In America, Leonard Bernstein, Zubin Mehta, Seiji Ozawa, Arthur Fiedler, and others have proven extremely successful in both these areas. Other great musical conductors, although extremely talented musicians, have unfortunately not been able to balance their efforts to direct music and raise funds.

Orchestral Musicians

Conductors are not always able to obtain the musical interpretations they want from the musicians under their direction. If the conductor is directing a school or community orchestra, the musicians may not have developed the skills necessary to deliver the sounds asked for. It is the responsibility of the conductor to choose literature within the reach of the musicians. Considerations of tempo must also be reevaluated for each performing group. The same work will take on different interpretive qualities with different musicians, and the musicians are critical tools in the building of a symphonic performance.

On the other hand, musicians in today's professional orchestras are very well prepared. For auditions they may be asked to perform any one of dozens of different selections from a variety of musical styles. To prepare for this they practice from books of orchestral passages **(excerpt books)** that include especially difficult or soloistic passages from standard orchestral literature. Many professionals have committed most of these excerpts to memory. As a result, they are well aware of the differences necessary between performances of, for example, Mozart and Mahler, or even early and late Beethoven.

excerpt books excerpts from orchestral music, by composer, for a specific instrument.

If a standard work is being performed today, why then, must the musicians rehearse if they already know their parts? The conductor has perhaps three or four rehearsals before a concert. The musicians rehearse to create a team unified by the interpretation of the conductor. Unless a work is very new or outside the standard literature, the musicians have already practiced their parts; in fact, many of them may have the parts memorized. World-class symphony orchestras are made up of exceptional technicians ready to respond to the direction of the conductor.

Musicians who play in an orchestra see only one notated part and must weave it into the whole. To perform a work where motives and themes are so important to the overall structure, the musician, with the aid of the conductor, must place emphasis on important melodies and rhythms. For example, the opening motive of Beethoven's Fifth Symphony is a vital building block, and when it appears in a musician's part it should be performed with understanding as to its relationship to the other parts. It may be an accompaniment idea in one place and a solo statement in another. The dynamic symbols written above and below the notes help with this interpretation, but there is no empirical interpretation. A *forte* may actually be louder in one performance than another, depending on how the other musicians are playing, the acoustics in the hall, the size of the orchestra, and the wishes of the conductor.

The musicians' ability to blend what they play with all the other sounds around them is critical. Unlike recording studios today, where musicians perform and record their parts without any of the other musicians around, orchestral musicians are required to listen, be responsive to the conductor, and place their sound into the total musical image.

Listening Notes

Listening alone will not introduce you to the many conducting styles and personalities of the brilliant conductors active today. Video recordings of symphonic concerts on television are broadcast periodically. Check your television guide and enjoy a concert where the conductor guides you through the performance. Notice if the conductor is working from a score or if it is memorized. Working without a score has become a status symbol to many conductors. Toscanini is partly responsible for this development. See if you can recognize any of the conducting patterns described in Chapter 4. See if there are moments where the conductor drops the patterns and becomes more expressive. Watch the response of the musicians to the motions of the conductor. Are the musicians paying attention to the directions? Watching concerts, and the conductor in particular, opens up a new visual way to understand the music.

Topic 5

THE INSTRUMENTAL SOLOIST

 ## The Soloist and the Orchestra

Seeing and hearing a virtuoso perform demanding music effortlessly is awe-inspiring. Anyone who has tried to play an instrument realizes the technical skill required to play even moderately difficult music; hearing virtuoso talent in light of a personal attempt at playing the same instrument is sensational. The premier form for virtuoso display is the **concerto.** The word *concerto* has been a part of music history for hundreds of years; the first secular concert work called a concerto is attributed to Torelli in 1686. The form was quickly adopted and developed by Corelli and Vivaldi. The first concertos were orchestral works featuring several soloists or a small ensemble within the orchestra.

We first encountered these orchestral concertos in our study of the Baroque period with the work of Vivaldi. Review the example of *The Four Seasons* in Chapter 7; much of the drama of the **concerto grosso** came from the virtuosic displays of the soloists and the contrasting dynamic levels between the soloists and the orchestra. The concerto grosso commonly pitted the tone colors of two, three, or four soloists against a full orchestral backdrop, perhaps the most famous being the *Brandenburg* Concertos by J. S. Bach. His six concerto grossi featured

concerto grosso
a form in which a soloist or ensemble is contrasted against a string orchestra or full orchestra.

■ *251*

many different instruments from various instrumental families. The second concerto in particular combined the most diverse of instrumental soloists: the trumpet, flute, oboe, and violin.

In the Classical period the concerto retained the three-movement structure of the concerto grosso but featured only one soloist. These works were often written by composers who were themselves great soloists. The most notable composer/performers in this period were Mozart and Beethoven. Their mastery of this form and their superior ability to improvise brilliant **cadenzas** set standards by which others would compose and perform.

cadenza
an unaccompanied solo that is very free rhythmically and melodically. Cadenzas are most commonly associated with the concerto form.

> ### The Virtuoso
>
> A cadenza generally appears in the first movement but sometimes the last. It traditionally follows a dissonant chord played by the orchestra. The soloist continues with exciting technical displays of skill, playing fast scales and arpeggios. The cadenza usually develops material presented earlier in the movement. The orchestra waits in silence until the soloist is finished. The signal ending the cadenza is customarily a long trill, after which the orchestra finally resolves the earlier dissonant chord.

The structure of the classical solo concerto is three movements. The scherzo or third movement associated with the four-movement symphony was deleted. The first movement generally follows the sonata-allegro form with the orchestra stating the themes before the soloist. The middle movement is slower and offers contrast, requiring highly developed interpretive skills. The favorite structure for the last movement is the rondo form. Of course, there are notable exceptions to this standard structure.

Of the next two examples, Haydn wrote three distinct movements while Mendelssohn smoothly connected the movements without stopping. Later, in the case of Liszt, the movements not only continue without stopping, they share thematic material.

Although the piano was a favored instrument for concertos, other solo instruments intrigued composers as well. One of the most popular solo concertos from the Classical period is Haydn's Trumpet Concerto in E-flat Major. Haydn wrote the work for a friend who had recently invented a trumpet with keys. The work, one of the first concertos for the modern trumpet, was nearly forgotten. Written in 1800, it was not published until 1929. Since that time it has become a staple in the concerto world.

Itzak Perlman performing at the Frederic Mann Auditorium in Tel Aviv

Listening Notes

Joseph Haydn, Trumpet Concerto in E-flat Major (1800).
Third Movement: Allegro

This movement benefits from two very powerful forms, the rondo and the sonata-allegro forms. See Chapter 4 for traditional diagrams. The structure of this movement is modified as follows: Exposition (A B A B′ A), Development (using material from both A and B), Recapitulation (A B″), Coda.

The themes of the third movement are light and tuneful, thus the return of the melody after the development section is satisfying and rewarding. The two themes are first presented in the orchestra and are repeated by the trumpet. Haydn shows a knowledge of the solo instrument; the themes are well-suited to the trumpet, enhancing the tonal colors and articulations specific to the instrument.

0:00	Violin section (soft) introduces the first theme (A), the orchestra follows immediately with a loud statement.
0:32	Build to a very stable cadence followed by a short pause.
0:35	The trumpet plays the first theme accompanied by a full orchestra.
1:01	Second thematic idea (B) is built around a dialogue between the orchestra and the soloist. The trumpet ends with fanfare figures.
1:41	The first theme (A) returns in rondo fashion.
1:57	The short development begins with immediate modulations of the first theme, fast violin figures, trumpet plays fanfare figures again. Decrescendo.
2:23	The first theme (A), recapitulation.
2:39	The second theme (B″) is presented by the trumpet but with several modifications. The octave leaps and broken chords are very difficult techniques for this instrument.
2:55	All sections of the orchestra soften ending the recapitulation.
3:22	Coda, sudden dynamic changes, irregular harmonic cadence, short silence, humorous and surprising ending.
4:50	Crescendo to the end.
5:02	End.

The writings of Haydn and Mozart helped to define the solo concerto. There was, however, an inevitable shift in priorities in the concertos of Beethoven in that the orchestra became a more dominant force. The balance between solo virtuosity and orchestral strength further intensified the drama already inherent in the concerto. With the increased size of the orchestra, concertos in the Romantic era blossomed into large emotionally charged structures.

Mendelssohn, like Haydn, wrote a concerto for a friend, in this case a violinist. And again, like Haydn, he invested the time to understand the instrument and its possibilities. Writing a virtuoso work without the ability to perform it oneself is a difficult task in itself. Mendelssohn's Violin Concerto in E minor sounds very difficult, but for a virtuoso it is not as intimidating as it might sound. Needless to say, performers love this kind of composition. The opposite would be to perform a concerto that sounds easy but is extremely difficult to play. Such a concerto, reportedly, is the Second Piano Concerto by Brahms.

Felix Mendelssohn
(1809–47)

DATELINE	BIOGRAPHY

1809 Felix Mendelssohn was born and raised in a wealthy and culturally active environment. Although his grandfather Moses Mendelssohn was a Jewish philosopher, the children were brought up in a Christian home.

1812 The family moved to Berlin and Felix and his sister, Fanny, began formal musical training under Carl Zelter, the head of the *Singakademie.*

1818 At the age of nine Felix made his debut as a concert pianist. By age twelve he was composing trios, quartets, sonatas, concertos, and operettas. His mother, Leah, organized musical gatherings at the family home, and Felix was able to debut his works with his own private orchestra and an audience of Berlin's artistic elite.

1826 At age seventeen Mendelssohn created a masterpiece when he wrote the overture to Shakespeare's *A Midsummer Night's Dream.*

1829 Mendelssohn found a copy of Bach's *St. Matthew's Passion;* he was so impressed by Bach's writing that he organized an orchestra and conducted the piece. This performance spawned a revival of Bach's music eighty years after his death.

1833 Mendelssohn became the town musical director and conductor at Dusseldorf.

1835 He was appointed conductor of the Gewandhaus Orchestra in Leipzig, and the orchestra grew to be the finest in Europe under his direction. Mendelssohn was one of the first conductors to stand in front of the orchestra to conduct.

1837 He married Cecile Jeanrenaud.

1841 Felix and Cecile moved to Berlin, where Felix became the musical director of the Academy of Arts established by Kaiser Friedrich Wilhelm IV.

1843 Mendelssohn opened his own music conservatory in Leipzig and employed Robert Schumann as an instructor.

1847 Mendelssohn died in Leipzig at the age of thirty-eight. Several factors contributed to his death, including general ill health, severe depression after the death of his sister, Fanny, and simple exhaustion from overwork.

Listening Notes

Felix Mendelssohn, Violin Concerto in E Minor, op. 64 (1844).
First Movement: Allegro molto appassionato

Unlike the Haydn Trumpet Concerto, this work starts immediately with the soloist. This is not the only variance introduced by Mendelssohn in this work; he took control of the cadenza both in its performance and its structural placement in the work. Cadenzas normally appeared at the end of the movement before the coda. However, Mendelssohn placed it at the end of the development section and used it to dramatically signal the recapitulation. He wrote out the cadenza rather than allow the soloist to improvise. Thus there is a brilliant segue when the orchestra joins the soloist for the recapitulation. Evidenced by the dramatic mood and tempo changes within the movement, this work is clearly in the Romantic style.

0:00	Exposition. The first theme appears with the solo violin following a short orchestral chord.
0:29	The soloist moves through fast-flowing melodic passages.
0:59	The orchestra plays the theme; short soloistic statements between chords in the orchestra, cadence.
1:30	Transition theme, first in the violins and then by the soloist.
1:45	The soloist moves up and down over a very large range. The orchestra joins, the soloists uses double-stops (two notes at once), decrescendo.
2:49	Second theme is peaceful and moves to the relative major. The soloist plays a single note in accompaniment as the clarinet states the theme.
3:01	Solo violin states the second theme.
3:50	The violinist returns to the first theme, the texture becomes more active. The tempo once again increases.
4:39	The orchestra plays chords (trills), the soloist plays soloistic passages in between.
5:00	The development starts with the transition theme (soloist), then the violins.
5:31	The soloist moves quickly through broken chord passages while the orchestra plays short fragments of the first theme.
5:36	The tempo and texture relaxes.
6:12	Crescendo leading into the cadenza.

6:22	The cadenza follows an unstable orchestral chord; the soloist first plays broken chords ending in the high range at the end of each phrase. Low trills ascend through broken chords still to very high notes. A rapid broken chord figure is established by the soloist and joined by the orchestra.
7:51	Recapitulation, first theme (orchestra) followed immediately by the transition theme.
8:39	Second theme, woodwinds, soloist again plays sustained note then takes over the theme.
9:46	Soloist again flies into soloist passages. After a pizzicato accompaniment figure the orchestra crescendos.
10:31	Double-stop technique returns.
10:39	Orchestral chords separated by soloist displays return.
10:57	Coda. Tempo increases, final chords.
11:38	End (a single sustained note in the bassoon is held connecting the first and second movements).

 *Full Circle*

The concerto grosso of the Baroque period developed into the solo concerto of the Classical period and finally into the orchestral concerto as in Bartók's *Concerto for Orchestra* studied in Chapter 10. This work is called a concerto because of the soloistic nature of the instruments within the orchestra; it is in essence a return to the orchestral concertos of the Baroque era. Modern concertos continued to experiment with different combinations of soloists and orchestra. The orchestra itself was also changing. For example, Arthur Bliss wrote a concerto for an interesting combination of piano, tenor voice, xylophone, and strings in 1933. Ellen Zwilich's *Concerto Grosso 1985* is another intriguing work written in the spirit of an orchestral concerto. There is no specific soloist; there are five movements and the theme is based on a theme from Handel's Sonata in D for violin. With this work the term *concerto* seems to have come full circle from the Baroque era.

The flexibility of the modern concerto is further evident in another of Zwilich's works *Concerto for Trumpet and Five Players*. The instrumentation calls for flute/piccolo, bass clarinet/clarinet, percussion,

Ellen Taaffe Zwilich
(1939–   )

DATELINE	BIOGRAPHY
1939	Ellen Taaffe was born in Miami, Florida, on April 30.
1957	She studied music at Florida State University; one of her mentors was the composer and piano virtuoso Ernst von Dohhányi.
1972	She worked in New York City as an usher at Carnegie Hall and played violin in the American Symphony Orchestra.
1975	Taaffe studied composition at Julliard with Elliott Carter and Roger Sessions, two prominent composers in the educational world.
1976	The successful performance in Boston of her String Quartet brought her major recognition.
1982	Zwilich's First Symphony was premièred at Lincoln Center by Gunther Schuller and the American Composers Orchestra; this piece earned her a Pulitzer Prize in 1983, the first one awarded to a woman in the field of music composition.
1984	This year she produced several major works, including *Celebration, Prologue and Variations, Concerto for Trumpet and Five Players,* and *Double Quartet.*
1985	Her *Concerto Grosso 1985* was commissioned by the Washington Friends of Handel in commemoration of the 300th anniversary of Handel's birth; it was performed for the first time in spring of 1986 by the Handel Festival Orchestra at the Kennedy Center in Washington, D.C.
1988	The New York Philharmonic commissioned the work *Symbolon* for its 1988 tour of the Soviet Union; the world première took place at Bolshoi Hall in Leningrad with Zubin Mehta conducting. It was the first American symphonic work to be premièred in the Soviet Union.
1989	Zwilich wrote *Concerto for Trombone and Orchestra,* premièred by the Chicago Symphony, that highlighted an instrument for which concertos are seldom written.

Listening Notes

Ellen Taaffe Zwilich, *Concerto Grosso 1985. Subtitle: "to Handel's* Sonata in D *for violin and continuo, first movement"*

As the subtitle suggests, this work draws its inspiration from an organic set of motives from a violin sonata by Handel. The work consists of five movements, all of which are based on the melodic influence of Handel. The motives are flexible, and in the hands of Zwilich, sound at times tonal and other times free from any specific tonal center. This concerto has no single soloist but does draw on the tradition of contrast. The interesting aspect of this work is the weaving of sounds and sonorities from the Baroque tradition with twentieth-century melodic ideas. The musical ideas borrowed from Handel supply the melodic content of both textures. The use of a harpsichord in the orchestra gives the music a nostalgic link with the Baroque era. Instrumentation and melody provide additional quotes from Handel's day. Zwilich displays an eloquent control of her craft in this work that travels so easily between centuries.

0:00 Three long unison notes open the movement.

0:19 The motive is played in the upper strings. The melodic shape sounds far more like the twentieth century than like Handel.

0:28 Theme repeats; long, low note continues as the only accompaniment.

0:36 Harpsichord and low strings enter playing a continuo-like accompaniment. The melody in the upper strings sounds like a contemporary movie theme but soon moves to more Baroque ideas, including trills.

0:57 Return of the more modern melody again over long sustained notes. It is passed around the orchestra.

1:16 Return to baroque texture, oboe solo.

1:33 The theme enters again, moves quickly through the woodwinds.

1:49 Strings restate the theme that transforms into the Baroque melody.

2:04 Traditional Baroque cadence. Last note is sustained in the lower strings as the upper strings again quote the theme.

2:11 A static section where the melodic motion is frozen. Fragments of the theme are played by the strings, a sustained chord continues.

2:33 Brief rolled chords by the harpsichord and a long sustained chord held by the winds and strings end the movement.

contrabass, and piano. The solo trumpet is accompanied by an amazing cross section of textures and colors. This work retreats to the three-movement structure typical of Classical and Romantic concertos; however, the orchestra is replaced by a chamber group.

The 1965 composition *Piano Concerto* by Elliott Carter integrates three contrasting elements. In this two-movement work the orchestra and piano soloist are musically immiscible; there is, however, a concertino group of seven instrumentalists that acts as an intermediary between the musical ideas presented in the orchestra and the conflicting ideas of the pianist. Carter raised contrast to yet another level of complexity and intellectualism. The term *concerto* has remained fluid for centuries and continues to reappear as new forms in which contrasting musical ideas and sounds excite and surprise.

The Soloist in Chamber Music

trio sonata
a sonata with three musical parts. The two higher melodies are performed by two soloists while the continuo players perform the third part.

continuo (basso)
the performance of a figured bass by a lute or keyboard reinforced by a cello.

In chamber music a parallel structure for soloists arose in the development of the **sonata.** Before the Baroque period the sonata merely meant that the music was played and not sung as in cantata. Violin sonatas were first to dominate the musical world. Corelli and Purcell brought violin sonatas and **trio sonatas** to new heights (see Chapter 7). They were themselves violinists and favored the instrument. For this same reason Vivaldi focused his attention on solo violin works.

Although the term *sonata* broadly covered many instrumental works, it slowly evolved into a three-movement work similar to the concerto. The major difference was that the accompaniment was supplied by a **continuo** or a keyboard instrument in lieu of an orchestra. The exception to this convention was the keyboard sonata; harpsichords and pianos were capable of supplying their own accompaniment. Instruments such as the flute, violin, or clarinet could not add the harmonic interest capable of a keyboard. There are, however, brilliant exceptions where solo instruments perform sonatas without any accompaniment; for instance, the unaccompanied violin sonatas of Bach and, in the early twentieth century, Max Reger.

The single-movement sonatas of Scarlatti in the Baroque era exemplify the early ambiguity of a sonata's larger structure. Piano sonatas borrowed their structure from the multimovement keyboard suites of the Baroque era. The number of movements slowly settled on three or four. The third movement or scherzo was dropped by the eighteenth and nineteenth century when the three-movement structure became the favorite.

Arthur Rubenstein

At the same time the construction of the piano improved, giving the instrument more brilliance and projection. This interested composers who themselves played the piano. Beethoven was both a talented pianist and composer and wrote many works for piano. All in all, he wrote five piano concertos, thirty-two solo sonatas, and other chamber works involving piano.

Listening Notes

Ludwig van Beethoven, Piano Sonata *(Appassionata), op.* 57 (1804).

First Movement: Allegro assai

The expressive qualities of this sonata tend to place it in the Romantic rather than the Classical period. This sonata has the balance and clarity of Classical music as well as the rich development typical of the Romantic composer. Notice the soft personal moments that are interrupted by explosive accents. The brilliant orchestral mind of Beethoven is evident in this solo sonata. It is easy to imagine the piano as a miniorchestra, performing percussive sounds and singing melodies. Beethoven's personal style is evident in the sweeping mood changes and sudden dynamic changes.

This sonata is in three movements with no break between the last two. The first movement, in the sonata-allegro form, is in F minor and is very serious. The second theme is similar to the first rhythmically but is in the relative major. Notice the virtuoso moments at the end of the development section and again at the end of the movement. Like his Fifth Symphony, the ending is expanded to include an additional development section and a second coda.

0:00	**Exposition.** First theme, very soft.
0:21	Four-note motive, repeated, last time loud.
0:43	Melodic trill idea alternates with loud block chords.
0:57	Transition theme, repeating note supplies forward motion and accompaniment.
1:21	Second theme, repeating chord accompaniment.
1:31	Sudden stop and a series of trills and long descending scale.

1:52 Aggressive closing idea, soloistic display softens and slows to a cadence.

2:24 **Development.** Fragments of the first theme and melodic trill idea.

2:54 Modulation with active accompaniment figure; first theme continues throughout.

3:21 Transition theme with repeating note returns with variation and modulation.

3:53 Second theme is now developed, crescendo.

4:18 Long series of arpeggios.

4:30 Four-note motive from the first theme group is accented several times.

4:42 **Recapitulation.** First theme is accompanied by a low repeating note.

4:58 Melodic trill idea, and four-note motive returns.

5:14 Sudden outburst of the block chord idea, repetitions move the idea higher and higher.

5:37 Transition theme with repeating note.

5:59 Second theme, with a repeating low note in accompaniment.

6:16 Sudden stop, ascending trills, long descending scale.

6:35 Coda parallels the closing idea of the exposition but moves into a new developmental section.

7:00 Development of the first theme.

7:14 Moves to developing the second theme.

7:25 Brilliant display of arpeggios moving to the extreme high register, down and back up again.

7:56 Four-note motive, repeated softer and softer.

8:14 Suddenly loud, faster tempo, the opening of the first theme is played in various ranges, momentum slows, dynamic level falls.

9:05 End.

Topic 6

STRING QUARTETS

Chamber ensembles are, by definition, small groups of musicians that perform in intimate settings. They range in size from as few as one soloist with an accompanist to as many as fifteen or twenty musicians in a small orchestra. Chamber music is concert music for small rooms. No ensemble has been as enduring as the string quartet, a favorite format for composers since the late 1700s. String quartets have two violins that play in the treble range, a viola in the alto range, and a cello in the tenor/bass range. These four stringed instruments are capable of producing unique soloistic sounds as well as lush, blending sonorities. The character of the ensemble is a product of the composer's musical skills and the sensitivity of the performers.

 ## Historical Background

Haydn was among the first to write for a quartet of strings. The first quartets of Haydn were dancelike, derived from dance suites and collections of movements called **divertimenti.** Although his op. 1 (1755–60) is now considered to be for string quartet, it was probably

divertimenti
a collection of dancelike forms performed by small string ensembles. They were the predecessors to the modern string quartet.

trio sonata
a sonata with three musical parts. The two higher melodies are performed by two soloists while the continuo players perform the third part.
continuo (basso)
the performance of a figured bass by a lute or keyboard reinforced by a cello.

played by a small string orchestra. The **trio sonatas** of the Baroque era were fading in popularity. The trio sonata, like the quartet, had four performers; however, the **continuo** part took two of the players, with cello and harpsichord supplying a bass line and chords. The developing quartet did not require a continuo as the equalization of all four voices took place.

The independence of each instrument came about slowly. In his early sets of quartets, op. 9 and op. 17 (1768–71), Haydn favored the first violin part with more difficult passages. The other parts assumed a role of accompaniment to the more soloistic first violin part. Haydn created this imbalance partly to carry on the homophonic tradition of divertimenti dance styles and partly because he took advantage of an exceptionally talented musician playing the first violin part. With op. 20 the equality of each part began to materialize, bringing about a unified texture built on the sharing of melodic lines.

Haydn first showed tendencies toward developmental writing in his quartets and eventually expanded them in his symphonies; developmental writing eventually led to the formulation of the sonata-allegro form. The string quartet did not have, however, the vast array of tone qualities available in a full orchestra. The quartet was held to more subtle changes in tone quality. The use of pitch range, dynamic range, plucking sounds **(pizzicato),** bowing sounds **(arco),** and other highly developed articulations comprised the arsenal of sounds available in his string quartets. He eventually wrote eighty-four quartets throughout his long life. Under Haydn's guidance, the string quartet flowered, establishing a well-defined identity for others to imitate and develop over the next two hundred years.

pizzicato
plucking a stringed instrument rather than bowing it.
arco
bowing a stringed instrument as opposed to plucking the strings.

Listening Notes

Joseph Haydn, String Quartet in E-flat, op. 33, no. 2 ("The Joke") (1781).
Fourth Movement: Finale: Presto

Haydn's early quartets are distinguished by their wit and freshness. There are six quartets in op. 33. This selection is the last movement of the second quartet, nicknamed "The Joke." This movement is a rondo with an ebullient theme. Haydn purposely wrote a confusing ending to this movement so that "the ladies would not begin talking before the music finished." The joke appears at the very end of the movement. Haydn

Music in Performance

A scene from Richard Wagner's opera *Götterdämmerrung*
(Robert McElroy/Woodfin Camp & Associates.)

Luciano Pavarotti
(F. Orglia/Sygma)

Kiri Te Kanawa performing in *Othello*
(Jack Vartoogian)

The Mormon Tabernacle Choir
(Alex Webb/Magnum Photos Inc.)

Violinist Nigel Kennedy and his poodle
(M. Pelletier/Sygma)

A scene from Andrew Lloyd Webber's *Phantom of the Opera*
(Clive Barda/Woodfin Camp & Associates)

Michael Jackson
(Sygma)

Mick Jagger and Tina Turner
(Ken Regan/Camera 5)

A family hoedown in Golden, Colorado
(James Cook/Time Syndication)

A member of 2 Live Crew filming "Banned in the USA"
(J.B. Diederich/Woodfin Camp & Associates.)

A music video in production
(Chuck Fishman/Woodfin Camp & Associates.)

prevents a normal ending from taking place. In the coda, the tempo suddenly moves to a serious *Adagio,* in striking contrast to the frivolous rondo theme. After only a few measures, the rondo theme returns; however, it is broken up by two measures of silence. With all momentum shattered, there are four measures of rests followed by two final measures of the theme. The result is confusion. Is the movement over?

Notice the balanced texture of the four instruments. Although the first violin still plays a dominant role, the independence of the four solo voices is nearly complete. The cello is confined to bass line activity while the second violin plays duets with the first violin or joins the viola and cello in accompaniment.

0:00	Rondo theme, short and light. The first violin is very active and the others provide accompaniment.
0:08	Repeat.
0:15	New material B.
0:32	First theme A.
0:39	New material C, activity level increases. This section ends with the second violin playing a duet with the first violin.
0:55	A.
1:02	New material. The cello stays on the same note, repeating it while the first violin assumes all melodic activity. The accompaniment joins the first violin in regularly spaced accents. This section is more developmental.
1:31	A followed by material from B above.
1:55	A followed by material from C above.
2:25	Tempo slows to a cadence.
3:03	Several more attempts at starting the theme are broken with short silences.
3:15	Two measures of silence.
3:20	Last attempt at the theme.
3:22	End.

The classical string quartet reached its zenith with Beethoven at the beginning of the Romantic period. His later quartets are profound and weighty works. His mature style is evident in the last five quartets and a fugue, op. 133 (1825), which was originally intended as a finale to his op.

130. These quartets are considered some of the most intellectual writing of his career. Written during his third period, they represent a firm footing in the Romantic style. He demanded aggressive virtuosity from the players to produce rich, full sonorities from the four parts.

Listening Notes

Ludwig van Beethoven, String Quartet in C-sharp minor, op. 131 (1826).

First Movement: Adagio, ma non troppo e molto espressivo

The last quartets of Beethoven are introspective, concise, and structurally unique. This work, for instance, blurs the traditional cadences between movements, giving the work a grand scheme. This fugue, while true to its polyphonic form, spells out a profound theme. Notice the interplay of the four voices. Beethoven maintains the integrity of each part in a fugal texture. The traditional structure that Haydn and Mozart helped to define was expanded by Beethoven to seven movements in this quartet. He had little interest in conforming to traditional structures; he freely spun out musical ideas that in turn defined larger structures. Unique large structures are a reflection of Beethoven's compositional style.

0:00	First violin plays the fugue subject. Notice the fourth note, which has a heavy accent. Similar accents will be heard throughout the movement.
0:12	Second violin plays the answer.
0:24	Viola enters with the subject.
0:37	The cello is the last to enter with the answer.
0:49	Short episode.
1:19	All parts move from low to high registers.
1:52	Pedal point (short), cello holds a long note, smooth modulation follows.
2:14	New key area, modulation again follows moving to another key area.
2:34	The rhythmic texture increases, cello remains the same while the other three parts start moving twice as fast (eighth notes).
2:57	All parts move again to a very high register.
3:25	The two violins play a duet while the viola and cello stop.
3:43	The viola and cello take over the duet.

4:17	All four parts again play at the same time; the key area returns home to C# minor.
4:40	A new eighth-note activity begins with the two violins, the viola plays the fugue subject. The subject and the eighth-note activity move from part to part.
5:06	The cello plays the subject, making each note twice as long as normal (augmentation).
5:42	The rhythmic texture becomes more complicated.
5:54	The climax of the movement has the largest pitch range thus far; the cello is on its lowest notes while the first violin plays very high notes.
5:59	The last accented note occurs, the range decreases and the dynamics soften.
6:10	End.

In the Romantic period, composers such as Schubert, Schumann, and Brahms explored avenues to develop rich sonorities and increase levels of dissonance and rhythmic complexity. Articulations were expanded to incorporate a more animated **tremolo** with thickening techniques such as **double-stopping** (playing two notes at once).

With the writings of Bartók the string quartets of the twentieth century reflected how durable tonality and the sonata form are. His six quartets, written between 1908 and 1939, push the limit of tonality to its extreme. The melodies, although very angular, are powerful. In addition, extended performing techniques were becoming more prevalent. The new virtuosity required of twentieth-century performers is evident in these quartets.

tremolo
the vibrato motion of a pitch. The pitch moves slightly higher and lower, adding animation to the note.
double-stopping
playing two notes at once on a stringed instrument.

Listening Notes

Béla Bartók, String Quartet no. 2, op. 17, (1915–17).
Second Movement: Allegro molto capriccioso

This selection is usually titled as being in A minor; however, the work is really centered around the note A. There is no typical harmonic structure to suggest a tonality of A minor, but there is, however, a repetitive use of the note A around which many of the musical ideas are based. There are tonal passages as well as bi-tonal passages (two key areas at once). Bartók's research into his native folk music also affects the modal harmonies that appear throughout all the movements.

The second movement is in rondo form and is very dissonant. The material is highly developmental, making theme recognition difficult. The rhythmic activity generates an energetic texture. Notice the rich and contrasting sonorities, a product of stark dissonances and ingenious scoring. Although the movement is marked *allegro* it fluctuates in tempo. The texture shifts dramatically and activity levels change, making it sound as if the tempo has slowed. Notice how difficult it is to anticipate the rhythmic pulse. See if you can find metric groupings.

0:00 This movement begins with a combined texture of bowing and pizzicato.

0:06 Energetic texture. Melody, first in the violin, borrows inflections from Hungarian folk music.

0:50 Cadence.

0:51 New melody (similar texture) is passed around through all the parts.

1:20 Ascending melodic idea.

1:32 Dissonant chords.

1:42 Independent melodic lines create a polyphonic texture.

2:00 New texture.

2:05 Repeating notes return, similar to the opening texture.

2:45 Tempo slows.

2:55 Cadence, new thin texture.

3:10 Short unaccompanied solo passages are answered by the others. Pizzicato and bowing texture.

3:36 Solo violin followed by tutti rhythms, tempo slows again.

3:55 Solo violin (pizzicato accompaniment.)

4:06 A long ascending melody is spelled out by each part in short solos, starting with the cello.

4:40 Energetic texture returns, followed by tutti rhythms.

5:08 Very independent lines, highly polyphonic.

5:25 Cadence, tutti.

5:35 Return to repeating note idea.

6:09 Dissonant chords (tutti rhythm).

6:25 Solo violin statements are followed by tutti chords.

6:42 Slow building of energy, fast repeating figures, busy texture but soft.

7:00 Unison rhythm, coda.

7:24 Unison ending.

7:46 End.

String quartets slipped easily into the world of atonal sonorities as evidenced in the five string quartets of Schoenberg. Melodies became even more angular, and the local rhythms defied any regular metric pattern. The separate voices in these quartets gave intensity and life to melodic ideas that seem more rhythmic than tuneful.

The Turtle Island String Quartet

String Quartet in Transition

Because of their subtlety and refinement, string quartets have rarely found mass appeal. However, the quartet has recently made the transition to another stylistic arena without losing its integrity, and the flexibility and endurance of the string quartet is once again evident in a more commercial setting. The Turtle Island String Quartet is an unusual group in that it is comprised of four composer/arrangers with solid traditional music backgrounds and well-developed improvisation skills. Their transition into the popular market has been swift and decisive.

Listening Notes

Darol Anger, *Street Stuff* (1989) performed by the Turtle Island String Quartet.

This selection is a hybrid of jazz, gospel, and Classical styles. The composer is a violinist in this performance. All the musicians have impressive improvisational skills that incorporate jazz inflections and accents. The string quartet texture remains intact. The four voices are equally melodic at times; however, the cello is often relegated to playing strict rhythmic bass lines typical of a **walking** bass found in **swing.** The interaction of the players is traditional to Classical quartet performance, the melodic interpretation is traditional to jazz, and the improvisation is traditional to virtuoso performance. Notice the traditional textures not associated with jazz. The blend of textures is fluid and natural.

0:00 Introduction, crescendo on two repeating notes.

0:07 Melody begins with sounds associated with a hoedown and folk fiddling, cello plays a bass line (bowed).

0:35 New texture, cello plays repeated notes.

0:57 First violin plays solo, others work together in accompaniment.

1:16 Double-time solo, most likely improvised.

1:26 Return to structured texture.

1:47 Walking bass figure, hand claps, swing feeling.

2:16 Texture change due mostly to the cello changing patterns.

walks, walking
a rhythmic-melodic pattern employed by a swing-style bass player. When a note is played on every beat of the measure and notes are organized into a scale, the impression is one of "walking" up and down the scale. A walking bass provides harmonic support for the rest of the ensemble.

swing
a style of playing two notes within a beat. A classical musician interprets the duration of each note as equal; a jazz musician makes the first note longer than the second. The result is a swinging, dancelike feeling of long-short, long-short.

2:23	Cello bows a jazz walking bass line, swing intensifies.
2:34	Solo cadenza, block chords articulate phrases.
3:01	Crescendo, tremolo accompaniment to solo.
3:10	Cello solo.
3:20	Violin starts the coda, the others enter with a chord that is made active by tremolos. The chord rises in pitch while a dog barks until the final chord.
3:46	Dog bark, end.

Contemporary composers still look to the string quartet as a medium for experimentation and development of musical thought. For example, the first computer-generated composition, *Iliac Suite* (1957) by Lejaren Hiller, was written for the string quartet. Another work, *Coconino: A Shattered Landscape for String Quartet* by Roger Reynolds, was first fleshed out through computer composition and eventually scored for string quartet. Reynolds, winner of the 1989 Pulitzer Prize, like other contemporary composers, continues to find the string quartet a vibrant medium for developing and expressing compositional thought.

Topic 7

SOUNDS FROM THE UNITED STATES

Music in the United States cannot be characterized by a single style. In fact, the multiplicity of styles in America typifies its music. However, like any country, the borrowing of its own folk music makes its concert music unique. American styles, influenced by Western European and African music, have been developed by individuals who have been fascinated by the sounds around them. Prior to the twentieth century, American composers were overshadowed by Europeans; with the emergence of cultural sounds such as blues, gospel, and jazz, a new blend of European and American music brought several American composers into prominence. In the case of Aaron Copland, those sounds were associated with images of the Old West. Charles Ives flavored his music with quotes from Protestant hymns and patriotic songs. George Gershwin found a unique niche somewhere between classical and commercial music styles. Meanwhile, Duke Ellington used jazz to develop a unique sound. By looking at these four twentieth-century composers, we will see the very diversity that comprises the sounds of the United States. These composers worked at approximately the same time but with strikingly different personal styles. It is such uniqueness and freedom of spirit that typifies the American composer.

Nationalism has been a part of music history for years. There has always been a temptation to quote one's past. The use of folk material is the essential ingredient for a nationalistic classification, and using compositional techniques associated with a country is not enough. The sound of the culture is vital to such a classification. Composers and compositions such as Charles Ives's *Variations on America,* Aaron Copland's *Rodeo,* or George Gershwin's *Porgy and Bess* are clear examples of nationalism through the use of folk and cultural music from America's recent past.

One of the most innovative composers of the early twentieth century was Charles Ives, whose music is filled with early American themes. The music is so different that he cannot be categorized by any school of composition. He has become the definition of American uniqueness. He wrote uniquely structured works, such as his Second Piano Sonata (the *Concord* Sonata); each movement, a musical portrait, is titled after an American writer, "Emerson," "Hawthorne," "The Alcotts," and "Thoreau." He builds the work around the famous motive from Beethoven's Fifth Symphony. Ives was also a gifted literary writer, as evidenced by the essays that accompany the *Concord* Sonata, titled *Essays Before a Sonata.* The essays do not speak of the music; they are commentaries on the individuals for which the movements of the sonata are titled. There are two additional and rather provocative essays about music and its creation.

Ives wrote five symphonies and other orchestral works full of surprising and imaginative textures. His *Three Places in New England* portrays a childhood memory of two marching bands marching in different directions playing different music. This work re-creates the environmental effect of several activities occurring at once. The dissonance is excitingly real.

Ives was free of convention and wrote music that changed quickly from extreme dissonance to sentimental consonance. His music, like his life, is diverse but hinged around a firm and emotional background in the church. He used hymns in his works as a point of security in dramatic contrast to unstable dissonant textures. For example, the final answer to his *Unanswered Question* is a simple statement of an old hymn. Patriotic themes were also a favorite source for his writings; he freely quoted songs such as "Columbia, the Gem of the Ocean" and "Yankee Doodle." In other works for organ or chorus he used two tonal areas simultaneously, creating a **polytonal** texture (*Variations on America,* written for organ, are both emotionally and intellectually conceived).

Although Ives was a very private person, he is remembered as a colorful individual. He was talented in business. He was instrumental in establishing life insurance in this country and wrote an effective book on selling. He worked on compositions that could never be completed. For

polytonal
the simultaneous performance of two different key areas. This can be accomplished with an orchestra or with a single keyboard instrument.

Charles Ives
(1874–1954)

DATELINE	BIOGRAPHY
1874	Charles Ives was born in Danbury, Connecticut. His father, George, was a music teacher who had conducted an Army band during the Civil War; he taught Charles to play piano, violin, and cornet and instructed him in harmony, counterpoint, and ear training, exposing him to many unusual and experimental sounds.
1888	Ives became organist at the First Baptist Church in Danbury, the first of many organist jobs he would hold during his lifetime.
1894–98	He studied at Yale University, taking classes from Horatio Parker, who discouraged Ives from composing unconventional pieces.
1898	After graduation, Ives moved to New York and got a job as a clerk for the Mutual Life Insurance Company; believing that music would never bring him financial security, he worked his way up in the insurance business while continuing to compose on the weekends.
1908	He married Harmony Twichell, daughter of a Hartford minister.
1909–15	He wrote Piano Sonata No. 2, which includes four movements written for New England authors Emerson, Hawthorne, the Alcotts, and Thoreau; this was printed in 1922, preceded by an explanation entitled *Essays Before a Sonata.*
1918	At the age of forty-four, Ives suffered a heart attack from which he never fully recovered; he was already a prosperous insurance executive and continued to compose, although most of his music was not well known until late in his life.
1920s	Ives continued to compose pieces based on American folk and popular music; the sounds of jazz, military marches, patriotic songs, and revival hymns can be heard in many of his songs, piano works, chamber music, and choral works.
1939	This year marked the first New York performance of the *Concord* Sonata; Ives was sixty-four years old.
1947	He won the Pulitzer Prize for Symphony No. 3, which had been written in 1911; he replied gruffly that he was ''too old for prizes.''
1954	Although Ives is considered by many composers to be the father of American music, many of his works were not performed until after his death this year in New York.

Listening Notes

Charles Ives, *General William Booth Enters into Heaven* (1914).

This song was originally written for piano and voice, but it is often performed with orchestral accompaniment. There are musical pictures of drums, banjos, and trumpet fanfares. Throughout, the texture is inventive and energetic. The musical curve of this work is similar to the flow of the church services in which Ives grew up. These services would dwell on the hopelessness of the human condition and how powerless everyone is. The last activity of the service would be the singing of an invitational hymn where everyone once again feels strength and rest. Much of Ives's music had this sense of drama. Dissonance and tension would build, only to find rest in simplicity and strength.

    The poem by Vachel Lindsay is focused on one of the founders of the Salvation Army, General William Booth. The text and melodic fragments from the hymn ''Are You Washed in the Blood of the Lamb'' become the refrain of this song, used to rally the troops to protect the poor and oppressed. Another hymn, ''Cleansing Fountain,'' becomes the march of strength at the end. There are suggestions in the score for a chorus to yell ''Hallelujah!'' as the music builds in intensity. The moments of excitement are balanced by tender statements of the hymn.

0:00	Repeating chord imitates a bass drum.
0:17	Repeated chord accompaniment continues.
0:39	Piano begins to play different chords, all dissonant.
1:00	Piano plays unison melody with the voice with supporting chords.
1:19	New texture, angular melodic pattern in the piano; vocal melody is very independent of the piano.
1:43	Both the voice and the piano become more percussive.
1:52	Rhythmic flow becomes more angular. The pulse and musical flow are in conflict.
2:00	Shouts, climax of song, rhythm remains very angular.
2:28	''Are you washed''; tempo and activity dissolve and soften.
2:46	Melody and accompaniment become simple by comparison, less dissonant.
3:09	Repeat.

3:38	Transition to first texture.
3:56	Quote of hymn "Cleansing Fountain."
4:20	Resolution, calm, stability; piano plays traditional hymn setting.
4:44	Repeated dissonant chord fades.
4:57	End.

example, the *Universe* Symphony was to be performed by all humanity on every hill and dale. Although this was an impossible task, he still worked on it. His writing style sparked experimental and nontraditional tendencies in later composers. As a New England transcendentalist, businessman, writer, and composer, Ives takes a unique position in American history.

The music of Gershwin crosses over three different music traditions. Patrons of classical music find his music sophisticated, intelligent, and immediately appealing. The commercial world applauds his genius of song. The jazz world takes his songs as standards for improvisation. His music is so definitive that others who use similar stylistic techniques are immediately compared to the Gershwin sound. His unique musical style is familiar to perhaps more Americans than that of any other American composer. The work that established Gershwin as a significant composer of concert music was *Rhapsody in Blue* in 1924. Commissioned by Paul Whiteman, it was originally written for a jazz band; however, it is most commonly performed today by an orchestra and solo piano. This piece incorporates many of the jazz elements of the day but is not jazz in the strictest sense. Neither does it conform to the expectations of traditional solo concertos. The form of this composition does not follow any traditional concerto structures. It is, however, jazz-flavored concert music full of rich melodies and harmonies.

Gershwin combined his distinctive style with folklike sounds in one of America's most famous operas, *Porgy and Bess.* The work is colorful, using syncopations and blue notes to intensify the soaring melodic lines. Because of the uniqueness of its musical style and the subject matter, this opera initially had a difficult time finding a place in American music. This work deals with the lives and struggles of black Americans living in Charleston, South Carolina. To compose this work Gershwin researched the music and lifestyles of African Americans. He built realistic characters with believable personalities dealing with problems similar to those found in most earlier romantic operas.

George Gershwin
(1898–1937)

DATELINE	BIOGRAPHY
1898	George Gershwin was born in Brooklyn and raised by his parents, who were Russian-Jewish immigrants. He grew up with little attention to music.
1908	After hearing a student play Dvořák's *Humoresque* on violin, he found the inspiration to teach himself to play popular songs on a neighbor's piano. He had his first serious piano lessons three years later, learning a wide range of piano literature.
1913	Gershwin left home at fifteen to work as a salesman in Tin Pan Alley, an area in Manhattan where the music industry was centered. He played songs for prospective buyers of sheet music. He continued to practice classical music to become a popular songwriter and was well aware of the vital relationship between classical and popular music.
1919	He wrote his first Broadway musical, *La, La, Lucille*. The next year he wrote a tremendously successful song, "Swanee," which was recorded by Al Jolson and sold millions of copies.
1920–30s	Gershwin composed a string of exciting and refreshing musicals, including *Lady, Be Good* (1924), *Funny Face* (1927), *Of Thee I Sing* (1931). His brother Ira usually supplied the lyrics. His compositions for the concert hall began in 1924 with *Rhapsody in Blue.* He continued to study composition and traveled to Europe to meet other composers such as Berg, Ravel, and Stravinsky.
1934	He began writing the opera *Porgy and Bess.* Although only mildly successful during his lifetime, it has since been performed all over the world and recently at the Metropolitan Opera.
1937	A wealthy man from his musical successes, he died of a brain tumor at the age of thirty-eight while living in Hollywood.

By 1930 Copland was already an extremely versatile composer. He wrote music typical of twentieth-century composers: dissonant, powerful, and concise. With the Depression, Copland, like many composers, moved stylistically to a more accessible music for the average concert-goer. It is not to say the music is not sophisticated or serious. He wrote

A scene from Gershwin's *Porgy and Bess*

A scene from Copland's ballet *Rodeo*

music for schools, radio and film, chamber music, opera, and symphony. His music is best remembered for its pictures of folklore. His ballets *Billy the Kid, Rodeo,* and *Appalachian Spring* appeared quickly, one after another (1938–44). The music from these ballets is commonly performed today in concerts without the accompanying dance. The music possesses percussive, syncopated rhythms associated with the twentieth century and Copland in particular but is tonal and melodic.

Listening Notes

George Gershwin, *Rhapsody in Blue* (1924).

This piece was originally written for Paul Whiteman's dance band in 1924 for a concert on Lincoln's birthday. It was intended to unite the world of popular music to the world of classical music. Gershwin was commissioned to write the work and appear as the piano soloist. The scoring for both the band and the orchestra was done by Ferde Grofé.

The piece opens with a clarinet trill and **glissando** that leads to a blues theme typical of Gershwin's writing. This opening statement has become a signature of his writing. The use of triplets gives the melody a swinging quality much like the jazz of the early swing era, the use of syncopation and dance rhythms adds to the jazz feeling of the music, and the use of the blues scale yields a decisive American sound.

This single-movement work falls into three large sections. Each section has brilliant virtuoso piano solos. These passages reflect a spirit of improvisation and are typical of Gershwin's own piano skills. The first section develops the opening blues theme, the second section is lively with rhythmic repetitions and syncopations, and the third section is slower, with a soaring theme. The orchestra closes the work in a short but powerful coda.

0:00 Low solo clarinet trill moved upward in a glissando arriving on the main theme. Notice the blues inflections.

0:40 The French horns play a new theme that will be used throughout the work.

0:53 Muted trumpet plays the first theme. The piano enters with another idea that will be developed later.

1:09 Full orchestra tutti.

1:20 Piano solo, no orchestral accompaniment, built on opening theme.

glissando
the continuous sliding up or down in pitch without distinct notes being heard. Trombonists can demonstrate the most obvious glissando when they slide smoothly between notes.

1:38	Display of technique increases.
1:50	Thick rich chords.
2:12	Bass clarinet joins the piano briefly (two times).
2:50	Developmental part, tempo increases.
3:20	March theme played by the full orchestra, the piano plays chords.
3:38	Echoes between the orchestra and piano.
3:55	Swing patterns intensify, snare drum, piano plays accompaniment ideas.
4:20	Clarinet returns and is followed by the march theme.
4:36	A combination of most of the themes fills the active texture.
5:00	Short clarinet solo is followed by a muted trumpet that uses a plunger mute. Full orchestra develops themes.
6:27	A long rhapsodic piano solo begins.
7:03	Modulation and theme development.
7:20	Swinging melodic pattern, tempo slows.
7:50	Opening theme. Horns in accompaniment.
8:19	Tempo almost stops.
8:49	Solo single-note melody (low range). It is repeated with a very simple block chord accompaniment.
9:50	Rapid accompaniment figure begins another display of flashing technique.
10:54	Orchestra plays a romantic theme, lush scoring; no piano.
11:35	Solo violin.
12:28	New livelier texture.
12:53	Piano plays the theme.
13:28	Animated rhythmic accompaniment.
13:42	New repeated-note texture.
14:43	Orchestra enters with low brass and builds to a very dissonant chord.
15:16	Tempo increases.
15:42	Climax. Piano plays the original theme in full chords.
16:13	Coda.
16:41	End.

Aaron Copland
(1900–90)

DATELINE	BIOGRAPHY

1900 Aaron Copland was born in Brooklyn, New York, the son of Russian-Jewish immigrants. His sister gave him his first piano lessons, and by the age of fifteen, he had decided to become a composer.

1918 He graduated from high school and studied harmony and counterpoint with Rubin Goldmark.

1921 He traveled to Paris and became the first American to study with Nadia Boulanger, a master teacher who influenced composers from several countries; she later performed his Symphony for Organ and Orchestra (1924) with the New York and Boston Symphony Orchestras.

1925–27 Upon his return to the United States Copland was inspired to compose strictly American music. The influence of jazz, particularly blues and ragtime, is evident in his *Music for the Theater*. He was twice awarded the Guggenheim Memorial Fellowship.

1930s Copland used jazz, revival hymns, cowboy songs, and American folk tunes to create his compositions; the ballets *Billy the Kid* (1938) and *Rodeo* (1942) were based on American West themes.

1930 He won RCA Victor's Award of $5,000 for his composition *Dance Symphony*.

1939–40 His music was brought to the general public with the film scores for *Of Mice and Men* and *Our Town*.

1942 His *Lincoln Portrait* and *Fanfare for the Common Man* reflected his American patriotism during World War II. Copland became an advocate for contemporary American music, teaching and lecturing at colleges and universities, writing for music journals, and supporting other composers through the American Composers Alliance.

1945 Copland was awarded the Pulitzer Prize for the ballet *Appalachian Spring*, written for Martha Graham.

1949 He won an Academy Award for the score of the motion picture *The Heiress*.

1950s He began using serial technique in his compositions, having been influenced by Stravinsky; he also began his career as a conductor.

1964 He revised and published his book *What to Listen for in Music,* a compilation of his lectures on music. In 1968 he revised an earlier work called *Our New Music* and published it under the title *The New Music 1900–1960.*

1970s Copland traveled as guest conductor, organized concerts of American music, lectured, and wrote about music; he was sent by the U.S. State Department as a musical ambassador to work with composers in South America.

1990 He died in December.

Listening Notes

Aaron Copland, ''Hoe-Down,'' excerpt from *Rodeo* (1942).

Four excerpts from the ballet *Rodeo* are commonly performed as a suite of dances as concert music. They are ''Buckaroo Holiday,'' ''Corral Nocturne,'' ''Saturday Night Waltz,'' and ''Hoe-Down.'' The last dance, ''Hoe-Down,'' is derived from an Old West folk song called ''Bonyparte.'' Notice the syncopation and the use of woodblocks and drums to provide bright percussive contrast to the string orchestra.

0:00 Introduction, cymbal crash, fanfare, strings and brass dialogue.

0:13 Fanfare repeats.

0:18 Strings play melody, wood blocks play irregular rhythms. Notice the accents in unexpected places.

0:33 Rhythm starts and stops in unpredictable places.

0:36 Hoedown theme, xylophone and strings. Notice the ringing notes (open strings) that do not change pitch; this is typical of ''fiddling'' in this folk style.

1:06 Full orchestra.

1:14 Return to the xylophone and strings.

1:31 Trumpet solo, rim shots on the snare drum.

1:39 Oboe solo followed by a violin and clarinet unison solo. Trumpet rejoins the soloistic texture.

1:55 Brass and strings dialogue.

2:02 Full orchestra.

2:15	New rhythmic feeling, wood blocks.
2:25	Tempo slows, trombone plays lower and lower notes.
2:41	Sudden return to string and xylophone theme.
2:53	Full orchestra.
3:00	Coda.
3:14	End.

Duke Ellington
(1899–1974)

DATELINE	BIOGRAPHY

1899 Edward Kennedy Ellington was born in Washington, D.C., into a middle-class family. His regal air earned him the nickname "Duke" while he was still in grade school.

1909? After he was hit accidentally with a baseball bat, his mother decided that piano lessons would be much less dangerous and insisted that he study music.

1916 During high school, Ellington formed his first band and began playing at dances. He was a shrewd businessman and owned his first Cadillac and a house before the age of twenty.

1923–27 Ellington took his band to New York and worked at the Kentucky Club, where the group was well received.

1927–32 The Ellington band became world famous while playing at the Cotton Club in Harlem; Ellington began writing and arranging for the band.

1926–40 Irving Mills served as manager for the Ellington band, arranging for bookings and recordings on several labels.

1930 Ellington's career began to take off; he hired Ivy Anderson as vocalist, increased the size of the band to fifteen pieces, including Johnny Hodges on saxophone and Cootie Williams on trumpet, and began composing specifically for this group.

1939 Ellington began a partnership with composer-arranger Billy Strayhorn, who wrote several songs for the band, including "After All," "Daydream," and the band's theme song, "Take the 'A' Train." Together they wrote "Satin Doll."

1943–50 The Ellington band performed yearly concerts at Carnegie Hall in New York City, introducing a new composition at each performance. Ellington's reputation as a songwriter grew with the popularity of tunes like "Mood Indigo," "Sophisticated Lady," and "In a Sentimental Mood."

1950 Although Ellington continued to write and perform on stage and in movies, the popularity of his band declined; in 1956 the band made a comeback at the Newport Jazz Festival, and once again, he was back on top.

1960s Ellington wrote a number of suites with African, Far Eastern, Middle Eastern, and West Indian themes; he continued to perform with traditionalists as well as new-wave musicians.

1965–73 He wrote three sacred concerts; the first one was performed in San Francisco's Grace Cathedral, the second in New York, and the third was premièred at Westminster Abbey in London. Already suffering from lung cancer, Ellington continued to tour with the band.

1974 The Duke continued his hectic work pace up until three months before his death in New York City.

Jazz developed in America as an art form unique to the United States. It is a history of performances, not detailed compositions. Musical ideas were most commonly hammered out in an improvisatory environment. With the advent of the dance bands in the 1940s came a need for arrangers and composers to organize the activity of many musicians. Duke Ellington was just such a composer/arranger, pianist, and band leader. His compositions, however, relied on the improvisational skills of performers such as Johnny Hodges and Cootie Williams to add unique instrumental colors. Rather than thinking of instruments alone, Ellington built compositions around the sounds of individuals.

Ellington was a prolific composer; he copyrighted 952 compositions, including three sacred concerts, twenty-one suites, three shows, three movie scores, and a ballet. He was perhaps the first composer in jazz to write across such a wide spectrum of styles. His music is loose and free and allows for long improvisations. Because he built many of his compositions around specific individuals, if those people left the band, the music was retired. Some of his songs, such as "Sophisticated Lady," were compared to Debussy because of a similarity in chord construction. His harmonic vocabulary was an important part of his identity.

Listening Notes

Duke Ellington, *Sophisticated Lady* (1933).

This composition fascinated both jazz and classical musicians. The rich chords used to harmonize nearly every note of the melody was compared to the impressionistic sounds of Debussy. There is, however, little evidence that Ellington was influenced by the writings of Debussy. The extensive use of solo instruments minimizes the attention on the lush chords in the background. This example is typical of the innovative harmonic ideas that seemed to flow from the pen of Ellington.

0:00   Piano introduction.

0:09   Trombone plays melody; banjo is the predominant rhythm instrument.

0:26   Melody is repeated with more melodic embellishments.

0:52   Clarinet takes over the melody line; muted brass accompany.

1:15   Muted trumpet assumes the melody.

1:35   Sax plays a variation of the melody in full chords; clarinet plays the highest part.

2:18   Piano solo is typical of the stride piano style.

2:38   Alto sax melody uses inflections and trills to ornament the melody. Woodwinds accompany with chords.

3:00   Tempo slows.

3:08   End.

Composers in America are found in many places: at colleges and universities, in film production, musical theater, jazz bands, commercial and rock performance, and at home simply writing songs. The diversity is remarkable and exciting. These four composers evidence the diversity of sounds found in American music. Copland quoted sounds of early Americana; Ives, Gershwin, and Ellington were examples of the idiom itself.

Topic 8

ETHNO-MUSICOLOGY

If you were asked to select one single piece of music to be played for students studying music around the world, and it had to represent the North American culture, what would it be? Considering the music we have studied so far, such a piece may not exist. There is really no single example of "our music" that could reflect the many cultural/ethnic backgrounds found in America. The diversity in our culture is responsible for its richness and complexity.

By examining other cultures we see our own world in a new light. Although there is a wide spectrum of musical styles around the world, there remains a sense of global unity in the arts. If we, as music students, learn to see value in the many styles in our own culture, we can learn to see the value in cultures throughout the world.

We have listened to music from over a 1,000-year period. Not all the sounds were familiar or likable; however, through study they have become more understandable. All this music has had a direct impact on our culture. The music we study next will be but an infinitesimal glimpse of the world. It will, nevertheless, suggest a basis for sounds that appear in the art and folk music of other cultures throughout their history. **Ethnomusicology** is the study of musical styles associated with specific ethnic groups. Even within cultures that seem homogeneous to outsiders, there are strata and subgroupings that escape our immediate

ethnomusicology
the study of music of different ethnic groups in light of tradition and culture.

■ *287*

attention. Ethnomusicologists work with details specific to each culture, tracing heritage and development.

 ## *Music from Other Cultures*

Although non-Western music shares the same components (rhythm, melody, and form) as Western European music, the priorities may be very different. For example, melody in one culture may be of the utmost importance, while rhythm may dominate in another. Whatever the priorities, familiarity and exposure make the music understandable and enjoyable. At first, music from other cultures may sound fascinating, even strange, because we lack meaningful association to tradition. Those parts of the music that contain sounds similar to the music from our culture will naturally make more sense to us.

Through soundtracks from movies, we have been given an idea of some of the sounds particular to other cultures. We must be aware, however, that the music used in soundtracks is not necessarily an honest representation of another culture's music. Many times it is written using familiar instruments and scales with melodic and harmonic alterations to give "the impression" of another country. Like most stereotypes, however, there is likely to be a modicum of truth in what we hear.

 ## *Folk Music: Unique Sounds from Unique Cultures*

Over the last twenty years the world of sound has become more integrated because of the growth in audio and video communications. It is difficult to be surprised by musical sounds different from ours because documentaries and satellite communications bring the arts from other countries directly into our homes. Like Europe and America, each country has a unique musical development generated by its folk music. The older an ethnic culture, the more significant the roots of its folk music. When compared to what has developed over centuries in Asia or Africa, relatively young countries such as the United States have a very short history of folk music.

Aside from the songs of native Americans and the early European settlers, American music has developed alongside technology. As a result it has been recorded and transported all over the world in its very young state. To some extent, today's music in America is also the world's. Those cultures that developed prior to this accelerating technology enjoy a more intimate musical tradition full of meaning and expression. In many countries folk music remains a vital part of its heritage and ethnic identity.

Folk music is shaped, transformed, and communicated largely through **oral tradition.** The music, once heard and memorized, is passed on to anyone who wishes to listen. The composer or originator, in most cases, remains unknown. Songs were used in preliterate societies to communicate history, society rules, and morals. In highly developed musical styles, as found in India and China, music played an important role in religion and philosophy. The significance of music is, therefore, tied directly to the cultures' needs and beliefs. All aspects of a culture—language, literature, religion, family, and governance—contribute to understanding that culture.

oral tradition
in the folk tradition, information, history, and culture were passed from generation to generation verbally. Many cultural traits are still communicated in this manner.

Perhaps it is unfair to look only at the folk music of a culture to understand music around the world. However, from folk music comes the organic material that has fed the developing art music associated with any culture. We saw with Ives, Copland, Gershwin, and Ellington (Topic 7) that America's musical heritage is a blend of music imported from Europe, jazz, and now rock. We cannot forget, however, that America has another important musical tradition that nearly disappeared, songs of the native American. We can only speculate that such nearly forgotten music exists in every culture. As in America, many cultures are not always aware of their own musical roots.

Dividing the Octave into Scales

The influence of folk music on the development of art music is profound; however, the level of influence varies from country to country. In China, for instance, the sounds of its native music permeate its opera performances. Chinese opera sounds very different from Western European opera due primarily to the difference in scale system. In many cultures the octave is divided differently. Our Western European ear is accustomed to twelve equal divisions in the octave. In China a **pentatonic scale** (five notes) is the basis for much of the characteristic "Oriental sound." Japanese melodies are also built on a variation of the pentatonic scale. In Africa three-note scales **(tritonic)** and seven-note scales **(heptatonic)** are combined with melodic patterns using whole steps and half steps. The most complex scale patterns are found in India where notes of a scale are divided by distances less than a half step. These **microtonal** scales lie far outside our listening experience. Many in our culture have difficulty perceiving such small intervals.

pentatonic scale
a scale with only five notes in the octave; a fundamental scale in Oriental music.
tritonic scale
a three-note scale used in African music.
heptatonic scale
a seven-note scale used in African music.
microtonal scale
scales that have intervals less than the half step.

Sounds from Several Cultures

Following is a series of listening examples showing the unique sounds of several cultures. In each case the folk music is a small but significant part of that culture's musical and social identity. Notice the similarities and differences of all these examples. Over the years each culture adopted sounds it liked and dropped those it disliked. It is interesting to see that sounds dropped from Western European music still exist in other parts of the world.

Japan

Listening Notes

koto
a Japanese harplike stringed instrument.

sho
a mouth organ with pipes similar to a pipe organ; a traditional Japanese instrument.

Japan (Gagaku): Imperial Sho Koto Chant.

This selection is performed by male singers intoning a slow, low traditional dance. They are accompanied by the **koto,** a plucked stringed instrument, and the **sho,** a mouth organ with small pipes. The sho plays a unison melody four octaves higher than the singers. The dissonant sound you hear is deliberately produced by playing the sho slightly out of tune against the singers. As the parts go in and out of tune, a feeling of tension and release is achieved. The koto is the primary source of percussive rhythm.

Japanese musicians performing in traditional dress on traditional instruments

 *Rhythm*

The basic heartbeat of music, rhythm, is another element that varies dramatically from country to country. Music in Africa, India, and Latin America has contrasting, complex rhythms that are played against one another. These combinations are called **polyrhythms.** The rhythmic patterns in American music are very simple compared to those found in India and Africa. Our cultural heritage is based on melody and harmony supported by regular, repeated rhythmic patterns. Only in the twentieth century has the concept of extended patterns and **modulated rhythm** (shifting meter) been fully developed in America. Other cultures focused on rhythmic polyphony rather than the melodic polyphony that dominated Western composition.

polyrhythm
the simultaneous use of two or more contrasting rhythms. Such rhythms often conflict with and blur the beat.

modulated rhythm
the constant movement from meter to meter in a short period of time. There is no regular pattern of beats.

 Harmony

Harmony is primarily a Western development. The most basic of all harmonic concepts is a **drone,** as heard in the bagpipes of Scotland; one or two pitches are sustained to support a freely floating melody. The early stages of polyphony found in European music developed in a similar fashion in other cultures; that is, multiple melodies slowly becoming harmony. There are other sophisticated forms of harmony in folk music; for example, when a melody, sung in unison, is varied by each performer, it produces a combination of unique melodic ideas. Two simultaneous versions of the same melody create an improvised form of harmony called **heterophony.**

drone
a long sustained sound used to support melodies above. This is a very early form of harmonic development.

heterophony
singing a melody in unison but with unique melodic ornaments between performers. This is an improvised form of harmony particular to folk music.

 India

Listening Notes

India: Sanai Gath (Raga Kaphi).

The Indian instrument most familiar to Americans is probably the **sitar,** a large stringed instrument with movable frets. However, many other sounds are associated with traditional Indian music. In this case drumming sounds that accompany most melodic instruments are heard. The two drums used

sitar
a fretted stringed instrument used in India. The frets are movable, allowing for microtonal scales.

tabla
a traditional drum used in Indian music.
baya
a drum used in Indian music.
tala
a rhythmic cycle that is repeated by drums while a raga is improvised above.
sanai
a double-reed snake-charmer's pipe used in music from India.
raga
a pattern of notes or scale on which an improvised melody is performed; used in Indian music.

here are the **tabla** and the **baya.** Drumming patterns in India are based on very sophisticated rhythmic cycles called **talas.** A tala varies in complexity from two or three notes to very long patterns. The melodic instrument is the **sanai,** a double-reed snake-charmer's pipe. Notice the sliding effects between pitches. The notes for this melody come from a traditional melodic pattern called a **raga.** There are hundreds of different ragas on which to base a performance. The time of day, the day of the week, and the year often govern which raga is to be used. The octave in Indian music is divided into twenty-two notes. Each raga is a scale of pitches selected from this microtonal series. The chosen raga and tala are used to build long and complicated improvisations. Notice the drone that adds harmonic support to the flowing melody of the sanai.

Ravi Shankar playing the sitar, accompanied by a tabla (drums) and a tambura (a drone instrument)

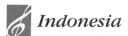

Indonesia

Listening Notes

Indonesia, Bali (Gender Wajang): Gamelan Orchestra.

This group of percussion instruments creates a surprising amount of melody. There are several types and sizes of tuned percussion instruments—gongs, bells, and xylophone—tuned to a pentatonic scale that makes it virtually impossible to create discordant note combinations. Notice how the dynamic levels shift throughout the selection. The texture is full of syncopated ideas within a very fluid tempo. The amount of improvisation varies. The accompaniment is generally very free with improvised ornaments and rhythms. The resonance of the music is pleasant to a Westerner's ears. The performance ends with an increase in tempo and melodic activity. This music influenced composers such as Debussy who admired the richness of its sonorities.

Balinese dancers with gamelan orchestra

China

Listening Notes

China: Hu-kin and Butterfly harp.

The **hu-kin** is a two-string instrument that is played with a bow. The bow is placed between the two strings, ready to move to the upper or lower string. The **butterfly harp** has short strings played by very small bamboo hammers. The two instruments play the same melody in unison. The melody is based on a pentatonic scale; the complexity of melodic shape is due partly to the microtonal ornamentation. Notice the long phrases and contrasting short phrases. The pattern of phrasing is in sharp contrast to the regularity of Western phrasing.

hu-kin
a two-string Chinese instrument played with a bow.
butterfly harp
a Chinese instrument with very short strings and played with small bamboo hammers.

A chinese instrumental ensemble performing on traditional instruments

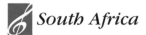
South Africa

Listening Notes

South Africa, Zululand: Flutes and Body Harp.

This performance is based on two simple repetitive melodic ideas of three notes each. When compared with the focused flute sound of Europe and America, the flutes are very breathy. The strings of the **body harp** are beaten with fingernails. The tone is produced by a calabash gourd that holds the bow-and-arrowlike harp. The chantlike repetitions have subtle variations in inflection; such a performance could possibly continue for quite a long period.

body harp
a bow-and-arrowlike harp with one to three strings found in South Africa. The strings are strummed with the fingernail.

A native Zulu war dance performed in South Africa

 *Native American*

Listening Notes

Navajo, American Indian: Ribbon Dance.

The unpitched instruments in this dance music are typical of the sounds used to accompany native American chant melodies. The drum and shaker or rattle were products of their immediate habitat; the drum was made from stretched animal skin and the shaker was made from beads strung around a gourd. The vocal quality is nasal, projecting easily through the percussion accompaniment. The melody is shared by a leader and two other singers who join in on the repeated phrases. The melodic pattern is a sophisticated balance of vocal **call-response.**

call-response
a musical dialogue between two musical statements; one musician states a phrase and the other fills in the gaps between the phrases.

A Plains Indian dance group walks from the ceremonial grounds after a performance at the Inter-Tribal Indian Ceremonial in Gallup, New Mexico

Topic 9

COMPOSING FOR MUSICAL THEATER

Musical theater has become a very popular part of American and European society. Since their beginnings in the late 1800s musicals have grown in scope and flair, incorporating many of the technological advances associated with stage and film. But at the heart of contemporary musicals is a plot communicated through song and empowered by music. The balance between words and music shifted at each stage of development. Unlike opera, understanding the words has always been a fundamental concern in musicals. Depending on the quality of the voices the size of the orchestra fluctuated. Voices in musical comedy are usually not as developed as in opera. Increased usage of amplification has allowed the size and volume of the pit orchestra to grow. Naturally, the singers also require amplification. Compared with the early musicals, the textures composed and performed today can be very dense and very loud.

The visual aspects of musical theater have developed along with the music. Lighting, costumes, and even location of the audience and performers have changed significantly. For example, in the musical *Starlight Express* (1984) the entire cast is on roller skates, moving through the stage and part of the audience on ramps. Musical theater today is a multimedia spectacle involving all branches of the performing arts: music, theater, visual arts, sound, and lighting.

Many musicals have been made into movies that differ dramatically from performances live on stage. Music performed live is immediate and cannot be redone if mistakes occur. Television and film can be edited into a "perfect" performance from piecemeal performances taped earlier. Composers must anticipate the various conditions for which the music is written. When a musical for stage is made into a movie, it requires more music and often a much larger orchestra. Stage productions and movie productions of the same work can and must vary considerably to accommodate the medium of performance.

minstrel shows
early American touring groups providing music and comedy.

burlesque
an early American form of entertainment with skits, gags, and music.

vaudeville
similar to minstrel shows. A source of popular entertainment in the early part of the twentieth century in America.

 ## The Development of Musical Theater

In 1866 a show called *Black Crook* opened the door to a new form of entertainment. It was perhaps the first musical to have a continuing plot to tie together a string of acts. Previously musical theater was primarily defined as **minstrel shows, burlesque,** or **vaudeville.** These shows had no story line; they were just a series of unrelated musical events. The mixture of opera, ballet, and operettas from Europe finally merged into an American form with the musical *The Book* in 1879. For the first time, the songs and dances were woven into a plot concerned with present-day

An early production of Florenz Ziegfield's *Showboat*

events. The term ***musical comedy*** became synonymous with the term *musical theater;* however, some of the later plots would prove to be less comic than dramatic.

The first notable composer to help define a new form of musical theater was George M. Cohan. His immediate predecessors, Victor Herbert and Sigmund Romberg, were immigrants who leaned heavily on the operetta traditions of Europe. Cohan's musical *Forty-Five Minutes from Broadway* in 1906 was instrumental in breaking ties with European tradition. Composer Jerome Kern further developed the American style in New York during World War I. When Kern teamed with lyricist Oscar Hammerstein II, the first mature American musical, *Show Boat,* was performed in 1927. George and Ira Gershwin followed with a political satire *Of Thee I Sing* in 1931, winning the Pulitzer Prize for drama. The 1920s and 1930s were fertile with composers and lyricists. Cole Porter and Irving Berlin joined Gershwin and Kern as leading composers of this period. The most famous team of the 1930s was composer Richard Rodgers and lyricist Lorenz Hart. The range of topics on which plots were built expanded greatly during this period, moving from themes of romantic love to subjects that were a little more controversial, even political.

The next major step in musical comedy came with Rodgers and Hammerstein's show *Oklahoma!* in 1943. Until this show the integration of plot, song, and dance was still uneven. *Oklahoma!* showed a new level of unity in both music and lyrics. Rather than a story with songs, the drama successfully integrated music and plot. The musicals most commonly performed by schools and community theaters today attest to the enduring success of Rodgers and Hammerstein: *Carousel* (1945), *South Pacific* (1949), *The King and I* (1951), and *The Sound of Music* (1959).

Musical theater has often been the place where the impossible becomes the possible. As in opera, individuals are characterized by the music they sing. There are difficult transitions to make in every work that has both dialogue and music. How, for example, does one move from spoken text to singing? In opera the problem was solved by eliminating all spoken text and substituting **recitatives** to provide dialogue. American musicals, on the other hand, have spoken dialogue and must somehow move into song. In the early movie musicals the plot solved the problem. Think back on the number of Fred Astaire movies that were basically a love story about two performers. The blur between performance and personal life made for easy transitions. The musicals of the thirties and forties were dominated by plots about dancers and singers who had good excuses to sing and dance—that is, a show within a show.

musical comedy
a generic name for American musical theater.

recitative
a declamatory vocal style used to tell of action or to relate a text without repetition. It is accompanied by a basso continuo.

Rodgers and Hammerstein

Oklahoma! was instrumental in making the move away from shows about singers and dancers. The singing and dancing became expressive of the mood and condition of the actors and their roles.

West Side Story is a surprising mixture of plot and conditions. It is not a show about a show at all; on the contrary, it is about gang culture.

A scene from *West Side Story*

In the musical, the gangs sing and dance, which is not at all realistic. The music is the glue holding the drama together. Leonard Bernstein shapes the musical much like a symphonic composer oversees the development of motives and themes. In fact, the last scene is an overwhelming resolution of the musical tension built up through the last several scenes. Although the situation is hardly realistic, the drama is effective, woven together by motives and themes.

The words are sung to communicate and not sung with an operatic projection. Clarity of words is required to draw the listener into the plot. In contrast to opera, one is not required to know the plot in advance. It is communicated through the performance.

Leonard Bernstein
(1918–90)

DATELINE	BIOGRAPHY
1918	Leonard Bernstein was born in Lawrence, Massachusetts. At the age of eleven he began studying piano with a teacher who not only taught him technique but encouraged him to study musical scores and to compose.
1935–39	After graduating from the Latin School in Boston, Bernstein attended Harvard College, studying piano and composition.
1939–41	Bernstein studied conducting and orchestration at the Curtis Institute of Music.
1940–41	These summers were spent at the Berkshire Music Center at Tanglewood, where he became assistant conductor for Serge Koussevitsky, conductor of the Boston Symphony Orchestra.
1943	Bernstein was working as assistant conductor of the New York Philharmonic when the sudden illness of guest conductor Bruno Walter led to his public debut and instant acclaim as a brilliant conductor.
1944	His first real success as a composer came when the Pittsburgh Symphony introduced his work *Jeremiah* Symphony; this same year he wrote the score to the Broadway show *On the Town,* which was a huge success.
1945–48	Bernstein served as musical director and conductor of the New York City Center Orchestra; this led to appearances as guest conductor for orchestras all over the world.

1949 He performed as the solo pianist with the Boston Symphony, which performed his composition *The Age of Anxiety.*

1951 Bernstein married Felicia Cohn, a native of Costa Rica; they had three children.

1953 He became the first American-born conductor to perform at the La Scala opera house in Milan; this year also marked the debut of his second Broadway musical, *Wonderful Town.*

1954 His musical *Candide* was praised by the critics, but failed at the box office; a later revision in 1973 proved much more successful.

1957 *West Side Story,* music by Bernstein, lyrics by Stephen Sondheim, and choreography by Jerome Robbins, became a Broadway smash hit.

1959 In addition to his musical compositions and success as a pianist and conductor, Bernstein also wrote several books, including *Joy of Music* (1959), *Leonard Bernstein's Young People's Concerts for Reading and Listening* (1962), and *Findings* (1982).

1980–90 Bernstein continued to compose and conduct concert and theater music; his contributions to the music world have been well recognized. His honors include fifteen honorary degrees, nine Grammy awards, eleven Emmys, the Kennedy Center Honors, and the Lifetime Achievement Award from the National Academy of Recording Arts and Sciences.

1990 He died of pneumonia in October of 1990 only four days after announcing his retirement.

Listening Notes

Leonard Bernstein, "Cool" from *West Side Story* (1957).

book (musical)
the words to a musical
comedy.

Lyricist Stephen Sondheim wrote this libretto (called a **book**) based on Shakespeare's *Romeo and Juliet.* The setting is New York where territorial rights are being fought over by a Caucasian gang and a Puerto Rican gang. The ex-leader of the Sharks falls in love with the sister of the Puerto Rican gang leader. The music is based on jazz styles that matured in the 1940s and early 1950s. The experience gained by Bernstein as conductor of the New York Philharmonic undoubtedly helped him produce a brilliantly orchestrated score.

This scene is both a ballet and a song (ensemble). Some of the gang members are scared and some are angry while others are trying to cool them both down. The orchestra sounds more like a contemporary jazz band than a symphony. The rhythms swing and the dancing is based on jazz movement. In 1957 the music and dance appeared aggressive and contemporary. It was a break from the more traditional orchestrations typical of this time in musical theater. There is dialogue, dance, and ensemble sections in this song. The texture varies considerably. The writing is sophisticated and enduring.

0:00 Introduction. Scoring is typical of the cool jazz style—vibraharp, piano, muted brass.

0:11 Voice enters; notice the finger snaps as part of the rhythm.

1:00 Ballet segment begins, string bass remains the harmonic and rhythmic support, pizzicato.

1:04 Solo muted brass lines and accents.

1:20 Growling brass, instrumentation like the introduction, drummer plays ride pattern on the high-hat.

1:53 Strings enter with solo woodwinds.

2:00 The texture becomes more and more polyphonic. Notice the low bass melody and heavy accents.

2:25 Drum solo filled in with brass section shouts. The instrumentation is now more traditional to the big jazz bands.

2:51 Notice the varying instrumentations and how the swing intensifies.

3:17 Last verse with loud big band fills.

3:33 Return to the first instrumentation with finger snaps.

3:56 End.

Musical theater since the 1920s has been a reflection of the times. It has never been more evident than with the musicals starting in 1964 with *Fiddler on the Roof*. The story follows the plight of Jewish oppression during the Russian Revolution. The music has been adopted by Jewish Americans as their own. This production focused on aspects of the ethnic diversity, a statement with which all Americans can identify. Following this production came political/social works such as *Hair* (1967) and the 1950s rock 'n' roll musical *Grease* in 1972. These works are time pieces in American pop art. The statements seem dated today but were relevant to their time due to the interpretive and persuasive nature of the plots. More recently, *A Chorus Line*, the longest running show in history, showed the plight of dancers in a competitive world. The individuals in the chorus line are trying to survive in a very competitive performance environment. Each hopeful auditioner expresses the need to perform, in spite of his or her personal problems. The plot returns to a show about a show.

Musical theater is generally reflective of society; however, there are examples where they involve more controversial topics such as *The Three-Penny Opera* (1928) by Bertolt Brecht with music by Kurt Weill. This modern version of the 1728 English **ballad opera** *The Beggar's Opera* deals with the subculture of beggars and thieves, portraying a very cynical outlook on society. This work has been successful in both America and Europe.

Except for the miraculous successes of an English writer, Andrew Lloyd Webber, the popularity of musical theater has suffered over the last few years. His talents have kept his musicals playing for years simultaneously in London, New York, and Los Angeles. His expensive productions are flashy and spectacular, with strange, unbelievable plots and settings; however, they are infectious in their newness. A cast of cats or a cast on roller skates are made believable and fun.

Over the years musical theater has, at times, required large voices; however, the need for words and believability usually required a more natural-sounding voice, one that is easily understood. Musicals rarely incorporated the operatic voice. Voices for musical theater and opera are trained differently; when compared to the expansive opera voice, vocal range and flexibility in musicals are limited. In 1987 Andrew Lloyd Webber, in collaboration with lyricist Charles Hart, produced *The Phantom of the Opera* where the subject matter required the use of operatic voices. This work enjoys a unique association with both opera and musical theater. Although it has not been adopted by the operatic community, it is ambitious both musically and technically when compared with more traditional productions of musical theater. Operatic voices and a large orchestra are required.

At times the comparison with serious opera is unquestionable; other times the comparison with contemporary commercial song is equally unquestionable. For this reason *The Phantom of the Opera* has successfully drawn fans of both opera and popular music. There is a new balance between sung and spoken dialogue. Spoken dialogue is reduced to a minimum; as a result, the music never stops. There is no time in this work where the orchestra is not actively contributing to the emotional development of the plot. In this work recitative is used successfully for the first time in musical theater. Lines of text are set without rhyme or

ballad opera
a light and often humorous dramatic form of opera performed specifically in England.

A scene from *Phantom of the Opera*

regular phrasing. The text drives the flow of the music. In this respect this work is more an opera than a musical.

Another comparison to opera is the **ensemble finale** where, like Verdi, four or five individuals sing separate and overlapping lines. Each expresses a different emotion and sings a different text. At these moments it is important to know in advance what is taking place in the plot. There is little chance to decipher the words successfully. These ensembles are clearly patterned after models from nineteenth-century opera. The association to classical music is paralleled by an equal association to contemporary rock styles. The works of Lloyd Webber are products of a well-trained classical musician with a strong affinity for rock. His writing follows in the tradition of the musicals *Hair* and The Who's *Tommy* where traditional styles fuse with popular styles.

ensemble finale
the final scene of an operatic section where several singers perform at the same time but sing independent texts and often express different moods; for example, Italian opera.

Andrew Lloyd Webber
(1948–   )

DATELINE	BIOGRAPHY
1948	Andrew Lloyd Webber was born in London. He grew up in a bohemian flat in London's South Kensington district, began studying violin at age three, and later took up piano and horn.
1957	John Lill, a British concert pianist who lived with the Lloyd Webbers at the time, encouraged his interest in concerts and the opera; by the age of nine, he had composed his first song.
1960	Lloyd Webber's aunt took him to see the stage production of *South Pacific,* and he became enthralled with the idea of composing for musical theater.
1962	Andrew won a scholarship to London's Westminster School and while there began producing student shows.
1965(?)	While attending Magdalen College at Oxford, he met and formed a partnership with lyricist Tim Rice, a law student with a strong interest in rock music.
1967	The partnership produced its first successful hit with *Joseph and the Amazing Technicolor Dreamcoat*, originally written for London's St. Paul School; rave reviews by a music critic led to a recording contract.
1971	The Lloyd Webber/Rice rock musical hit, *Jesus Christ Superstar*, told the story of the last seven days of Jesus through the eyes of Judas Iscariot and produced some number one hit songs, including "I Don't Know How to Love Him." This same year Andrew married Sarah Tudor Hugill; they had two children.
1976	*Evita*, the story of Juan and Eva Perón, was meant to be an allegory reflecting the political situation in England in the mid-1970s; after the success of this show, the partnership with Tim Rice was dissolved. They reunited in 1986 to write a show for Queen Elizabeth's sixtieth birthday.
1981	Lloyd Webber's first success on his own was *Cats*, which became another smash hit in the United States and England; his obvious musical talent plus an extraordinarily keen business sense had turned him into a multimillionaire.
1982	The death of his father, an organist, led him to write *Requiem* using the liturgical text of the Latin Mass; from this work came the hit song and video "Pia Jesus."

1983 Lloyd Webber divorced his first wife; the next year he married soprano Sarah Brightman, who had performed in the cast of *Cats*.

1984 *Starlight Express*, a fantasy rock musical performed entirely on roller skates, became another box-office success.

1987–8 Lloyd Webber's wife, Sarah, starred in his operalike musical, *The Phantom of the Opera*.

1990s Lloyd Webber continues to write and produce shows (*Aspects of Love*, 1990); his London-based production company, the Really Useful Group, produces shows, records, and videos and owns its own studios and theaters.

Listening Notes

Andrew Lloyd Webber, Act I, Scenes 4 and 5 from *The Phantom of the Opera* (1987).

As you listen to this excerpt, notice the various levels of vocal technique. There are extremes between full operatic voice and spoken dialogue. The use of microphones placed on each lead singer allows for this contrast. Scene 4 is the journey to the labyrinth underground where the Phantom lives. The orchestration is dominated by electronic synthesizers. Christine, one of the singers in the opera being staged above, is mesmerized by the music of the Phantom and becomes the vehicle for his music. In Scene 5 the Phantom persuades her to become the expression of his music:

"You alone
can make my song take flight—
help me make the music of the night . . ."

Christine is caught in a conflict between her lover Raoul and the hypnotic control of the Phantom. Notice the orchestral control throughout these two scenes.

Scene 4: "The Phantom of the Opera"

0:00 Introduction, pipe organ, synthesized drums and bass. Christine and the Phantom are in a boat on an underground lake.

0:18 Christine sings, accompaniment continues.

1:02 Phantom sings the second verse. Similar accompaniment, but with a larger orchestra.

1:46 Verse three, Christine sings and the Phantom ends the phrase. Notice the sound effects in the accompaniment.

2:02 They sing in unison.

2:21 Interlude with sound effects.

2:39 The Phantom begins the next verse; they sing in unison to end the verse.

3:15 Notice the dissonance in the accompaniment. Rhythm patterns remain rigid, the Phantom speaks lines while Christine sings melodic lines but without words.

4:12 Climax ends leaving the sound of the pipe organ and the Phantom.

Scene 5: "The Music of the Night"

0:00 Phantom sings, low strings and harp accompany.

0:29 Cello finishes the line (it will be sung at the end of the song).

0:41 More traditional orchestration, light woodwinds, strings, string bass playing pizzicato. Contrasts with the electronic setting of the previous scene.

1:44 Word painting for the word *soar*.

2:02 Return to original melody. Notice the string glissando. The orchestra begins to swell.

2:41 French horn solo, full string section.

3:02 Climax.

3:25 Last statement of the melody.

4:04 Full orchestra concludes the verse.

4:29 The Phantom ends the scene softly. Notice the surprising chord in the final cadence.

5:09 End.

Topic 10

COMPOSING IN THE STUDIO

The recording studio is now a common environment for composers and performers in most contemporary styles. Every group that records must now perform to microphones as well as to live audiences. The pressure of performance is still present; in fact, the pressure for a perfect performance is greater than in a live situation because any flaw will be noticed with each repeated listening. There is one comfort: Errors can be redone. However, the time to rerecord is expensive. Recordings must sustain many listenings. Errors seem to grow in volume each time the recording is played. Musicians in the studio are called to play in an isolated environment. There is no audience with which to communicate. The microphone becomes an extension of the performer and the product is stored on tape.

Many musicians are not suited to perform in both live and studio situations. Some studio musicians today never perform live. Some musicians blend the two experiences; that is, they have prerecorded music to which they play or sing. It is not uncommon today to have the entire performance on stage prerecorded and the soloists **lip sync.**

lip sync
mouthing the words to a prerecorded tape.

By looking at two contemporary composers who have grown up during this transition from live performance to recorded performance, we can appreciate how music production has changed in the last fifty years. Henry Mancini and Quincy Jones were both involved in jazz and commercial music. Their personal styles have deviated from one another considerably; however, they both have shown tremendous endurance and understanding of the composer's role in the many aspects of studio music.

 ## New Concepts in Notation and the Lack of It

Since the invention of the phonograph, studio recording has involved both concert and commercial music. Classical concert music is often recorded during a performance in front of an audience with the musicians reading traditional notation; the composer is rarely involved. Commercial songs, on the other hand, are rarely notated in the same way. Most groups rehearse with the composer, and through **collective composition** build a final product. The studio often serves as an environment for composition and performance. Classical music, on the other hand, rarely uses the studio to "work out ideas" or develop performance relationships.

collective composition musicians working together to complete a composition by playing ideas specific to their instruments; rhythm sections are most commonly involved in this process.

Through the early 1970s the process of recording film scores reflected the notational tradition of classical music; musicians arrived at the studio prepared to play whatever was placed in front. In these cases musicians were hired for their reading skills rather than for their improvisational skills. Only the rhythm section was asked to produce musical ideas in light of the shorthand notation supplied by the composer.

Mancini typifies the diverse abilities of studio composers. He has shown the flexibility to compose both original music and imitative music. He, like other studio composers such as Oliver Nelson and Lalo Schifrin, is capable of writing music that replicates almost any style. Composers for film and television are required to produce chameleonlike musical sounds quickly and accurately.

mix (mixed) the process of blending instruments together into a musical whole. In the modern studio, mixing is performed electronically by engineers. In orchestras and ensembles, mixing is performed by the performers themselves.

Because the studio is a controlled environment, instruments that are difficult to hear in live performance can be heard easily. A flute and electric guitar can be made equals in volume in a studio. Because the instruments are recorded separately the balance between instruments is not determined until all the parts are **mixed** together by the audio engineer. Even the softest sound of a flute can compete with the loudest sound of a full brass section. The control is now in the hands of the engineers, not the instrumentalists. Mancini was one of the first to take advantage of new instrumental combinations available through studio manipulation. For decades his orchestrational abilities produced some of the most popular sonorities in commercial music.

Henry Mancini
(1924–   )

DATELINE	BIOGRAPHY

1924 Henry Mancini was born in Cleveland to Italian immigrants. The family soon moved to Pennsylvania where his father worked in the steel mills. He began flute lessons at eight years old and piano at twelve; he later played in the Sons of Italy band with his father.

1937 Mancini was first flutist in the Pennsylvania All-State Band; during his high school years he began writing out jazz band arrangements taken off Artie Shaw and Glenn Miller albums.

1938–40 Mancini studied piano, theory, and composition with Max Adkins in Pittsburgh.

1941 After high school Mancini entered the Music School of the Carnegie Institute of Technology; he also spent a short time at Juilliard School of Music before being drafted into the Army.

1945 After World War II he was hired as pianist and arranger for the Glenn Miller Band.

1947 He married Virginia O'Connor, a vocalist with the Meltones, Mel Torme's group; they had a son and two daughters.

1947–51 These years were spent doing freelance work for singers and jazz groups.

1952–58 After relocating to Hollywood, Mancini worked for Universal Studios writing film scores, including *The Glenn Miller Story* (1954) and *The Benny Goodman Story* (1956).

1958 Mancini met and began collaborating with director Blake Edwards, writing television themes for shows such as ''Mr. Lucky'' and ''Peter Gunn.'' The theme song to ''Peter Gunn'' and the subsequent album earned him his first two Grammys.

1960 He returned to motion picture work and began writing prolifically for movies including *Breakfast at Tiffany's* (1961) and *Days of Wine and Roses* (1962); both ''Moon River'' and the ''Theme from Days of Wine and Roses'' earned him Oscars.

1960–80 Mancini's credits include over 100 movies, sixty albums, four Oscars, twenty Grammys, and seven gold records. Some of his more well-known film scores include *Charade*, *Victor/Victoria*, and *The Pink Panther* and all of its sequels. During these years he continued to record his music and conduct his own orchestra.

1970s Mancini had the honor of serving as guest conductor for orchestras all over the world, including the London Symphony. He has conducted several Academy Award presentations.

1980s Mancini lives in Los Angeles and continues to write and arrange music for films and television; he is possibly the most prolific writer of commercial music to date.

Listening Notes

reverb
the echo effect that is now produced by digital signal processors; early reverb came from the room or hall in which the music was performed.

effect
the process of changing the original sound of an instrument. The most common effects are echo, delay, and chorus.

signal processing
to take a recorded sound and alter it using various musical effects such as reverb or delay.

third stream
jazz that incorporates elements of classical music such as modern classical sounds, orchestral instruments, and/or classical composing techniques.

cool jazz
a post-bebop style that softened some of the aggressive elements of bebop. The melody was played in a more comfortable range, the rhythm section used fewer explosive sounds, and the tempos were more relaxed than in bebop. Also called West Coast jazz.

Henry Mancini, ''A Cool Shade of Blue'' (1959).

Exotic instruments heard in this selection were rarely used until the late 1950s. The alto flute in the introduction, the duet between the alto sax and alto flute, strings playing pizzicato, soft vibraphone solos, and a twenty-piece string section are just a few of the colors Mancini developed in the studio. In addition to the many instrumental colors, notice the rich echo effect of early studio recordings. The instruments sound vibrant as if they are in a very large hall. **Reverb** (echo) was the first **effect** to be used extensively in the studio. Today many forms of **signal processing** are available to enhance the natural sound of acoustic instruments. Electronic effects are a natural extension of the practice of using mutes for strings and brass. They are all attempts to shape and redirect the tone of an instrument.

The underlying style of this piece leans heavily on **third stream** and **cool** or **West Coast** jazz (see Chapter 11). Mancini was an important contributor to these jazz styles. He used a more subdued rhythm section than typical of bebop, and he wrote most of the melodic lines in comfortable ranges where they are most resonant. These sounds were very popular in the commercial music market. This music is typical of soundtracks for movies in the 1960s.

0:00 Alto flute introduction.

0:06 Bass and drums enter.

0:13 Melody played by alto flute and alto saxophone in unison.

0:26 Strings enter.

0:40 String section takes over the lead, muted trombone figures in background.

0:54	Trombone section playing the same rhythm but different notes (solo).
1:04	Improvised piano solo, strings accompany, bass and drums continue jazz patterns.
1:35	Alto flute solo, improvised.
2:01	Muted trombones (unison) dialogue with a solo guitar.
2:28	Vibraharp solo, sustained chords in accompaniment first by woodwinds, then by strings.
2:56	Single trombone note and fall, bass solo (walking patterns), drums become more animated.
3:10	Return to the original melody and scoring.
3:37	Coda.
3:44	End.

 ## *The Studio Musician: Multitrack Recordings*

Composing, rehearsing, and recording music has changed dramatically in the last thirty years. Music no longer has to be performed with all the musicians playing at the same time. With the development of **multitrack recording** techniques, musicians can be brought into the studio to perform their parts in turn rather than together. The music is **layered** up from the fundamental rhythm section to the soloists. At each stage the musicians enter the studio and perform to the previously recorded **tracks.** The communication between musicians that had been a necessary part of all ensemble performances moved in a new direction. The first performers to record must be aware of what will be recorded later; the subsequent performers must respond to what they hear, knowing that they will not be able to influence the parts already recorded on tape.

 ## *Production Techniques*

It is the role of a producer to guide and coordinate the composer, musicians, and technical engineers so that the final project represents a "total package" and not a "sum of the recorded parts." Quincy Jones has been involved for years in the studio as a composer, performer, and producer. His knowledge of the market and all the aspects of production

multitrack (recording)
the process of recording individual parts separately and mixing them together at a later time. Modern studios have as many as thirty-two or more tracks available to record and mix later.
layered
recording instruments separately and mixing together later. Each instrument is a layer of the total sound.
tracks
the individual recording of parts to be combined later (mixed) for a total ensemble. See multitrack recording.

has made him one of the most successful producers in history. He has taken near stars and catapulted them into stardom. He used his traditional musical background together with his composing and performing skills. Comparison to the musical activities of composers such as Mozart, Beethoven, and Wagner is not inappropriate. Jones is an improviser, performer, and composer. He is in touch with the active musical market like Beethoven was. They both used the marketplace to produce works both new and unique. The performers for whom Jones has contributed production skills read like a Who's Who of commercial music: James Ingram, George Benson, The Pointer Sisters, Michael Jackson, and many more.

Quincy Jones
(1933–   )

DATELINE	BIOGRAPHY
1933	Quincy Jones was born in Chicago. His family moved to Seattle when Quincy was ten years old.
1947	He began playing trumpet and had his first trumpet lessons in 1950 with Clark Terry, who was in Seattle playing with the Count Basie Orchestra.
1951	Jones attended Berklee School of Music in Boston on a scholarship.
1952–53	He toured as a trumpeter with the Lionel Hampton Big Band.
1954–56	Jones worked for the Dizzy Gillespie band as director and arranger, also playing in the brass section.
1957	After moving to Paris he studied writing and arranging with Nadia Boulanger and worked for Barclay Records; he won several European awards for composing, arranging, and conducting.
1959	Jones was hired as musical director for the Harold Arlen blues opera *Free and Easy* and took the jazz orchestra from this show on tour in 1959 and 1960.
1962	After returning to the United States Jones became musical director of Mercury Records; he was the first African American to hold a job as vice-president in charge of artists and repertoire.
1963	Jones had his first big hit when he produced Lesley Gore's "It's My Party."

1965 He began writing film scores, beginning with *The Pawnbroker*; he worked with Ray Charles, a friend from his Seattle youth, on the score of *In the Heat of the Night*, a combination of country, pop, soul, jazz, and electronic free form. His television credits include ''Sanford and Son,'' ''Ironside,'' ''I Spy,'' and ''Roots.''

1969 Jones signed with A & M Records and produced a series of jazz funk albums; he became mentor, producer, and arranger for such artists as James Ingram, Al Jarreau, and Chaka Khan.

1974 Jones suffered two brain aneurisms, and subsequent surgeries kept him inactive for over a year.

1980s Jones found huge success as producer of Michael Jackson's top-selling albums *Thriller* and *Bad*.

1985 He produced and organized the African aid hit single, ''We Are the World.''

1989 Production of the album *Back on the Block* reaffirmed Jones's prominence in the world of studio music.

Listening Notes

Quincy Jones, ''The Places You Find Love'' from the album *Back on the Block* (1989).

This album hosts more soloists and performers (over 200) than might first be expected. No single group records all the songs. The level of specialty is extraordinary. There are synthesizer programmers listed for each part of a drum set; for example, an individual may be given a credit for a snare drum sound. They are listed as performers because it is their sounds that are being played or programmed into the performance. All the songs on this album combine acoustic sounds with rigidly programmed electronic sounds.

The performances range from rap to lush instrumentals, funk, jazz/rock, and ballad. There is even a song ''Wee B. Do InIt'' where the rhythm section sounds are made up of head scratches (shaker), chest slaps (bass drum), tongue clucks (cross-stick snare), and other percussive body sounds. The band is called the Human Bean Band.

''The Places You Find Love'' is a Swahili translation along with African lyrics. Listen to the multitude of sounds and see if you can determine what is programmed and what is acoustic. Notice how the rigid rhythmic patterns support the free, sometimes improvised solo lines from the lead singers (Siedah Garret, Chaka Khan.)

0:00	Introduction. Drum sounds and echo effects on voices.
0:28	Solo voice, keyboard, bass, bongos, bass drum. The texture is very clear and simple; more synthesized sounds slowly creep into the texture.
1:10	String sounds.
2:06	Chorus, rhythm section intensifies.
2:29	Return to original texture.
3:20	Chorus and accompaniment become very thick again, soloist improvises above.
3:45	Swahili chorus takes the lead.
4:18	Instrumental interlude (synthesized).
4:49	Return to chorus, descant solo.
5:12	Vamp ending continues, improvised vocal solo above the full choral texture.
6:00	The chorus becomes dominant, ends in a recitation.
6:25	End.

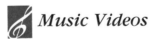 Music Videos

The studio has grown in concept with the advent of music video. When a song is expanded into video it can take on many different expressions. The most obvious setting of a song is to film a performance, but video soon outgrew the concept of "almost a concert" and began producing videos that were interpretive of the text. The tradition of word painting reached new heights. Videos have always tried to express the lyrics; however, with the technological advances of the last few years, videos have taken on tremendous proportions. Michael Jackson, for example, has produced videos that have the scope of a "mini-movie." He produced politically stimulating statements against world hunger with "We Are the World" and "Man in the Mirror." In contrast to these videos he has produced high-energy scenes depicting a myriad of topics, from the horror video "Thriller" to the street scene of "Beat It."

Because of the tremendous possibilities offered musicians in recording studios, competition in the commercial market has intensified dramatically. The cost of recording one song and video can exceed thousands or even millions of dollars. The chance for new talent to find exposure has been diminished considerably because of the cost factor. The number of people needed to produce a recording and/or video is remarkable when one considers the relatively small number of people needed to produce a concert only 100 years ago. The talent required to produce an album of twelve songs is larger than most executives enjoy:

- Producer
- Associate Producer
- Engineers
- Technical Director
- Creative Services Personnel
- Production Coordinator
- Contractor
- Mixing Engineers
- Visual Artists
- Musicians
- Facilities and Equipment Directors
- Wardrobe and Makeup Staff
- Titling and Editing Assistants

The positions listed above further expand with larger productions. For example, the album *Back on the Block* produced by Quincy Jones has a technical staff alone of twenty-one people. The musicians involved total nearly 200. The diverse talents on this album speak highly of Jones's tremendous organizational abilities and his enormous musical clout. Notice the number of names associated with the next album you listen to. The days of one artist controlling all the aspects of a commercial production are gone.

GLOSSARY

Absolute music   instrumental music not associated with a poem, story, or title. The music is not meant to be interpretive of any literary element.

A cappella   choral music performed without accompaniment.

Accent   a note that is played louder to make it stand out from the notes before and after it.

Accidentals   symbols placed in front of a note to move the pitch up or down by a half step. A sharp moves the pitch up, a flat moves the pitch down, and a natural sign removes the flat or sharp.

Aleatory, chance music   other terms for indeterminate music.

Allegro   stylistic term meaning fast or lively.

Amplitude   the volume of a sound. Amplitude is measured by the height and depth of its wave form.

Answer   the statement in a fugue that overlaps the original subject. It follows and overlaps each statement of the subject.

Arco   bowing a stringed instrument as opposed to plucking the strings (pizzicato).

Aria   a lyric and often demanding vocal work used in opera, oratorios, and cantatas.

Ars nova   "new art." This fourteenth-century style is typified by a popular polyphonic motet style using stories of village life and texts in the vernacular.

Articulation markings   symbols above or below a note to indicate special treatment such as ***legato*** (smooth and attached) or ***staccato*** (separated, detached).

Artificial intelligence   a computer environment where decisions in creation and direction are determined by software. These systems develop and expand simple ideas into complex structures.

Art song   a setting of a poem by an established literary writer. The most common languages for these songs are Italian, French, and German.

Atonal, atonality   music associated with the twentieth century where the tonality or key area is avoided.

Ballades   see **character pieces.**

Ballad opera   a light and often humorous dramatic form of opera performed specifically in England.

Ballet (fa-la-la)   a popular English madrigal style in the Renaissance. The homophonic verse is followed by a polyphonic refrain of fa-la-la.

Bar lines   the vertical lines in the music staff creating units of music called measures.

Basso continuo   see **through bass.**

Basso ostinato   see **ground bass.**

Baya   a drum used in Indian music.

Beat   a rhythmic pulse. A strong, regular beat is fundamental to all dance music.

Bel canto   a vocal style that displayed virtuosic techniques associated with the da capo form. The vocalist improvised complicated ornaments to display vocal prowess.

Binary form   a formal structure using theme repetition and contrast (A B or A A B B).

Blues, country and city   a vocal style that used blue notes and inflections. Country blues is a free and less disciplined style of blues. City blues is more structured and involves several musicians playing accompaniment.

Body harp   a bow-and-arrowlike harp with one to three strings found in South Africa. The strings are strummed with the fingernail.

Bombs, dropping bombs   a bebop drumming technique. Bombs are accented notes that do not correspond with other rhythmic ideas in the ensemble. They supply energy and excitement.

Boogie-woogie   a blues piano style where the left hand repeats a rhythmic melodic pattern (ostinato) that supplies the harmony. The right hand improvises above.

Book (musical)   the words to a musical comedy.

Bridge (B)   the contrasting section in a song form (A A′ **B** A). This contrasting section has a different chord progression and melody.

Burlesque   an early American form of entertainment with skits, gags, and music.

Butterfly harp   a Chinese instrument with very short strings and played with small bamboo hammers.

Cadence   the end of a musical idea. It can be the end of a phrase, theme group, or movement.

Cadenza   an unaccompanied solo that is rhythmically free in both pulse and meter. Cadenzas are most commonly associated with the concerto form.

Call-response   a musical dialogue between two musical statements; one musician states a phrase and the other fills in the gaps between the phrases. In early American religious traditions it was called "lining out": A leader would sing a line of text and the congregation would respond with the same line.

Camerata (Florentine)   a group of composers and poets who gathered in 1575 to develop a new dramatic relationship between music and text.

Canon, canonic   a musical form in which a melody is followed by and overlaps the same melody; also called a "round." A familiar canon is "Row, Row, Row Your Boat."

Cantata   a musical piece that is sung. The church cantata was a short dramatic work with solos and chorus sections.

Cantus firmus   a melody, most often a Gregorian chant, used as the lowest part, the **tenor.** Other parts were written above, creating a form of polyphonic music.

Castrati   male singers who sang soprano or alto roles in opera because of castration before puberty.

Chamber music   another term for ensemble music. It is designed to be played in smaller rooms where large choirs and orchestras would not be suitable. Chamber music usually has only one individual on each part.

Chanson   literally, "a song"; the French equivalent of the German Lied.

Character pieces   short, miniature single-movement works for piano. Common character pieces from the nineteenth century are nocturnes, études, polonaises, mazurkas, impromptus, ballades, preludes, and intermezzi.

Chorale   a four-part homophonic composition; traditionally, a Lutheran hymn sung by a congregation in church.

Chorale prelude   an organ work based on a Lutheran chorale melody.

Chord   the simultaneous sounding of three or more notes. In tonal music, chords have specific harmonic relationships to one another, and chords are used to accompany melodies.

Chorus   a section in an oratorio, opera, or cantata performed with several singers on each part.

Chromatic   the use of half steps in melodies and chords, suggesting movement from one key area to another.

Coda   the musical extension at the end of a movement or performance. It can be very short or quite long and developmental.

Collective composition   musicians working together to complete a composition by playing ideas specific to their instruments; rhythm sections are most commonly involved in this process.

Collective improvisation the process where several musicians improvise a melodic or rhythmic part that combines to form a unified, polyphonic texture; for example, Dixieland.

Comic operas very popular operas written in England, Italy, and Germany. Comic operas were not considered a part of the serious opera tradition.

Comping, comps a rhythmic activity supplied by the chording instruments and the drummer to help fill in the texture. The left hand of the pianist supplies chords that complement the melodic activity. A guitarist comps with chords sounding much like the pianist's left hand. The drummer uses the snare drum, playing rhythms similar to those used by the pianist and the guitarist.

Concertino group in a concerto grosso the solo group, in contrast to the orchestra or ripieno group.

Concert master the assistant to the conductor of an orchestra. Traditionally, the first chair violinist is automatically the concert master.

Concerto (solo) a three-movement work featuring a soloist accompanied by the orchestra.

Concerto grosso a form in which a soloist or ensemble is contrasted against a string orchestra or full orchestra.

Concert overture an overture played on the concert stage. The overture is not the introduction to a literary work or opera.

Conductor the musician in front of an orchestra or choir who uses hand, arm, and body motions to direct the interpretation of the music.

Consonance the pleasing sound of two or more notes. Consonant sounds are stable and do not create tension.

Consort a small ensemble of musicians playing instruments from the same family.

Continuo (basso) the performance of a figured bass by a lute or keyboard reinforced by a cello.

Contrapuntal a polyphonic writing technique. Melodic parts are overlapped with different rhythms so that each maintains a unique identity.

Contrast one of the primary techniques used to construct binary and ternary forms. Contrasting themes or melodies add interest and spur a sense of return when the original melody reappears.

Cool jazz a post-bebop style that softened some of the aggressive elements of bebop. The melody was played in a more comfortable range, the rhythm section used fewer explosive sounds, and the tempos were more relaxed than in bebop. Also called West Coast jazz.

Countersubject a melodic statement performed in duet fashion with the answer in a fugue. It is a complementary melody and supplies motives and complexity to the texture.

Crescendo a gradual increase in dynamic level from soft to loud.

Crossover a jazz style where jazz and rock combine with the newest of commercial instruments and recording techniques.

Cue a visual motion given by the conductor to instruct a performer of an entrance or needed musical effect.

Da capo aria a form A B A′ for soloists to sing emotionally intense melodies that were commonly ornamented on the repeat of the A section.

Dance repeated rhythms that support or suggest movement.

Decrescendo a gradual decrease in dynamic level from loud to soft.

Development the middle section of a sonata-allegro form. Thematic material is modulated, broken down into smaller units, and changed and developed.

Disco a dance style typified by a heavy bass drum on each beat of the measure. A contemporary style of the late 1970s.

Dissonance a combination of notes that seems unrelated or harsh. Too many dissonant sounds make most listeners uncomfortable.

Divertimenti a collection of dancelike forms performed by small string ensembles. They were the predecessors to the modern string quartet.

Dodecaphony see **serialism.**

Dominant (V) the chord built on the fifth degree of the scale. It requires resolution to the tonic chord.

Doubling two or more voices or instruments playing the same melody at the same time.

Double-stopping playing two notes at once on a stringed instrument.

Drone a long sustained sound used to support melodies above. This is a very early form of harmonic development.

Dry recitative a vocal form with only continuo accompaniment as opposed to orchestral accompaniment.

Duplum the part written above the tenor or cantus firmus in early polyphony.

Dynamics various volume (loudness) levels, as well as gradual changes in volume. Italian terms describe the various volume levels between *piano* (soft) and *forte* (loud).

Effect the process of changing the original sound of an instrument. The most common effects are echo, delay, and chorus.

Electronic music music generated through tape manipulation and/or computer software.

Ensemble a small group of musicians each performing independent parts.

Ensemble finale the final scene of an operatic section where several singers perform at the same time, but sing independent texts and often express different moods; for example, Italian opera.

Envelope the four elements that make up the sound of a note: attack, decay, sustain, and release (ADSR). **Attack** is the sound of a note as it begins, **decay** is the sound of a note as it softens quickly immediately after the attack, **sustain** is the time a note sings after the attack and short decay; **release** is the ending of the note.

Episodes melodically free sections in a fugue.

Ethnomusicology the study of music of different ethnic groups in light of tradition and culture.

Études see **character pieces.**

Excerpt books excerpts from orchestral music, by composer, for a specific instrument.

Experimental/theoretical music music based on theories where the outcome is not determined. This music explores sounds and their relationship to the musical arts.

Exposition the first section of the sonata-allegro form in which two themes (or theme groups) are presented, the first in the tonic and the second in the dominant or relative minor.

Figured bass a system of small numbers written above a bass note to indicate the intervals needed to build the desired chord.

Fixed idea a recurring theme (specific to Berlioz's *Symphonie fantastique*). It appeared, although transformed, in each movement of this program symphony.

Flat to lower the pitch of a note by half a step. The symbol is ♭.

Free jazz a modern jazz style that questions traditional melodic and harmonic rules. Performers are free to play anything at anytime they feel is musical.

Frequency the length of a sound wave or the number of vibrations per second. Every pitch has a specific frequency; for example, the note A above middle C vibrates 440 times a second.

Fugue a musical form that uses subjects, answers, and countersubjects in an overlapping manner. It is related to a very complicated round or canon.

Fundamental pitch the primary pitch. The lowest pitch heard in an overtone series is the fundamental, and also the loudest, pitch.

Fusion a jazz style where elements of jazz and rock fuse into a new identifiable style.

Glissando the continuous sliding up or down in pitch without distinct notes being heard. Trombonists can demonstrate the most obvious glissando when they slide smoothly between notes.

Grave a stylistic term indicating the mood and possible tempo of a performance; very slow, seriously.

Gregorian chant a form of medieval chant (monophony). There are several collections of chant, and Pope Gregory I assembled this collection. Other collections are named after the individual who collected them or after the location where they were collected, for example, **Ambrosian** and **Byzantine** chants.

Ground bass   a repeated melody in the bass (passacaglia) that supports melodies above; also called **basso ostinato.**

Half step   the smallest distance or interval between two notes in Western European music.

Hard bop   a bebop style with elements of blues along with a less angular sense of melody. Also called straight-ahead jazz.

Harmonic extensions   notes that are dissonant to a chord's fundamental three notes but are still theoretically related to the chord.

Harmonic rhythm   the frequency and regularity of chord changes in a composition. A pulse is established by the regular movement from one chord to another.

Harmony   the result of sounding two or more different notes at the same time to build chords; also the progression of chords and their relationship to one another.

Harpsichord   the most dominant keyboard instrument in the Baroque period. Strings are plucked when a key is depressed.

Heptatonic   a seven-note scale used in African music.

Heterophony   singing a melody in unison but with unique melodic ornaments between performers. This is an improvised form of harmony particular to folk music.

Homophony   a single melody supported by chords rather than by additional melodies.

Hu-kin   a two-string Chinese instrument played with a bow.

Imitation   repeating a melodic idea or entire melody immediately in another part; for example, a round. Imitation was used extensively in the Renaissance.

Impressionism   in music, a style at the turn of the twentieth century emphasizing tone color, sonority, and image.

Impromptus   see **character pieces.**

Improvisation   the instantaneous creation of music. Players improvise melodies, harmonies, bass lines, and rhythms. Texture is improvised by all the musicians working together.

Indeterminate music   partially composed music. The performer is required to make decisions while playing. The level of decision-making varies considerably, from choosing what note to play to deciding what the overall structure will be.

Intermezzi   see **character pieces.**

Interval   the distance between two notes.

Intonation   accuracy of pitch. Good intonation or being "in tune" is the exact sounding of a specific pitch without being slightly above or below the standard.

Inversion   playing a melody upside down. Each interval of the melody is reversed; for example, up a third instead of down a third. Used in fugues and serial composition.

Key, tonal area   one note is more stable than any other, and the key is defined by this note. All other notes in the same key are less stable and eventually lead back to the primary note. The key area establishes a **tonality** where all notes and chords are related to the tonal area or single note.

Keyboard (visual)   the arrangement of keys on a piano or synthesizer.

Key signature   a group of ♭'s or ♯'s representing the tonal area of a song; for example, the key of A, or the key of B-flat. The key signature is written on the staff at the beginning of a composition.

Koto   a Japanese harplike stringed instrument.

Layback   melodies played slightly behind the beat; the effect imparts a feeling of improvisation to a solo.

Layered   recording instruments separately and mixing together later. Each instrument is a layer of the total sound.

Leitmotifs   motives associated with a person, act, or object. Leitmotifs are a unifying feature of Wagnerian opera; they develop and change as the characters change.

Libretto   a text designed specifically to be set to music.

Lied   a German art song. These songs disappeared after the Renaissance but reappeared in the nineteenth century.

Lip sync   mouthing the words to a prerecorded tape.

Liturgical Mass   Both parts of the Mass, the Ordinary and the Proper, are set to music. The Mass has been used as a formal structure for large sacred music works.

Madrigal   a secular poem about love, popular in the Renaissance, set in a polyphonic texture with contrasting homophonic sections. Word painting was prevalent.

Madrigalisms   specific words or feelings are emphasized musically. Associated with word painting.

Major   a mode based on a scale. This mode is the most familiar mode in our culture today. When compared with the minor mode it seems bright and lively.

Mazurka   see **character pieces.**

Measures   small equal units of a composition that contain a determined number of beats. Measures are separated in written music by vertical bar lines.

Measured rhythm   a notational system associated with the School of Notre Dame that established a more precise form of metered rhythm.

Melisma   singing several notes per syllable. Some melismas are very long with many notes sung using one syllable of text.

Melody   a logical series of notes that expresses a musical thought; angular melodies, which are not very singable, are considered just as melodic as the tuneful melodies common to simple folk songs. There are two basic types of melodies; **conjunct** melodies move by step and small intervals, and **disjunct** melodies move by larger skips.

Meter   the number of beats grouped in each measure. For example, 3/4 meter means 3 quarter notes per measure; 6/8 means 6 eighth notes per measure, and so on. Various meters form the bases of dance forms; for example, a waltz is written in groups of 3 (3/4 time), and cha-cha is in groups of 4 (4/4 time).

Microtonal   scales that have intervals less than the half step.

MIDI   acronym for Musical Instrument Digital Interface. This process transmits data between several electronic instruments so that they all communicate and play together.

Miniatures   short works in the Romantic era such as art songs and single-movement piano compositions.

Minimalism   a trancelike style of the twentieth century. The music has very narrow ranges in dynamics, texture, or rhythm, is very repetitive, and stays constant for long periods.

Minor   another mode based on a scale. It sounds darker than the common major mode.

Minstrel shows   early American touring groups providing music and comedy.

Minuet and trio   a dance form derived from earlier suites. This three-part form (A B A) remained a part (the third movement) of the symphony and string quartet until it was modified and replaced by the scherzo and trio form.

Mix (mixed)   the process of blending instruments together into a musical whole. In the modern studio the mixing is performed electronically by engineers. In orchestras and ensembles the mixing is performed by the instrumentalists.

Mode, modal   a scale of whole steps and half steps. There are seven common modes, including the major and minor scales.

Modified strophic form   two or more verses of an art song set to the same music but additional verses set to new music.

Modulated rhythm   the constant movement from meter to meter in a short period of time. There is no regular pattern of beats.

Modulation   the movement from one key area to another.

Monody, monodic style   a new vocal technique of solo voice and basso continuo developed by the Camerata.

Monophony   a single melody with no other musical accompaniment; for example, a Gregorian chant.

Motet   polyphonic settings of a Latin text. An essential part of Renaissance music, they are sacred choral works but are not part of the Mass.

Motion   comprised of rhythm, meter, and tempo. Music moves forward in patterns of beats and at various speeds. These elements define the motion of the music.

Motive a small musical unit made up of a short identifiable rhythm encompassing a few pitches. The most famous motive is the opening of Beethoven's Fifth Symphony.

Motown a name for the musical style that emanated from Detroit. It is a black rock style with a strong emphasis on rock rhythms.

Movement a self-contained structure that is only part of a larger work. For example, a symphony has four separate movements.

Multitrack (recording) the process of recording individual parts separately and mixing them together at a later time. Modern studios have as many as sixty-four tracks available to record and mix later.

Musical comedy a generic name for American musical theater.

Musical space the range of sound filled by the music elements motion, pitch, harmony, texture, and tone.

Musical theater a dramatic production based on everyday themes featuring vocal and instrumental sounds that relate to traditional musical styles.

Music dramas a self-proclaimed name for Wagner's operas. He considered them larger in scope than other operas.

Musicology the study of musical styles, both historically and theoretically.

Music video a video production that accompanies or interprets a song.

Musique concrète music composed from recorded and electronically affected acoustic sounds and tape manipulation.

Muted darkening or softening the tone of instruments by using mutes. Brass instruments place mutes in the bell while strings use wooden clamps on the bridge.

Neoclassicism music of the early twentieth century inspired by the restraint and control exhibited in the eighteenth century. This style was partially a response to the overly emotional music of the late nineteenth century.

Neoromanticism a style that borrows musical ideas of the nineteenth century to compose in the twentieth century.

Nocturnes see **character pieces.**

Octave the distance (in terms of pitch) between two notes with the same letter name. For example, from the note C up to the next note named C is one octave.

Opera a large-scale work featuring an orchestra and vocalists acting out a dramatic theme or story.

Opera buffa opera that was entirely sung (Italian) but still part of the comic opera tradition. Recitative was used instead of spoken dialogue.

Opéra comique French comic opera that was based on satire. These operas developed into a more realistic form in the late nineteenth century; they were not equal in scope to grand opera of the same period.

Oral tradition in the folk tradition, information, history, and culture were passed from generation to generation verbally. Many cultural traits are still communicated in this manner.

Oratorio a large vocal and instrumental dramatic work based on a sacred subject. Like opera it has arias and recitatives; however, there is no staging or dramatic acting.

Orchestration the process of assigning instruments to musical ideas. Orchestration is part of the compositional process, important to the mood and spirit of a work.

Ordinary the part of the liturgical Mass that is performed every service.

Organum a two-part form of early polyphony. Each part is sung in parallel either at a fourth, fifth, or octave apart. There are three forms of organum: parallel, free, and melismatic.

Ornament a melodic device that accentuates a melodic idea. Found in every style of music, ornaments are either rehearsed or added freely by the performer, depending on the style.

Ostinato a repeated, usually short, rhythmic musical figure. In boogie-woogie it is an eight-note pattern.

Overture the opening instrumental selection that precedes a music drama or theatrical work. See **concert overture.**

Overtone series the combination of pitches that are based on the same fundamental pitch. Every note has several related pitches, or overtones, from low to high, that vibrate at the same time.

Passacaglia a contrapuntal style. Variations are written over a repeating bass line (ostinato).

Passion a dramatic sacred work, using arias, recitatives, and choruses as found in oratorios, that characterizes the suffering and death of Christ.

Pedal point the long sounding of a low note on a pipe organ while melodies move freely above. The most common placement of a pedal point was at the end of large sections or works.

Pentatonic scale a scale with only five notes in the octave; a fundamental scale in Oriental music.

Phrase the musical equivalent of a spoken phrase, clause, or sentence; a melodic statement with a recognizable beginning, middle, and end.

Pianoforte, piano the dominant instrument in music since the nineteenth century. The instrument is named for its ability to play both loudly (*forte*) and softly (*piano*).

Pitch the highness or lowness of a note, dictated by the speed of its sound vibrations.

Pizzicato plucking a stringed instrument rather than bowing it.

Point of imitation the moment a new phrase begins where each part enters using the same melodic idea. The entrances are staggered, creating a thick polyphonic style.

Polonaise see **character pieces.**

Polychoral motet a motet that is performed by more than one choir or group of instruments.

Polyphony the performance of two or more melodic parts that are independent and relatively equal in melodic content.

Polyrhythm the simultaneous use of two or more contrasting rhythms. Such rhythms often conflict with and blur the beat.

Polytonal the simultaneous performance of two different key areas. This can be accomplished with an orchestra or with a single keyboard instrument.

Preludes the opening movements in suites and fugues in Baroque instrumental music. They are most commonly associated with the pipe organ.

Primitivism in music, a twentieth-century style inspired by primitive works of art, where music is combined with rhythmic and melodic angularity.

Program music music based on some literary element, either a poem, story, or title. The music is interpretive of the story or mood presented in the program.

Proper the part of the liturgical Mass that represents the various religious seasons, as opposed to the Ordinary, which remains the same throughout the year.

Raga a pattern of notes or scale on which an improvised melody is performed; used in Indian music.

Ragtime a compositional form based on European dance forms. It later became a style used for improvisation on the piano.

Range the distance between high notes and low notes on an instrument. Also the distance between loud and soft, fast and slow.

Recapitulation the last section of a sonata-allegro form in which the two primary themes (or theme groups) are restated in the tonic key after the development.

Recitative a declamatory vocal style used to tell of action or to relate a text without repetition. It is accompanied by a basso continuo.

Reform opera a form of serious opera where the difference between recitative and aria was softened. It recaptured some of the audience lost to oratorios and ballad opera.

Repetition repeating melodies to build familiarity and stability. Composers use repetition and contrast to build large formal musical structures.

Requiem mass a mass for the dead.

Retrograde playing a melody or tone row backwards or in the opposite direction.

Retrograde-inversion playing a melody or tone row backwards and upside down at the same time.

Reverb the echo effect that is now produced by digital signal processors; early reverb came from the room or hall in which the music was performed.

Rhythm the regularly recurring pulses or beats that are arranged into regularly recurring groups consisting of multiples of two or three pulses that establish meter. Rhythm refers to the frequency of chords and the activity of the melody, hence harmonic rhythm and melodic rhythm.

Rhythm and blues a rhythmic dance form of the blues. It led to the development of rock 'n' roll.

Riff a melodic motive used in jazz to build larger melodic structures.

Ripieno group in a concerto grosso the orchestral or tutti group, in contrast to the solo group (concertino).

Ritornello the orchestral section that contrasts the solo sections in a concerto grosso.

Rondo a formal structure in which the first theme is restated between a series of new themes (A B A C A D A).

Rubato "robbed time." In the piano style of Chopin, the right hand would pull and push against the regular rhythm being played in the left hand, suggesting a sense of rhythmic freedom.

Russian Five five composers who worked together in hopes of producing a music style representative of their Russian heritage rather than the music imported from Europe.

Sampling the re-creation of existing wave forms. Any sound can be analyzed and its wave form plotted. The synthesizer can then read out this code and from it re-create an exact copy of the original sound.

Sanai a double-reed snake-charmer's pipe used in music from India.

Scale any of several sequences of pitches dividing an octave into whole steps and half steps. The octave has twelve half steps, which is the **chromatic scale.**

Major and minor scales are built by using a combination of whole steps and half steps.

Scherzo and trio a musical form designed after the minuet form. Scherzos are usually followed by a trio that returns to the scherzo themes.

School of Notre Dame a twelfth-century musical style that devised a clear form of measured rhythm similar to the metered music of today.

Scored the process of placing each instrument into the musical texture. See **orchestration.**

Segue means to continue to the next musical section without stopping.

Sequenced music as the product of electronically processing all the musical parts of a composition. The parts are played separately and stored as data in a computer. The data are combined and organized by the computer to be played together later.

Serialism a modern classical system for writing music. Devised by Schoenberg, it arranges the twelve tones of the octave into a tone row or series. Because all twelve notes of the octave are used, tonality is destroyed. Atonal composition is also called twelve-tone technique or dodecaphony.

Series notes, rhythms, and dynamics can be used to build a serial composition and can provide an order for melodic and rhythmic activities. The series can be played forward, backwards (retrograde), upside down (inversion), and upside down and backwards (retrograde-inversion) or can start on a different pitch (transposition).

Sharp to raise the pitch of a note by half a step. The symbol is ♯.

Sho a mouth organ with pipes similar to a pipe organ; a traditional Japanese instrument.

Signal processing to take a recorded sound and alter it using various musical effects such as reverb or delay.

Sinfonias instrumental musical sections in early opera.

Singspiele a German form of comic opera. It is based on folk topics and songs.

Sitar a fretted stringed instrument used in India.

The frets are movable, allowing for microtonal scales.

Sonata   an early term used to describe instrumental music. There are two kinds of sonatas: the secular da camera and the more serious sacred da chiesa. Later in history the term refers to a three-movement solo work, a soloist with piano accompaniment.

Sonata-allegro form   the primary large structure used for the first movement of a symphony. Themes are expounded, developed, and recapitulated.

Sonata da camera   secular instrumental music.

Sonata da chiesa   sacred instrumental music.

Song, song cycles   art songs from the nineteenth century. Cycles were a series of poems set to music that related some common story.

Soul   a blues style defined by the black musical tradition of slow rock (1970s) that emanated from Detroit (Motown).

Sound poetry   a literary style of writing words and/or syllables for their sound alone. The meaning of the text may be irrelevant to the performance of the recitation.

Sprechstimme   a singing technique used in the twentieth century. The voice half-sang and half-spoke the melody. The result is similar to very animated speech.

Standards   songs from musicals, jazz, or commercial music that are used as a basis for jazz improvisations. They are standards because most jazz players know them and they are standard to the literature.

Stops   the levers or buttons used to open a rank of pipes on an organ so that the air can go through them when a key is depressed.

Stride   a highly improvisatory, technically developed form of ragtime piano.

String quartet   a musical group comprised of two violins, viola, and cello. String quartets share the same compositional form as symphonies.

Subject   the first statement in a fugue. Once answered by another part, it enters again in a third part.

Suite   a group of highly styled dance forms. Suites were written for small ensembles, harpsichord, and orchestra.

Swing   a style of playing two notes of equal value within a beat. A classical musician interprets the duration of each note as equal; a jazz musician makes the first note last longer than the second. The result is a swinging, dancelike feeling of long-short, long-short.

Symbolism   a literary style of the late nineteenth century that inspired many impressionists.

Symphonic poem   a single-movement work for orchestra based on a poem, story, or title.

Symphony   a large four-movement work for orchestra that developed in the eighteenth century.

Syncopation   placing an accent on a normally unaccented part of the beat or measure. For example, a Viennese waltz is counted "ONE, two, three," but a syncopated jazz waltz sounds like "go-PARK-the-car."

Synthesizer   a tone generator, often a keyboard. Using a synthesizer, sounds imitating acoustic instruments or new and unique wave forms are created.

Tabla   a traditional drum used in Indian music.

Tact, taktus   the up-and-down motion made by early conductors intended to guide the musicians rhythmically.

Tala   a rhythmic cycle that is repeated by drums while a raga is improvised above.

Tape manipulation   used to affect recorded sounds. Tapes can be slowed down, sped up, run backwards, or cut and reassembled in a different order.

Tempo   the speed of a musical composition. The basic rhythmic pulse can be slow or fast or change gradually between fast and slow.

Tenor   the lower part (cantus firmus) in early polyphony.

Ternary form   a three-part formal structure using contrast and repetition of themes (A B A or A A B A).

Terraced dynamics   a technique used in the Baroque era to change dynamics. More players or more stops on the organ were added, resulting in sudden rather than gradual dynamic changes.

Texture   the activity level of the musical elements. When the activity is high, the texture is thick; when the activity is low, the texture is thin. Dynamics and range also affect the texture.

Thematic transformation changing the theme to take on a different character or personality each time it returns in the movement or work.

Theme a unique and identifiable melody. Extended works rely on themes for unification.

Theme and variations a formal structure of a single work or movement of a larger work. Once a theme is stated, it is varied to the point of obscurity and is usually restated at the end of the selection.

Theme group a tonal area that takes the place of a single theme in a sonata-allegro form.

Third stream jazz that incorporates elements of classical music such as modern sounds, orchestral instruments, and composing techniques.

Through bass the continuous-sounding bass line that underpins much of the music of the Baroque period; also called **basso continuo.**

Through-composed form music without repetitive sections for different verses. Although the text of a song is strophic, the music may be different for each verse.

Time signature the two numbers at the beginning of written music indicating the number of beats per measure and what note value will be counted as one beat; for example, 3/4, 6/8, 4/4.

Toccata a flamboyant introductory organ piece that precedes a fugue.

Tone the sound quality of an instrument or voice. For example, the tone of a voice may be nasal, shallow, full, or deep.

Tone poem see **symphonic poem.**

Tone row an ordering of the twelve notes in an octave. The row will be the basis of a serial composition.

Tonic (I) the chord built on the first degree of the scale. It has a feeling of rest and completion.

Total serialism an extended use of serialism. In addition to using pitches in a series, dynamics and rhythms are also serialized.

Tracks the individual recording of parts to be combined later (mixed) for a total ensemble. See **multitrack recording.**

Transitional sections appear between themes or theme groups and help introduce new material. They can be developmental in nature with motivic interplay and modulation.

Transitional themes short melodic sequences or motives that provide melodic progression between larger thematic areas.

Transposition to rewrite or play musical notation in another key. In serial composition, starting the row on another pitch.

Tremolo the vibrato motion of a pitch. The pitch moves slightly higher and lower, adding animation to the note.

Trio sonata a sonata with three instrumental parts. The two higher melodies are performed by two soloists while the continuo players perform the third part.

Tritonic scale a three-note scale used in African music.

Tune up bringing two or more instruments in agreement on pitch. Once instruments are tuned, the music can better be controlled by the musicians.

Tutti means everyone plays. In the concerto grosso, tutti is another term for **ritornello.**

Twelve-tone technique see **serialism.**

Vaudeville similar to minstrel shows. A source of popular entertainment in the early part of the twentieth century in America.

Venetian School composers who wrote and performed music in the late sixteenth century using the polychoral style. The works required multiple choirs of voices or instruments.

Verismo a movement centered around realism in the late nineteenth century. Operas (such as Puccini's) depicted realistic emotional situations incorporating a wide range of emotions.

Virtuoso a performer who excels above all the others; a technically superior musician.

Wah-wah pedal the pedal used by guitarists to vary the level of distortion and volume from their guitar amplifier. It can sound like vocal inflections.

Walks, walking a rhythmic-melodic activity employed by a swing-style bass player. When a note is played on every beat of the measure and notes move in a scale pattern, the impression is one of "walking" up and down the scale. A walking bass provides harmonic support for the rest of the ensemble.

West Coast jazz   see **cool jazz.**

Whole-tone scale   a scale without half steps. Major and minor scales both have half steps and whole steps.

Word painting   a word stressed musically to make it stand out from the words before and after it. The emphasis is made to interpret the special meaning of the word.

PHOTO CREDITS

■ *331*

TOPIC 1   Page 206: (detail) Gemalde von Franz Schams (1823–1883). Archiv fur Kunst und Geschichte, Berlin. Page 207: Hans Namuth. Page 210: Art Resource. Page 211: Bettmann Newsphotos. Page 214: Gemalde von Franz Schams (1823–1883). Archiv fur Kunst und Geschichte, Berlin. Page 217: Frank Driggs Collection.

TOPIC 2   Page 218: (detail) Bettmann Newsphotos. Page 225: Omikron/ Photo Researchers, Inc.

TOPIC 3   Page 228: Bettmann Newsphotos. Page 233: © 1981 Jim Caldwell. Page 234: New York Public Library. Page 239: Bettmann Newsphotos.

TOPIC 4   Page 243: (detail) Bettmann Newsphotos. Page 246: Bettmann Newsphotos. Page 247: Jack Vartogian.

TOPIC 5   Page 251: Michael Putland/Retna. Page 253: Michael Putland/ Retna. Page 255: Omikron/Photo Researchers, Inc. 259: NYT Pictures. Page 260: Jerry Cooke, Life Magazine. © Time Warner, Inc.

TOPIC 6   Page 263: (detail) Jaques Chenet/Woodfin Camp & Associates. Page 269: Jaques Chenet/Woodfin Camp & Associates.

TOPIC 7   Page 272: (detail) Houston Grand Opera/Sherwin M. Goldman Productions. Page 274: New York Public Library. Page 277: Bettmann Newsphotos. Page 278: (top) Houston Grand Opera/Sherwin M. Goldman Productions; (bottom) New York Public Library at Lincoln Center. page 281: Robin Platzer. Page 283: Bettmann Newsphotos.

TOPIC 8   Page 287: (detail) Bettman Newsphotos. Page 290: Bettmann Newsphotos. Page 292: Loomis Dean/Life Magazine, © 1958, Time Inc. Page 293: Bettmann Newsphotos. Page 294: Hansel Mieth/Otto Hagel, Life Magazine, © Time Warner, Inc. Page 295: Time Magazine. Page 296: New Mexico Department of Development.

TOPIC 9   Page 297: (detail) Culver Pictures. Page 298: Culver Pictures. Page 300: (top) Frank Driggs Collection; (bottom) Fred Fehl/New York Public Library. Page 301: Sherry Suris/Photo Researchers, Inc. Page 305: Joan Marcus. Page 306: Jack Vartoogian.

TOPIC 10   Page 309: (detail) Bettman Newsphotos. Page 311: Bettmann Newsphotos. Page 314: Frank Driggs Collection. Page 317: Sygma.

Index